T0298821

Technology Entrepreneurship in Theory and Practice

Technology entrepreneurship refers to business activities that are based on new scientific insights and new technical developments. It describes the process by which enterprising teams and individuals convert new technical knowledge into products and services. It encompasses entrepreneurial pursuits in all fields of engineering and science where progress opens novel ways of creating value. Often these activities are based on intellectual property, although it may also make sense to consciously pursue an open technology strategy. Entrepreneurial activities in these domains lead to ventures with specific characteristics.

Technology Entrepreneurship in Theory and Practice compiles the essential research knowledge about principles and practices in technology entrepreneurship. Systematically presenting theory and practice for entrepreneurs coming from an engineering or scientific background, the authors assemble a comprehensive overview of the subject and enhance it with their expert viewpoints. The book compiles and summarizes available knowledge and approaches to enable engineers and scientists to develop entrepreneurial initiatives.

Technology Entrepreneurship in Theory and Practice will find an audience among technology entrepreneurs, engineers and scientists, entrepreneurship educators, executives, consultants, and policymakers worldwide.

J. Mark Munoz is a tenured Full Professor of International Business at Millikin University and a former Visiting Fellow at the Kennedy School of Government at Harvard University. He is the editor of the Routledge books, *The Economics of Cryptocurrencies* (2020), *Global Business Intelligence* (2017), and *Advances in Geoeconomics* (2017).

Orestis Terzidis heads the Institute for Entrepreneurship, Technology Management and Innovation (EnTechnon) at the Karlsruhe Institute of Technology (KIT). After receiving his PhD in Physics, he worked at SAP from 1998 to 2011, first as an application developer, and later as assistant to CEO Henning Kagermann and director and vice president of the SAP Research Center in Karlsruhe. In 2011, he joined KIT as a full professor.

Technology Entrepreneurship in Theory and Practice

Perspectives in Science and Engineering

Edited by
J. Mark Munoz and Orestis Terzidis

Routledge
Taylor & Francis Group

LONDON AND NEW YORK

First published 2025
by Routledge
4 Park Square, Milton Park, Abingdon, Oxon OX14 4RN

and by Routledge
605 Third Avenue, New York, NY 10158

Routledge is an imprint of the Taylor & Francis Group, an informa business

British Library Cataloguing-in-Publication Data
A catalogue record for this book is available from the British Library

ISBN: 9781032376646 (hbk)
ISBN: 9781032376639 (pbk)
ISBN: 9781003341284 (ebk)

DOI: 10.4324/9781003341284

Typeset in Times New Roman
by codeMantra

Contents

List of Contributors   *vii*

PART I
Introduction   1

1 **Introduction: Technology Entrepreneurship**   3
   J. MARK MUNOZ AND ORESTIS TERZIDIS

2 **The Fundamentals of Technology Entrepreneurship**   7
   GUY W. BATE AND LISA CALLAGHER

3 **Entrepreneurial Competencies**   17
   DARSEL KEANE AND ROD B. McNAUGHTON

PART II
From Technology to Value   31

4 **IP Institutions and Strategic Implications for New Ventures with a Global
   Orientation**   33
   YUE XU AND YUMAO WANG

5 **From Technology Idea to Value Proposition**   46
   SARAH MANTHEY AND DILEK CETINDAMAR KONAZOGLU

6 **Product Development**   57
   SAADEDDINE SHEHAB, RACHEL SWITZKY, AND KEILIN JAHNKE

PART III
Strategy and Business Model   65

7 **Personal Values, Core Competencies, Entrepreneurial Vision, and Mission**   67
   PANAGIOTIS KYRIAKOPOULOS AND ALEXANDER TITTEL

8 **Designing the Business Model**   74
   LORENA BERRÓN CADENAS AND JUNE Y. LEE

9 **Challenges in Entrepreneurial Decision-Making under Uncertain
   Business Environments**   81
   MARCOS HASHIMOTO

PART IV
Entrepreneurial Marketing   89

10 **Market and Competitor Analysis**   91
    GÉRARD MARTORELL

11 **Customer Discovery and the Lean Startup Method**   105
    KATHLEEN R. ALLEN

12 **Pricing, Promotion, and Place**   113
    MARTIN KLARMANN, ANDREAS KLEINN, AND ORESTIS TERZIDIS

PART V
Funding a Venture   129

13 **Framing the Funding Challenge**   131
    ORESTIS TERZIDIS AND J. MARK MUNOZ

14 **Funding Process for Technology Ventures**   139
    CHRISTOPH P. WESSENDORF

15 **Understanding How Capital Providers Think**   147
    YU WEI YE

PART VI
Team and Organization   155

16 **Team Building – It Is All about People, the Mission, and Values**   157
    MARGARET A. GORALSKI AND KRYSTYNA GÓRNIAK-KOCIKOWSKA

17 **Entrepreneurial Leadership**   164
    EDWARD AGBAI

18 **Building an Organization**   175
    RAFAEL AUGUSTO SEIXAS REIS DE PAULA AND ROGER (RONGXIN) CHEN

Index   *185*

Contributors

Dr. Edward Agbai is an author and Associate Professor of Leadership and Organizational Governance in the School of Entrepreneurship at Emmanuel University, Raleigh, North Carolina, USA. He has published 11 books and over 50 peer-reviewed articles.

Kathleen R. Allen, PhD, is an entrepreneur, consultant, and author specializing in the commercialization of new technologies. She has authored more than 15 books in the field of entrepreneurship and technology.

Guy Bate is the Director of the Master of Business Development (MBusDev) program and a Professional Teaching Fellow in innovation and strategy at the University of Auckland Business School. He holds PhDs in both Management and Biomedicine and has 20 years of consultancy and management experience in the pharmaceutical, biotechnology, and health technology industries.

Lorena Berrón Cadenas is a Research Associate at the University of San Francisco School of Management and B2B Product Manager in the tech industry. She holds a BS in Biomedical Engineering from Tecnológico de Monterrey and an MS in Entrepreneurship and Innovation from the University of San Francisco.

Lisa Callagher is a Senior Lecturer in Innovation and Entrepreneurship at the University of Auckland. Her research focuses on the processes of innovation, specializing in cooperative organizing. Her research has been published in specialized outlets like *R&D Management*, *IEEE Transactions in Engineering Management*, and general journals, including *Organizational Studies*, *Management Learning*, and *Journal of Management Inquiry*.

Dilek Cetindamar Konazoglu is a Professor of Contemporary Technology Management in the School of Computer Science at the University of Technology Sydney. Her main interest and research topics are digital transformations, entrepreneurship, and technology & innovation management.

Roger (Rongxin) Chen is at the University of San Francisco. His work focuses on strategy and innovation, with emphasis on new venture development and corporate innovation.

Dr. Margaret A. Goralski is a Professor at Quinnipiac University. She teaches strategy, writes about *Artificial Intelligence & the UN Sustainable Development Goals*, and serves on the UN PRME NA (Principles of Responsible Management Education North America) Steering Committee. Goralski is the UN PRME NA Global Working Group Liaison.

Dr. Krystyna Górniak-Kocikowska is a Professor Emerita of Philosophy at Southern Connecticut State University in New Haven. One of her areas of interest is the question of ethical problems pertaining to the creation, developments, and applications of digital technologies, including generative AI.

Dr. Marcos Hashimoto is the Managing Director of the Turner School of Entrepreneurship and Innovation at Bradley University, with a PhD in Business Administration and author of four books. He founded three companies and co-founded two social organizations. Previously to the academic career, he worked for 18 years for large American Corporations in Brazil, including Citibank and Cargill.

Keilin Jahnke is a Teaching Assistant Professor at the Grainger College of Engineering, University of Illinois at Urbana-Champaign. She teaches courses on international engineering, innovation, creativity, and design thinking, helping students develop effective strategies to identify and define problems, navigate the design process, and create innovative solutions.

Darsel Keane is the Director of the University of Auckland Business School's Centre for Innovation and Entrepreneurship. She is currently completing her PhD, focusing on measuring the entrepreneurial mindset and how to develop it through entrepreneurship education and extracurricular activities.

Martin Klarmann is currently a Professor of Marketing at the Karlsruhe Institute of Technology (KIT). He is the Head of the Marketing & Sales Research Group and Co-Director of the Institute of Information Systems and Marketing (IISM). Before, he worked as professor of marketing and innovation in the School of Business and Economics at the University of Passau.

Andreas Kleinn is a Researcher at the Institute for Entrepreneurship, Technology Management, and Innovation (EnTechnon), Karlsruhe Institute of Technology (KIT). He is also the founding partner of the marketing and consulting company Klai GmbH.

Panagiotis Kyriakopoulos is a Research Fellow at the Enterprise Research Centre of Warwick Business School. He holds a PhD in Management from the Adam Smith Business School, University of Glasgow. He has published papers in leading international refereed journals such as the *Journal of Business Research*.

June Y. Lee is an Associate Professor of Entrepreneurship and Innovation at the University of San Francisco School of Management. She received her MS and PhD degrees in Management Science from Stanford University.

Dr. Sarah Manthey holds a PhD from the Institute of Entrepreneurship, Technology Management, and Innovation, where she developed the Technology Application Selection Framework, designed to assist researchers in exploiting and commercializing new technologies. She has advised and coached aspiring startups and is an experienced lecturer and coach in the field of technology entrepreneurship.

Gérard Martorell is an Associate Professor of Entrepreneurship and Capstone Projects at Xi'an Jiaotong Liverpool University (XJTLU), China, and is associated with many universities globally. He has founded five startups, holds three patents on biocides, and has more than 23 years of experience in marketing and general management of big transnationals.

Rod B. McNaughton is a Professor of Entrepreneurship and the Academic Director of the Centre for Innovation and Entrepreneurship at the University of Auckland Business School. His research on the rapid internationalization of knowledge-intensive new ventures aims to influence policymaking, guide startup strategies, and inform educational programs to improve the growth and success of SMEs.

J. Mark Munoz is a tenured Full Professor of International Business at Millikin University a former Visiting Fellow at the Kennedy School of Government at Harvard University. He is the editor of the Routledge books, *The Economics of Cryptocurrencies* (2020), *Global Business Intelligence* (2017), and *Advances in Geoeconomics* (2017).

Rafael Augusto Seixas is a Professor of Innovation and Technology Management at the Federal University of Minas Gerais, Brazil. His research area focuses on resources for innovation, venture capital funds, agile methodologies, and organizational innovation.

Saadeddine Shehab is the Associate Director of Assessment and Research at the Siebel Center for Design, University of Illinois at Urbana-Champaign. His research primarily focuses on students' collaborative problem-solving processes and the teacher's role in STEM classrooms that integrate design-based learning.

Rachel Switzky is the Inaugural Director of the Siebel Center for Design at the University of Illinois at Urbana-Champaign. The Siebel Center for Design is dedicated to practicing, modeling, and teaching design thinking, leveraging human-centered design principles to reimagine the campus, community, and the world at large.

Orestis Terzidis heads the Institute for Entrepreneurship, Technology Management, and Innovation (EnTechnon) at the Karlsruhe Institute of Technology (KIT). His research interests focus on educating entrepreneurs and supporting them in the various aspects of their endeavors.

Alexander Tittel holds a PhD in Economics and Management from the Karlsruhe Institute of Technology (KIT). His research focuses on entrepreneurship education, particularly in entrepreneurial competencies and using Ikigai in educational settings.

Yumao Wang, MD, is senior editor, holds a Major in Pharmaceutical Chemistry and graduated from Peking Union Medical College (PUMC). Since 2012, he has been working with Intellectual Property Publishing House Co., Ltd., and studying Intellectual property coursework held by Cardozo-CIPTC. He published a book series about Intellectual Property of Pharmaceutics.

Christoph P. Wessendorf is an accomplished tech entrepreneur and execution-driven senior manager with a deep passion for technology. He holds a doctorate from the Karlsruhe Institute of Technology (KIT), where his research focused on the valuation of early stage technology ventures.

Dr. Yue Xu is a Senior Lecturer in Cardiff Business School. She is an active and passionate researcher on the topic of outward direct investment by emerging market multinational firms. She published in journals and books widely exploring institutional theories, FDI theories, and recently the impact of digital technology on business environment.

Yu Wei Ye is a PhD candidate in the interdisciplinary specialization of Strategy, Innovation, and Entrepreneurship. Before pursuing her PhD, Yu Wei accumulated substantial industry and management experience in the financial industry.

Part I

Introduction

1   Introduction

Technology Entrepreneurship

J. Mark Munoz and Orestis Terzidis

1.1 Introduction

Technology has become an important business driver and economic contributor around the world. The global technology industry is valued at $5.2 trillion, with the US contributing about 35%, Asia 32%, and Europe 22%. In the US alone, the sector added over 264,000 jobs to 12 million workers in the tech industry in 2022 (Flynn, 2023).

Technology comes in different variations and forms, including fields such as mechanical engineering, medical engineering, information and communication technology, manufacturing, and electronics. Likens (2022), in a PWC report, cited eight high-potential emerging technologies as artificial intelligence, augmented reality, blockchain, drones, Internet of Things, robotics, 3D printing, and virtual reality.

As technology gains prominence in business and society, entrepreneurs leverage their knowledge and technical expertise worldwide to create and build ventures. In fact, ventures around the world received over $415 Billion in funding in 2022 (CB Insights, 2023). Over 5 million start-ups were created in the US alone in 2022 (Tanzi, 2023).

Technology entrepreneurship refers to business activities that are based on new scientific insights and new technical developments. It is the process by which enterprising teams and individuals convert new technical knowledge into products and services (Shane and Venkataraman, 2000). It typically requires investing in an endeavor where people and other resources are utilized to create value (Bailetti, 2012). Technology is reconfigured to create a value proposition (Oestreicher-Singer and Zalmanson, 2013).

Its practice largely encompasses entrepreneurial pursuits in engineering and science, where progress opens novel ways of creating value. It constitutes a blend of different concepts and is closely aligned with the notion of innovation (Nacu and Avasilcai, 2014).

Entrepreneurs are increasingly drawn to technology enterprises (Hus et al., 2007). Activities relating to technology entrepreneurship are heavily anchored on intellectual property, although it may also make sense to pursue an open technology strategy consciously. Entrepreneurial activities in technological domains lead to ventures with unique characteristics. In the digital realm, its practice has been applied across multiple disciplines (Zaheer et al., 2019). By the nature of its contribution to some level of innovation and progress, positive economic impact may materialize (Szabo and Herman, 2012).

Technology ventures sometimes face the challenge of successful execution and may have a lower survival rate (Pisano, 2006; Nesheim, 1997). One of the key obstacles is the long duration of the path toward commercialization (Goldner et al., 2009). The knowledge and expertise of the start-up team on the impact of the technology on the market are important considerations for

DOI: 10.4324/9781003341284-2

venture success (Gruber et al., 2013). In addition, access to the right stakeholders is essential (Pahnke et al., 2015).

Technology entrepreneurship may be practiced in a variety of settings, ranging from young start-up firms to non-profit organizations to mature multinational corporations. The common criteria defining its practice are leveraging technology and resources with the intent of commercialization under the conditions of risk and uncertainty. Liu et al. (2005) highlighted the importance of structures and resources in technology entrepreneurship.

Technology ventures differ from other types of ventures due to their heavy reliance on technology. In a technology-reliant scenario, entrepreneurs must navigate multiple challenges simultaneously. For example, while they learn and develop their technology, efforts also have to be directed toward understanding consumers, the market, regulatory and legal environment, and competition, among others. In addition, innovation is necessary (Nacu and Avasilcai, 2014).

Similar to other types of ventures, the performance of technology ventures is affected by both the internal and external environment. The internal environment refers to the personnel, policies, technology systems, and procedures they have in place, while the external environment refers to customers, suppliers, investors, competitors, government, and other venture stakeholders. Entrepreneurs need to balance the demands of both environments carefully. Jelinek (1996) indicated the value of a coordinated effort in technology entrepreneurship.

As an enterprise is built, technology entrepreneurs need to plot out a successful mix of strategies to be successful, including value creation, business model development, talent acquisition and development, marketing, and fundraising. Nichols and Armstrong (2003) underscored the relevance of management in technology entrepreneurship.

The practice of technology entrepreneurship has its own mix of challenges and opportunities. The ability to learn, act, and apply in a simultaneous and timely manner, especially for those in the science and engineering fields, can provide a solid framework for success.

1.2 Book Objective

There is a scarcity of literature on technology entrepreneurship (Shane and Venkataraman, 2003; Zhang et al., 2008). Compiling the essential research knowledge about principles and practices in technology entrepreneurship is an important goal of this book. There is a need to systematically present theory and practice for entrepreneurs coming from an engineering or scientific background. This book aims to assemble a comprehensive overview of the subject and combine it with expert viewpoints to compile available knowledge and approaches, enabling engineers and scientists to develop entrepreneurial initiatives.

1.3 Book Organization and Future Directions

The pace, scope, and breadth of technology entrepreneurship will likely increase in the future. The insights and ideas from this book will help current and future entrepreneurs navigate a growingly complex and challenging environment and find pathways to success.

This book is designed as a resource for the identification and exploitation of opportunities in the field of science and engineering-driven ventures. Drawing on academic research and practitioner insights, the book offers clear conceptual frameworks and empirical findings and combines them with practical approaches that junior or experienced entrepreneurs may use. The aim is to combine an edited volume's variety and richness of perspectives with a consistent and integrated content architecture. In this way, the plan combines the depth of expert knowledge with a comprehensive view of the needs of scientists, engineers, executives, and entrepreneurs worldwide. The goal is to create a resource that supports readers in the development of the relevant entrepreneurial competencies.

The book will be of value to a multitude of audiences. Academics will find the featured approaches and cases helpful in theory development. Scientists and engineers will find fresh perspectives in the practice of entrepreneurship. Executives and entrepreneurs will find some of the ideas helpful in business planning. Government officials, policymakers, and consultants will be able to develop better policies and guidelines for the organizations they serve.

The book intends to expand the discussion of technology entrepreneurship globally and solicit contributors' views and expertise worldwide. As a result, this pioneering book project sets a solid foundation and framework for the practice of technology entrepreneurship. Furthermore, it provides the basis for future research on the topic.

The book is organized into six themes and 18 chapters: **Introduction** Chapter 1 Introduction (*J. Mark Munoz and Orestis Terzidis*), Chapter 2 Basic concepts and facts (*Guy Bate and Lisa Callagher*), Chapter 3 Entrepreneurial competencies (*Darsel Keane and Rod McNaughton*), **From Technology to Value** Chapter 4 Intellectual property *(Yue Xu and Yumao Wang)*, Chapter 5 From technology to value proposition (*Dilek Cetindamar Konazoglu and Sarah Manthey*), Chapter 6 Product development (*Saadeddine Shehab, Rachel Switzky, and Keilin Jahnke*), **Strategy and Business Model** Chapter 7 Values, Competencies, Vision, and Mission (*Panagiotis Kyriakopoulos and Alexander Tittel*), Chapter 8 Designing the business model (*Lorena Berrón Cadenas and June Y. Lee*), Chapter 9 Entrepreneurial decision making (*Marcos Hashimoto*), **Entrepreneurial Marketing** Chapter 10 Market and competitor analysis (*Gerard Martorell*), Chapter 11 Customer development and lean start-up (*Kathleen Allen*), Chapter 12 Pricing, placement and promotion for technology ventures (*Martin Klarmann, Orestis Terzidis and Andreas Kleinn*), **Funding a Venture** Chapter 13 Financing technology ventures (*Orestis Terzidis and J. Mark Munoz*), Chapter 14 Funding process (*Christoph Wessendorf*), Chapter 15 Capital provider perspective (*Yu Wei Ye*), **Team and Organization** Chapter 16 Team building (*Margaret Goralski and Krystyna Gorniak-Kocikowska*), Chapter 17 Entrepreneurial leadership (*Edward Agbai*), and Chapter 18 Building an organization (*Rafael Augusto Seixas Reis de Paula and Roger (Rongxin) Chen*).

Science and engineering constitute an important impetus toward humanity's and society's progress. The by-products of science and engineering can contribute to sustainable development in many diverse and impactful ways (Johnson and Schaltegger, 2020). Unlocking the potential of technical progress while mitigating possible undesirable effects is the key agenda of responsible entrepreneurship and innovation. It is equally important to understand the commercial viability of the undertakings. With the growing prominence of technology in our contemporary world, technology entrepreneurship that responsibly supports, nurtures, and enhances science and engineering will be vital for the next generations.

References

Bailetti, T. (2012). Technology entrepreneurship: Overview, definition, and distinctive aspects. *Technology Innovation Management Review*, 2(2), 5–12.

CB Insights (2023). State of the venture 2022 report. Accessed June 9, 2023. Available at: https://www.cbinsights.com/research/report/venture-trends-2022/

Flynn, J. (2023). 25 trending tech industry statistics. Accessed June 9, 2023. Available at: https://www.zippia.com/advice/tech-industry-statistics/

Golder, P. N., Shacham, R., and Mitra, D. (2009). Innovations' origins: When, by whom, and how are radical innovations developed? *Marketing Science*, 28(1), 166–179.

Gruber, M., MacMillan, I. C., and Thompson, J. D. (2013). Escaping the prior knowledge corridor: What shapes the number and variety of market opportunities identified before market entry of technology start-ups? *Organization Science*, 24, 280–300.

Hsu, D. H., Roberts, E. B., and Eesley, C. E. (2007). Entrepreneurs from technology-based universities: Evidence from MIT. *Research Policy*, 36(5), 768–788.

Jelinek, M. (1996). "Thinking technology" in mature industry firms: Understanding technology entrepreneurship. *International Journal of Technology Management*, 11(7, 8), 799–813.

Johnson, Matthew P., and Schaltegger, S. (2020). Entrepreneurship for sustainable development: A review and multilevel causal mechanism framework. *Entrepreneurship Theory and Practice*, 44(6), 1141–1173.

Likens, S. (2022). Eight emerging technologies and six convergence themes you need to know about. PWC. Accessed June 9, 2023. Available at: https://www.pwc.com/us/en/tech-effect/emerging-tech/essential-eight-technologies.html

Liu, T., Chu, Y.-Y., Hung, S., and Wu, S. (2005). Technology entrepreneurial styles: A comparison of UMC and TSMC. *Technology Management*, 29(1–2), 92–115.

Nacu, C. M., and Avasilcai, S. (2014). Technological ecopreneurship: Conceptual approaches. *Procedia-Social and Behavioral Sciences*, 124, 229–235.

Nesheim, J. (1997). *High-Tech Start-Up*. Saratoga: Electronic Trend Publication.

Nichols, S. P., and Armstrong, N. E. (2003). Engineering entrepreneurship: Does entrepreneurship have a role in engineering education. *IEEE Antennas and Propagation Magazine*, 45(1), 134–138.

Oestreicher-Singer, G., and Zalmanson, L. (2013). Content or community? A digital business strategy for content providers in the social age. *MIS Quarterly*, 37, 591–616.

Pahnke, E. C., Katila, R., and Eisenhardt, K. M. (2015). Who takes you to the dance? How partners' institutional logics influence innovation in young firms. *Administrative Science Quarterly*, 60(4), 596–633.

Pisano, G. (2006). *Science Business: The Science, Reality and Future of Biotech*. Boston: Harvard Business School Press.

Shane, S., and Venkataraman, S. (2000). The promise of entrepreneurship as a field of research. *Academy of Management Review*, 25(1), 217–226.

Shane, S., and Venkataraman, S. (2003). Guest editors' introduction to the special issue on technology entrepreneurship. *Research Policy*, 32, 181–184.

Szabo, Z. K., and Herman, E. (2012). Innovative entrepreneurship for economic development in EU. *Procedia Economics and Finance*, 3, 268–275.

Tanzi, A. (2023). Over 5 million new US start-up show covid-era boom has legs. *Bloomberg*. Accessed June 9, 2023. Available at: https://www.bloomberg.com/news/articles/2023-01-17/over-5-million-new-us-startups-show-covid-era-boom-has-legs#xj4y7vzkg

Zaheer, H., Breyer, Y., and Dumay, J. (2019). Digital entrepreneurship: An interdisciplinary structured literature review and research agenda. *Technological Forecasting and Social Change*, Elsevier, 148(C), 119735. https://doi.org/10.1016/j.techfore.2019.119735.

Zhang, G., Peng, X., and Li, J. (2008). Technological entrepreneurship and policy environment: A case of China. *Journal of Small Business and Enterprise Development*, 15, 733–751.

2 The Fundamentals of Technology Entrepreneurship

Guy W. Bate and Lisa Callagher

When thinking about technology, we often emphasize the work of well-established companies (e.g., large firms in industries such as software, pharmaceuticals, or aerospace engineering). However, we also need to recognize that many new technologies are developed and commercialized outside these corporate environments by scientists and engineers as technology entrepreneurs.

We can think of technology entrepreneurship as the range of capabilities and collaborative processes that permit the mobilization of new scientific and technological ideas, translating and transforming them into something (e.g., a new product or service) that creates, delivers, and captures value (Majdouline et al., 2022). This chapter introduces fundamental terms and concepts in technology entrepreneurship to offer a broad sense of such themes. Notable terms are italicized. Later chapters will then dive more deeply into these areas.

2.1 Introductory Themes

2.1.1 Innovation and Technology

The contemporary understanding of entrepreneurship originates in the notion of *creative destruction* coined by Joseph Schumpeter. He considered that economies experience constant change, where entrepreneurial action challenges existing market orders and disrupts competition (Schumpeter, 1942). Entrepreneurs embrace such changes to innovate and find new ways of generating value.

Today, the importance of technology entrepreneurship extends beyond just issues of market economies and competition. Technology innovation is vital to sustainable development in a complex contemporary world troubled by environmental, social, and economic concerns (Schaltegger & Burritt, 2018).

2.1.2 Technology Entrepreneurs

Successful entrepreneurs can recognize and seize opportunities that may not be evident to others. They are skilled in solving problems and generating creative solutions (Mitchelmore & Rowley, 2010). They develop a mindset that is comfortable with uncertainty and deviating from conventions, and they thrive through challenge (Kuratko et al., 2021). New ventures can struggle to survive, and failure rates are high (Soto-Simeone et al., 2020). So, resilience, perseverance, and a desire to learn, practice, and adapt are essential attributes (Mitchelmore & Rowley, 2010).

DOI: 10.4324/9781003341284-3

Notably, entrepreneurs also collaborate. Technology entrepreneurship is usually a team-based endeavor that brings together people with different knowledge, ideas, and perspectives (Bailetti, 2012). So, while team members share a passion for developing new technological opportunities, they usually have complementary experience spanning—for example—science, management, commerce, and finance. Entrepreneurial competencies and capabilities will be discussed further in Chapter 3.

2.1.3 Entrepreneurial Ecosystems

However, collaboration does not end at the team level. Given that technology entrepreneurship can be a source of societal value, several organization types (both public and private) work together in a mutually supportive manner. These collaborations can lead to the development of *entrepreneurial ecosystems*: environments that foster innovation, development, and growth by bringing together entrepreneurs, universities, incubators, venture capital firms, consultants, lawyers, and other contributors (e.g., Majdouline et al., 2022). Thriving geographic hubs for innovation, such as Silicon Valley, have emerged through such ecosystem development.

2.1.4 Uncertainty and Risk

Technology entrepreneurs operate in *uncertain* environments, which means entrepreneurial teams must bear *risk*. Indeed, some scholars suggest that successful entrepreneurs may more readily accept or accommodate risk than others (Cramer et al., 2002).

The economist Frank Knight distinguished between risk and uncertainty. In *uncertain* situations, the decision-maker cannot know or make any prediction in advance (referred to as unknowable information). In contrast, when it comes to *risk*, the decision-maker can estimate the *probability* of a particular outcome (Knight, 1921). Thus, entrepreneurs can, to some extent, manage risk through research and analysis, but uncertainty can only be coped with by preparing for contingencies. To help navigate these issues, scholars have attended to a variety of ways to analyze and categorize the risks and uncertainties associated with the technology (Kapoor & Klueter, 2021) as well as with the technology venture (Packard et al., 2017).

2.1.5 Effectuation

Technology entrepreneurship is not linear. Entrepreneurial teams do not necessarily start with concrete ideas or goals and then systematically work toward these. Instead, they often improvise, constantly assessing and reassessing how to use their strengths and whatever resources they have at hand (or can access) to develop opportunities and react creatively to contingencies. Saras Sarasvathy calls this an *effectuation* logic (Sarasvathy, 2009). A similar logic applies at the ecosystem level: the ecosystems in which entrepreneurial teams are embedded shape, and are shaped by, the geographically located resources at hand (Hubner et al., 2022).

While entrepreneurial processes are non-linear and iterative, successful entrepreneurs are usually quite thorough in deciding which new opportunities to pursue and how they should do this. Accordingly, Section 2.2 describes ways of exploring and evaluating new opportunities. Then, Section 2.3 considers the decisions involved in realizing value from these opportunities. Finally, Section 2.4 provides an overview of one crucial path for realizing value from technology—the new venture.

2.2 Exploring and Evaluating Opportunities

2.2.1 Sources of Opportunity

Scholars generally conceptualize opportunities in three ways: discovery, creation, and actualization (Ramoglou & Gartner, 2022). The *discovery view* asserts that entrepreneurship aims to recognize opportunities to profit, implicitly assuming that opportunities somehow exist in some latent form and await discovery. The creation view claims that opportunities are created by the actions of entrepreneurs, assuming that the actions (agency) of entrepreneurs are crucial (Alvarez & Barney, 2007). The discovery view is consistent with what technology innovation scholars describe as "technology push"—science- and research-driven developments of a technological nature drive innovation. In contrast, the assumptions of the *creation view* are more consistent with the "demand pull" idea in technology innovation, whereby unmet customer problems are met with opportunities created by entrepreneurs.

The third and emerging view conceptualizes opportunities as the actualization of profits by combining structural conditions and entrepreneurial actions through new ideas or products (Ramoglou & Tsang, 2018). This *actualization view* assumes a social constructivist perspective. It is consistent with technology innovation scholarship that shows technology push and market pull forces are on a continuum (Brem & Voigt, 2009), such that opportunities come about through an interplay between scientific ideas and changes in the market environment (Khilji et al., 2006). Here, technology entrepreneurs construct or shape favorable circumstances to profit from technology innovation.

2.2.2 The Value of an Opportunity

Opportunities exist because someone perceives them as offering value. But what do we mean by the *"value"* of an opportunity? Commonly, we refer to the potential *commercial* value. Entrepreneurs often thus express value in terms of future financial returns. However, broader economic, social, and environmental impacts are other ways to communicate value. Indeed, this is important as technology innovations have tremendous potential to contribute to a sustainable future (Schaltegger & Burritt, 2018).

2.2.3 Value Propositions

How do entrepreneurs think about creating value? One common means is defining a value proposition—a clear statement of who might gain value and how that might take place.

The notion of the value proposition is helpful as it brings together various considerations that span the pulls and pushes between market and technology (see above). Alexander Osterwalder has formalized these into the *Value Proposition Canvas*, a visual template that helps explore, shape, and refine value propositions (Osterwalder et al., 2015). Specifically, the canvas invites the entrepreneur to think through the *pains* that customers or stakeholders may experience and the *gains* they expect or need. The canvas, therefore, encourages entrepreneurs to consider ways to *create gains* that customers want and that *relieve (or remove) pains* that customers will pay to address.

2.2.4 Is It Worth It?

Technology entrepreneurs must also ask if the opportunity—based on its value proposition—is worth pursuing, given the investments required (Day, 2007). A key issue is the *market size* for the opportunity: is it big enough to warrant the necessary time and investment? If not, it may be better to consider other possibilities.

A technology may serve the *total addressable* (or total available) market (TAM). However, not all of this market may be reachable, so only part of the TAM may be the *target market* for the opportunity. This may be due to competition. Competitor technologies (available now or in the future) may limit the *market potential*. Each competitor will have its value proposition; it may therefore be important to consider competitive *positioning* as part of evaluating opportunities.

2.3 Exploiting Opportunities

2.3.1 Intellectual Property

Entrepreneurs will seek to protect the knowledge that underpins a technological invention or opportunity to limit the risk that it can be used (*appropriated*) by others. Once legally protected, the entrepreneurial team has *intellectual property rights* (IPRs) over this asset, which means that they hold a monopoly right to capture value and profit from their opportunity for a given period and in each jurisdiction. However, such protections require inventors to protect their rights through civil action. Thus, protecting IPRs requires an institutional framework to support such proceedings and the willingness of the inventor to defend their rights.

IPRs take several forms. *Patents* grant a period of *exclusivity* for the knowledge asset, which discourages competitors from making or selling competing intellectual property (but possibly only for specific applications or uses) for a defined period. *Trademarks* protect intangible assets such as the names and logos associated with products, services, and companies. *Copyrights* prevent others from copying or publishing *original works*, including books, music, and—importantly for some technology entrepreneurs—software products and computer code. In the case of copyright, while the original material is protected, the ideas underpinning it are not. The types of IPRs commonly used vary across sectors. Patents are common in chemicals, pharmaceuticals, and manufacturing sectors as they make clear the novel aspects of the invention to prospective buyers or licensors. In contrast, they are rare in other sectors like software, which are built on intangible ideas, the documentation of which would make them easy to copy (Orsenigo & Sterzi, 2010).

Finally, it is essential to note that intellectual property can also take on more informal forms. Entrepreneurial teams aim to keep their knowledge secret (i.e., *trade secrets*). As their organizations develop specific capabilities, they can hide their tacit know-how, making it harder for others to copy or imitate.

2.3.2 Business Models and Markets for Ideas

To profit from technological innovations, entrepreneurs must *create* value and *deliver* it to customers so that there is enough value to *capture* for themselves. Often, profit is the primary form of value capture, but organizations can use multiple mechanisms for this (Michel, 2014). These three elements (value creation, delivery, and capture) are the essence of the *business model* (Casadesus-Masanel & Ricart, 2010; Osterwalder & Pigneur, 2010; Shafer et al., 2005; Teece, 2010).

Not all entrepreneurs pursue products for end customers. Thus, the business model informs the difference between realizing value in a "product-market" or a "market for ideas" (Gans & Stern, 2003). In the former case, entrepreneurs will invest resources to develop, manufacture, and ultimately sell the product or service to the end-user *(customer)* and compete within the *product market*. In the latter case, the entrepreneurial team cooperates with *partners* to commercialize the technology. The team thus seeks to sell their *ideas* to other teams and companies (thus competing in the *market for ideas*) rather than to sell a finished product to customers (Natalicchio et al., 2014).

2.3.3 Business Model Options

Based on this thinking, there are some general business model options. First, the idea and knowledge—as captured and protected in a patent—can be *licensed* (a *license* being a grant of rights to commercialize) to another company (e.g., as part of a *partnership* or *alliance*). This other company then takes responsibility for developing and marketing the product or service (i.e., *creating* and *delivering* value into the product market). The entrepreneurial team (the *licensor*) *captures* value by receiving payments from the licensing company (the *licensee*).

These payments may take the form of *upfront payments, milestone payments* (associated with reaching agreed points in product development), or *royalties* (a proportion of sales or profit) when the technology reaches the product market. In addition, the entrepreneurial team may retain rights to specific uses for the technology to commercialize independently of the licensee. Alternatively, the entrepreneurial team can sell the IPRs (and potentially any associated business operations) to another company (an *acquisition*). In this case, the entrepreneurs capture value for themselves through this sale. However, they generally lose any future rights to commercialize the technology.

2.3.4 Business Model Design

Analytical tools are available to think more specifically about business model structure. For example, Osterwalder's *Value Proposition Canvas* (see above) and *Business Model Canvas* (Osterwalder and Pigneur, 2010) encourage entrepreneurs to think through vital elements for value realization. These elements are partners, activities, resources, value propositions, customer relations, channels, customer segments, cost structures, and revenue streams.

Some of these elements may be more relevant for established businesses than for technology entrepreneurs, so Maurya developed a *Lean Canvas*, which replaced "partners" with "problem", "activities" with "solution" "resources" with "metrics" and "customer relations" with "unfair advantage" (Maurya, 2022). The *Lean Canvas* aims to capture and consider the specific uncertainties and risks inherent in entrepreneurial activities.

2.3.5 Experimentation and Learning

Ries (2011) and Blank (2013) also discuss *lean* business model development methods. Working from the principles of the Business Model Canvas—together with those from lean manufacturing and agile software development—such methods encourage entrepreneurs to adapt the business model as they learn (*pivoting*). Consistent with *effectuation*, the value creation, delivery, and capture process is thus iterative. For example, in developing a technological solution or product, entrepreneurs first aim to meet the needs of early customers with a *minimum viable product*. They then learn from this process, refining products and business model components to serve changing and expanded markets. The ongoing experimentation and discovery process is analogous to work in science that checks assumptions against a null hypothesis (McGrath, 2010). A later chapter considers business model design and development in greater depth.

2.4 The Technology Venture

Establishing a new venture is the most common way of exploiting significant technological opportunities (Shane, 2001). New ventures support economic development, provide a substantial source of new and knowledge-based employment opportunities, and offer much-needed solutions to environmental and social problems (Schaltegger & Burritt, 2018). New ventures have thus long been a focus for entrepreneurship scholars and policy-makers for these reasons (Shepherd et al., 2021). Given the importance of the venturing path, this section offers some introductory detail. Later chapters will expand upon issues that include venture formation, funding, and organization.

2.4.1 *Plans and Pitches*

As we have indicated, technology entrepreneurship is based on learning, iteration, and experimentation. However, setting up and running a new venture requires careful organization and coordination. So, there are times when entrepreneurs need to be more prescriptive about evaluating, documenting, and presenting their business ideas (e.g., when they need to win support from potential investors, partners, collaborators, and future employees). Planning can also help founders take stock of their situation, share and coordinate knowledge, and reflect upon their position and future trajectory.

Thus, entrepreneurs will usually put together a *business plan*. A plan can be a detailed written report or a slide presentation. The range and depth of information covered will depend on the audience (for example, investors may need far more detail on financial elements than a potential partner might), but Table 2.1 lists some standard components. Zacharakis (2009) advises entrepreneurs to tailor their plans so that it presents a story to the reader that makes sense to them, given their specific motives and interests.

To gain support, the entrepreneurial team may use *pitching* to convincingly discuss and defend their business plan (or its elements) with others. Relatedly, the term *elevator pitch* refers to a summary story that presents a synopsis for supporting the venture. The idea is to gain initial interest from potential investors or collaborators (for instance, during a chance meeting) as a segue to further discussions.

2.4.2 *Resourcing the Venture*

As the venture moves along the commercialization pathway, new skills and knowledge will be required (Lubik & Garnsey, 2016). The founding team will need resources that are beyond their immediate control. Necessary capabilities may span, for example, management, finance, research and development, engineering, quality assurance, law, manufacturing, human resources, marketing, and sales.

There are various means to support this expansion. Entrepreneurs can choose to employ new staff (*hiring*), they can contract work to consultants or other suppliers (*outsourcing*), or they

Table 2.1 Some components of a business plan

Executive summary	*Market/competitor analysis*
The industry context and need	Entrepreneurial/founding team
The opportunity within this context	Organizational and resource needs
The technology	Uncertainties and risks
The value proposition	Financial plan for the venture

can develop the skills of existing staff (*training*) to the extent that such staff is available. The advantage of hiring (and training) is that resources can be committed to the venture, and skill development will strengthen the firm's operations. However, outsourcing may offer greater flexibility as the appropriate mix of skills can be brought into the organization as needed.

Building partnerships and managing effective networks of working relations with other firms can also facilitate access to complementary resources and skills (Paquin & Howard-Grenville, 2013). As the venture's needs and business model change over time, so will the balance between building internal resources and working with external parties (Lubik & Garnsey, 2016).

2.4.3 Financing

It may be some time before a venture can fund itself through profits (assuming it ever can). Therefore, access to money or external equity is critical. Indeed, running out of cash or failure to secure external equity are main reasons for new venture failure (CB Insights Research, 2021). So, what sources of financing are available?

Entrepreneurs can get others to loan them money (*debt financing*) (Shulman, 2009) or to invest in their business to gain a stake in its ownership (*equity financing*) (Bygrave, 2009). In the early stages, some entrepreneurs may self-finance or take on informal funding in the form of loans from family and friends. Others may engage in *bootstrapping* (i.e., they support themselves by "pulling themselves up by their bootstraps"). Bootstrapping involves funding the business by reinvesting cash from growing revenues. Government grants can support this process in that businesses must often commit in-kind resources and expertise to match public funding. Entrepreneurs may also secure equity finance from wealthy individuals (*angel investors*). This is called *seed funding*.

As a venture's financial needs grow, entrepreneurs may seek larger tranches of equity financing. This often comes from venture capital firms, which manage significant investment funds, or large firms who have corporate investment schemes. The level of investment required typically increases as the venture develops. Investors commonly refer to the incremental stages of investment as *Series A, Series B*, and *Series C* financing rounds. Depending on the business model choices as the venture unfolds, entrepreneurs might seek funding from other companies who then act as investors or are partners in strategic alliances. They may raise funds by listing on a public share market (an *initial public offering* or IPO) or by generating income through deals.

All types of investors want to know how they will extract their investments and their share of the profit. Ultimately, the entrepreneurial team and the investors who join them along the journey will look at exit strategies. Public listings and strategic sales offer pathways for investors to exit the venture.

2.5 Conclusion

Technology entrepreneurship involves developing and implementing new technological ideas through new business ventures to create, deliver, and capture value. It often requires collaboration among entrepreneurs, universities, incubators, venture capital firms, consultants, and other organizations and operates in uncertain environments that involve risk. Successful technology entrepreneurs are skilled in recognizing and seizing opportunities, generating creative solutions to problems, and collaborating with others. They also possess resilience, perseverance, and adaptability and must be willing to accept or accommodate risk. Technology entrepreneurship can have economic, environmental, and societal benefits and is vital to sustainable development.

Opportunities for technology entrepreneurship can arise through a mix of "technology push", where new scientific research and inventions drive new ideas, and "demand-pull", where entrepreneurs develop technological solutions to the identified customer or stakeholder problems. Entrepreneurs express the value of an opportunity in terms of its potential commercial value and its broader economic, social, and environmental impacts. Entrepreneurs can explore and refine their ideas for value creation using a tool such as the Value Proposition Canvas, which asks them to consider the pains and gains experienced by customers or stakeholders and the technological product or service that can address them. Entrepreneurs must also consider whether the opportunity is worth pursuing based on the investments required and the size and reachability of the market, including the potential competition.

Intellectual property refers to the knowledge assets entrepreneurs seek to protect to limit the risk of others using or appropriating them. This protection can include patents, trademarks, copyrights, or trade secrets. It grants the entrepreneurial team exclusive rights to capture value and profit from their opportunity for a defined period and in a specific jurisdiction. Technology entrepreneurship involves creating and delivering value to customers and stakeholders while also capturing value for the entrepreneurs. The business model for doing so can include competing in a product market or a market for ideas. In the latter case, the entrepreneurial team may license their ideas to another company or sell the intellectual property and potentially any associated business operations to another company. Alternatively, the entrepreneurial team may commercialize the technology through a venture firm or spin-off company. The business model also considers the value proposition, the target market, and the resources required to bring the technology to market.

Establishing a new venture is a common way entrepreneurs exploit significant technological opportunities. Doing so supports economic development, provides employment, and offers solutions to environmental and social problems. To gain support for their venture, entrepreneurs may create a business plan, a written or slide presentation outlining the business's details and potential. They may also have to pitch or present a summary story to potential investors or collaborators. Resources, including skills and knowledge, are necessary for the venture to expand and can be acquired through hiring, outsourcing, training, or building partnerships and networks with other firms. Financing is also critical and can be obtained through various means, such as personal savings, loans, grants, venture capital, and crowdfunding, and may involve negotiating equity stakes or royalty agreements with investors. The venture's legal structure and governance must also be considered, including intellectual property, contracts, and regulations. Later chapters will further develop these themes.

References

Alvarez, S. A., & Barney, J. B. (2007). Discovery and creation: Alternative theories of entrepreneurial action. *Strategic Entrepreneurship Journal*, 1(1–2), 11–26.

Bailetti, T. (2012). Technology entrepreneurship: Overview, definition, and distinctive aspects. *Technology Innovation Management Review*, 2(2), 5–12.

Blank, S. (2013). Why the lean start-up changes everything. *Harvard Business Review*, 91(5), 64–72.

Brem, A., & Voigt, K.-I. (2009). Integration of market pull and technology push in the corporate front end and innovation management—Insights from the German software industry. *Technovation*, 29(5), 351–367.

Bygrave, W. D. (2009). Equity financing: Informal investment, venture capital, and harvesting. In W. D. Bygrave & A. Zacharakis (Eds.), *The Portable MBA in Entrepreneurship* (pp. 161–195). John Wiley & Sons, Ltd.

Casadesus-Masanell, R., & Ricart, J. E. (2010). From strategy to business models and onto tactics. *Long Range Planning*, 43(2), 195–215.

CB Insights Research (2021). The top 12 reasons startups fail. https://www.cbinsights.com/research/report/startup-failure-reasons-top/

Cramer, J. S., Hartog, J., Jonker, N., & Van Praag, C. M. (2002). Low risk aversion encourages the choice for entrepreneurship: An empirical test of a truism. *Journal of Economic Behavior & Organization*, 48(1), 29–36.

Day, G. S. (2007). Is it real? Can we win? Is it worth doing? *Harvard Business Review*, 85(12), 110–120.

Gans, J. S., & Stern, S. (2003). The product market and the market for "ideas": Commercialization strategies for technology entrepreneurs. *Research Policy*, 32(2), 333–350.

Hubner, S., Most, F., Wirtz, J., & Auer, C. (2022). Narratives in entrepreneurial ecosystems: Drivers of effectuation versus causation. *Small Business Economics*, 59(1), 211–242.

Kapoor, R., & Klueter, T. (2021). Unbundling and managing uncertainty surrounding emerging technologies. *Strategy Science*, 6(1), 62–74.

Khilji, S. E., Mroczkowski, T., & Bernstein, B. (2006). From invention to innovation: Toward developing an integrated innovation model for biotech firms. *Journal of Product Innovation Management*, 23(6), 528–540.

Knight, F. H. (1921). *Risk, uncertainty and profit*. University of Chicago Press.

Kuratko, D. F., Fisher, G., & Audretsch, D. B. (2021). Unraveling the entrepreneurial mindset. *Small Business Economics*, 57(4), 1681–1691.

Lubik, S., & Garnsey, E. (2016). Early business model evolution in science-based ventures: The case of advanced materials. *Long Range Planning*, 49(3), 393–408.

Majdouline, I., Baz, J. E., & Jebli, F. (2022). Revisiting technological entrepreneurship research: An updated bibliometric analysis of the state of art. *Technological Forecasting and Social Change*, 179, 121589.

Maurya, A. (2022). *Running lean*. O'Reilly Media, Inc.

McGrath, R. G. (2010). Business models: A discovery driven approach. *Long Range Planning*, 43(2), 247–261.

Michel, S. (2014). Capture more value. *Harvard Business Review*, 92(10), 78–85.

Mitchelmore, S., & Rowley, J. (2010). Entrepreneurial competencies: A literature review and development agenda. *International Journal of Entrepreneurial Behavior & Research*, 16(2), 92–111.

Natalicchio, A., Messeni Petruzzelli, A., & Garavelli, A. C. (2014). A literature review on markets for ideas: Emerging characteristics and unanswered questions. *Technovation*, 34(2), 65–76.

Orsenigo, L., & Sterzi, V. (2010). Comparative study of the use of patents in different industries. *Knowledge, Internationalization and Technology Studies (KITeS)*, 33, 1–31.

Osterwalder, A., & Pigneur, Y. (2010). *Business model generation: A handbook for visionaries, game changers, and challengers*. John Wiley & Sons.

Osterwalder, A., Pigneur, Y., Bernarda, G., & Smith, A. (2015). *Value proposition design: How to create products and services customers want*. John Wiley & Sons.

Packard, M. D., Clark, B. B., & Klein, P. G. (2017). Uncertainty types and transitions in the entrepreneurial process. *Organization Science*, 28(5), 840–856.

Paquin, R. L., & Howard-Grenville, J. (2013). Blind dates and arranged marriages: Longitudinal processes of network orchestration. *Organization Studies*, 34(11), 1623–1653.

Ramoglou, S., & Gartner, W. B. (2022). A historical intervention in the "opportunity wars": Forgotten scholarship, the discovery/creation disruption, and moving forward by looking backward. *Entrepreneurship Theory and Practice*, 10422587211069310. https://doi.org/10.1177/10422587211069310

Ramoglou, S., & Tsang, E. W. K. (2018). Opportunities lie in the demand side: Transcending the discovery-creation debate. *Academy of Management Review*, 43(4), 815–818.

Ries, E. (2011). *The lean startup: How today's entrepreneurs use continuous innovation to create radically successful businesses*. Crown Business.

Sarasvathy, S. D. (2009). *Effectuation: Elements of entrepreneurial expertise*. Edward Elgar Publishing.

Schaltegger, S., & Burritt, R. (2018). Business cases and corporate engagement with sustainability: Differentiating ethical motivations. *Journal of Business Ethics*, 147(2), 241–259.

Schumpeter, J. A. (1942). *Capitalism, socialism and democracy*. George Allen & Unwin.

Shane, S. (2001). Technological opportunities and new firm creation. *Management Science*, 47(2), 205–220.

Shafer, S. M., Smith, H. J., & Linder, J. C. (2005). The power of business models. *Business Horizons*, 48(3), 199–207.

Shepherd, D. A., Souitaris, V., & Gruber, M. (2021). Creating new ventures: A review and research agenda. *Journal of Management*, 47(1), 11–42.

Shulman, J. M. (2009). Debt and other forms of financing. In *The Portable MBA in Entrepreneurship* (pp. 197–224). John Wiley & Sons, Ltd.

Soto-Simeone, A., Sirén, C., & Antretter, T. (2020). New venture survival: A review and extension. *International Journal of Management Reviews*, 22(4), 378–407.

Teece, D. J. (2010). Business models, business Strategy and innovation. *Long Range Planning*, 43(2), 172–194.

Zacharakis, A. (2009). Business planning. In William D. Bygrave and Andrew Zacharakis (Eds.), *The Portable MBA in Entrepreneurship* (pp. 109–136). John Wiley & Sons, Ltd.

3 Entrepreneurial Competencies

Darsel Keane and Rod B. McNaughton

3.1 Introduction

Entrepreneurial competencies – the skills, knowledge, and attitudes underlying successful entrepreneurial actions – are increasingly valued by founders, investors, employers, educators, and policymakers. Their interest stems from a growing appreciation of the benefits of entrepreneurial behaviour for society beyond founding companies (Mitchelmore & Rowley, 2010). While entrepreneurial competencies are crucial when founding a venture, they are also helpful when entering or re-entering the job market, launching new initiatives in established companies, for self-employment, or starting a cultural, social, or commercial venture (Bird, 2019).

Engineers and scientists often work on developing new technologies, products, or processes that have the potential to solve problems and create value. They have a unique science-led perspective and technical expertise. Entrepreneurial competencies can enhance these abilities by helping technology-oriented professionals discover unmet needs, identify potential users and stakeholders, solve problems creatively, and develop strategies for bringing their ideas to fruition. Entrepreneurial competencies also help engineers and scientists understand the business context in which they operate and how to effectively communicate and collaborate with others, such as business partners, investors, and customers. Similarly, they can help researchers collaborate with technology transfer offices, funders, and industry partners.

In the case of technology entrepreneurs, understanding, developing, and practising the competencies required to start, design, and grow a venture enhances their likelihood of success (Markman et al., 2002). If entrepreneurs know the required competencies, they can support themselves and their teams in developing or recruiting for them (Mitchelmore & Rowley, 2010). For investors and professional service providers, awareness and understanding of entrepreneurial competencies help them coach, mentor, and support entrepreneurs and their teams (Orser & Riding, 2003).

The benefits of entrepreneurship for economic development, innovation, competitiveness, and well-being are well-recognised (Lackéus, 2015). Consequently, policymakers and research organisations like universities look to increase the entrepreneurial competencies of their constituencies and staff to increase productivity, create more startups, and increase survival and growth rates (Mitchelmore & Rowley, 2010). They do this through diverse entrepreneurship education and support programmes. Consequently, there are a growing number of such programmes at all levels, from primary and secondary schools to tertiary education and among practising entrepreneurs in the community. Entrepreneurial educators work across disciplinary boundaries, helping engineers and scientists develop their entrepreneurial competencies alongside their technical knowledge and competencies.

This chapter introduces what engineers and scientists need to know about entrepreneurial competencies and how they can be developed through entrepreneurship education. It begins by

DOI: 10.4324/9781003341284-4

reviewing the meaning of competencies, followed by a summary of entrepreneurial competencies. Four entrepreneurial competency models are compared: EntreComp, 13 Entrepreneurial Competencies, KEEN Engineering Entrepreneurial Mindset and Skills, and the Entrepreneurial Competency Framework. Measuring entrepreneurial competencies is discussed, followed by how entrepreneurial competencies can be developed, especially in higher education.

3.2 What Are Competencies?

There is disagreement on the distinction between competence, competencies, and competency. These terms are often used interchangeably, as they are in this chapter. But other authors use them to mean different things. Additionally, words such as acumen, assets, capabilities, expertise, knowledge, resources, and skills describe similar concepts (Pennetta et al., 2023). Consequently, "competencies" is a fuzzy concept (Le Deist & Winterton, 2005).

In an attempt to bring definitional clarity, Komarkova et al. (2015, p. 30) noted that "knowledge and skills are common to both definitions of competence and competency and attitude, while usually directly related to the domain of competency, is increasingly becoming a crosscutting issue common to the two domains." Thus, they propose that competencies focus on actions, performance, and assessment, while competencies stress behaviours, motivation, and personal traits. The commonality between these perspectives is knowledge, skills, and attitudes.

This chapter adopts the European Parliament and Council's (2006, p. 13) definition of competencies as "…a combination of knowledge, skills, and attitudes appropriate to the context." The European Parliament and Council (2018, p. 7) further clarified each component:

- knowledge is the facts and figures, concepts, ideas, and theories that are already established and support the understanding of an area or subject,
- skills are the ability and capacity to carry out processes and use the existing knowledge to achieve results, and
- attitudes describe the disposition and mindsets to act or react to ideas, persons, or situations.

3.3 What Are Entrepreneurial Competencies?

Following this definition, entrepreneurial competencies are the specific combination of knowledge, skills, and attitudes required for successful entrepreneurship (Bird, 2019). However, like other competency sets, entrepreneurial competencies are fuzzy, with numerous definitions grounded in different disciplines, approaches, and notions of competence (Mitchelmore & Rowley, 2010).

Additionally, there is disagreement about the contexts in which entrepreneurial competencies are relevant and, thus, what constitutes successful entrepreneurship. The argument stems from the breadth of outcomes considered to be entrepreneurial. A narrow context focuses on forming new, often technology-based, ventures. However, entrepreneurship is increasingly broadly defined, focusing on value creation in many contexts. From this perspective, entrepreneurship "is when you act upon opportunities and ideas and transform them into value for others. The value generated can be commercial, cultural, or social" (Vestergaard et al., 2012, p. 13). Relatedly, there is growing evidence that the competencies needed to start a venture are helpful to a broad range of undertakings and career paths. Thus, entrepreneurial competencies are transferable (Bacigalupo et al., 2016).

While competencies are essential to getting things done, mindset – beliefs and habits of thought – are also influential, shaping perspectives and the approach to tasks and challenges.

Competencies focus on what a person can do, and mindset concerns how they think and perceive the world around them. Thus, entrepreneurial competencies and mindset impact effectiveness in different ways. Improving competencies helps people perform more effectively, while developing an entrepreneurial mindset helps them approach tasks and challenges more proactively and resiliently. Most entrepreneurship educational programmes seek to build an entrepreneurial mindset alongside more readily identified and measured competencies.

While there is no agreement on the definition of entrepreneurial competencies or the list of competencies included, research designed to identify and classify competencies has uncovered considerable overlap despite starting with different definitions of the construct. The following section summarises this work and compares four taxonomies or frameworks of entrepreneurial competencies.

3.4 Taxonomies and Frameworks of Entrepreneurial Competencies

Researchers have identified entrepreneurial competencies and grouped them in various ways (e.g., Man et al., 2002; Mitchelmore & Rowley, 2010; Rasmussen et al., 2011; Winterton, 2002). For this chapter, the nuanced differences between approaches and the taxonomies they produce are not as crucial as their commonalities and encouraging familiarity with core entrepreneurial competencies and popular classifications and frameworks. Thus, building and adapting on the work of Gianesini et al. (2018), four taxonomies are described and compared. Morris et al.'s (2013) 13 Entrepreneurial Competencies and Bacigalupo et al.'s (2016) EntreComp are retained from Gianesini et al. (2018) analysis due to their widespread acceptance and recognition as entrepreneurial competencies frameworks. KEEN and the Entrepreneurial Competence Framework are added as they are especially relevant to scientists and engineers because of their focus on technology entrepreneurship.

3.4.1 EntreComp

Perhaps the best-known framework of entrepreneurial competencies is EntreComp, with over 70 European initiatives using this framework (McCallum et al., 2018). EntreComp perceives entrepreneurial competence as an individual and collective capacity (Bacigalupo et al., 2016). EntreComp defines entrepreneurship as the overarching competence, with three underlying competence areas – ideas and opportunities, resources, and "into action." These, in turn, are broken down into 15 competencies, as in Table 3.1.

3.4.2 13 Entrepreneurial Competencies

The 13 Entrepreneurial Competencies model was created by identifying the "competencies that are most critical for entrepreneurial success" through a Delphi study of 20 successful entrepreneurs and 20 entrepreneurship educators (Morris et al., 2013, p. 353). Table 3.2 summarises the results.

3.4.3 KEEN Engineering Entrepreneurial Mindset and Skillset Framework

KEEN (Kern Entrepreneurial Engineering Network) provides a framework for developing entrepreneurially-minded engineers (KEEN, 2022). This framework comprises two elements – entrepreneurial mindset and skillset. An entrepreneurial mindset reflects three "Cs": curiosity,

Table 3.1 EntreComp competencies framework (Bacigalupo et al., 2016, p. 12)

Areas	Competences	Hints	Descriptors
1 Ideas and opportunities	1.1 Spotting opportunities	Use your imagination and abilities to identify opportunities for creating value	• Identify and seize opportunities to create value by exploring the social, cultural, and economic landscape • Identify needs and challenges that need to be met • Establish new connections and bring together scattered elements of the landscape to create opportunities to create value
	1.2 Creativity	Develop creative and purposeful ideas	• Develop several ideas and opportunities to create value, including better solutions to existing and new challenges • Explore and experiment with innovative approaches • Combine knowledge and resources to achieve valuable effects
	1.3 Vision	Work towards your vision of the future	• Imagine the future • Develop a vision to turn ideas into action • Visualise future scenarios to help guide effort and action
	1.4 Valuing ideas	Make the most of ideas and opportunities	• Judge what value is in social, cultural, and economic terms • Recognise the potential an idea has for creating value and identify suitable ways of making the most out of it
	1.5 Ethical and sustainable thinking	Assess the consequences and impact of ideas, opportunities, and actions	• Assess the consequences of ideas that bring value and the effect of entrepreneurial action on the target community, the market, society, and the environment • Reflect on how sustainable long-term social, cultural, and economic goals are and the course of action chosen • Act responsibly
2 Resources	2.1 Self-awareness and self-efficacy	Believe in yourself and keep developing	• Reflect on your needs, aspirations and wants in the short, medium, and long term • Identify and assess your individual and group strengths and weaknesses • Believe in your ability to influence the course of events despite uncertainty, setbacks, and temporary failures
	2.2 Motivation and perseverance	Stay focused and don't give up	• Be determined to turn ideas into action and satisfy your need to achieve • Be prepared to be patient and keep trying to achieve your long-term individual or group aims • Be resilient under pressure, adversity, and temporary failure

Table 3.1 (Continued)

Areas	Competences	Hints	Descriptors
	2.3 Mobilising resources	Gather and manage the resources you need	• Get and manage the material, non-material, and digital resources needed to turn ideas into action • Make the most of limited resources • Get and manage the competencies needed at any stage, including technical, legal, tax, and digital competencies
	2.4 Financial and economic literacy	Develop financial and economic know-how	• Estimate the cost of turning an idea into a value-creating activity • Plan, put in place, and evaluate financial decisions over time • Manage financing to make sure my value-creating activity can last over the long term
	2.5 Mobilising others	Inspire, enthuse, and get others on board	• Inspire and enthuse relevant stakeholders • Get the support needed to achieve valuable outcomes • Demonstrate effective communication, persuasion, negotiation, and leadership
3 Into action	3.1 Taking the initiative	Go for it	• Initiate processes that create value • Take up challenges • Act and work independently to achieve goals, stick to intentions, and carry out planned tasks
	3.2 Planning and management	Prioritise, organise and follow up	• Set long-, medium-, and short-term goals • Define priorities and action plans • Adapt to unforeseen changes
	3.3 Coping with uncertainty, ambiguity, and risk	Make decisions dealing with uncertainty, ambiguity, and risk	• Make decisions when the result of that decision is uncertain, when the information available is partial or ambiguous, or when there is a risk of unintended outcomes • Within the value-creating process, include structured ways of testing ideas and prototypes from the early stages to reduce the risks of failing • Handle fast-moving situations promptly and flexibly
	3.4. Working with others	Team up, collaborate, and network	• Work together and cooperate with others to develop ideas and turn them into action • Network • Solve conflicts and face up to competition positively when necessary
	3.5. Learning through experience	Learn by doing	• Use any initiative for value creation as a learning opportunity • Learn with others, including peers and mentors • Reflect and learn from both success and failure (your own and other people's)

Table 3.2 13 Entrepreneurial competencies (Morris et al., 2013, p. 358)

1	Opportunity recognition	The capacity to perceive changed conditions or overlooked possibilities in the environment that represent potential sources of profit or return to a venture.
2	Opportunity assessment	The ability to evaluate the content structure of opportunities to accurately determine their relative attractiveness.
3	Risk management/ mitigation	Taking actions that reduce the probability of a risk occurring or reduce the potential impact if the risk were to occur.
4	Conveying a compelling vision	The ability to conceive an image of a future organisational state and to articulate that image in a manner that empowers followers to enact it.
5	Tenacity/perseverance	The ability to sustain goal-directed action and energy when confronting difficulties and obstacles that impede goal achievement.
6	Creative problem solving/ imaginativeness	The ability to relate previously unrelated objects or variables to produce novel and appropriate or useful outcomes.
7	Resource leveraging	Skills at accessing resources one does not necessarily own or control to accomplish personal ends.
8	Guerrilla skills	The capacity to take advantage of one's surroundings, employ unconventional, low-cost tactics not recognised by others, and do more with less.
9	Value creation	Capabilities of developing new products, services, and/or business models that generate revenues exceeding their costs and produce sufficient user benefits to bring about a fair return.
10	Maintain focus yet adapt	The ability to balance an emphasis on goal achievement and the strategic direction of the organisation while addressing the need to identify and pursue actions to improve the fit between an organisation and developments in the external environment.
11	Resilience	The ability to cope with stresses and disturbances such that one remains well, recovers, or even thrives in the face of adversity.
12	Self-efficacy	The ability to maintain a sense of self-confidence regarding one's ability to accomplish a particular task or attain a level of performance.
13	Building and using networks	Social interaction skills that enable an individual to establish, develop, and maintain sets of relationships with others who assist them in advancing their work or career.

connections, and creating value. KEEN (2022a) describes entrepreneurially minded people as those who:

1 Are constantly curious about our changing world and employ a contrarian view of accepted solutions.
2 Habitually connect information from many sources to gain insight and manage risk.
3 Create value for others from unexpected opportunities, persist through, and learn from failure.

Skillsets reinforce this mindset within the three domains of opportunity, design, and impact. Table 3.3 lists the skills within these three domains.

3.4.4 Entrepreneurial Competence Framework

Tittel and Terzidis (2020, p. 20) undertook a review to create "a consolidated and classified list of entrepreneurial competencies for students with a technical engineering background, entrepreneurs, coaches, people responsible for intrapreneurship programs and accelerator programs in established companies and entrepreneurship support organisations." Table 3.4 presents the Entrepreneurial Competence Framework resulting from their research.

Table 3.3 KEEN skillset

Opportunity	Design	Impact
1.1 Identify an opportunity	2.1 Determine design requirements	3.1 Communicate an engineering solution in economic terms
1.2 Investigate the market	2.2 Perform technical design	3.2 Communicate an engineering solution in terms of societal impact
1.3 Create a preliminary business model	2.3 Analyse solutions	3.3 Validate market interest
1.4 Evaluate - technical feasibility - customer value - societal impact - economic viability	2.4 Develop new technologies (optional)	3.4 Develop partnerships and build a team
1.5 Test concepts quickly via customer engagement	2.5 Create a model or prototype	3.5 Identify supply chains and distribution methods
1.6 Assess policy and regulatory issues	2.6 Validate functions	3.6 Protect intellectual property

Finally, Table 3.5 synthesises the four taxonomies, identifying many similarities that may be core competencies. For example, all four have competencies related to spotting opportunities, creativity, planning and management, coping with uncertainty, ambiguity and risk, and collaboration and partnerships. KEEN and Tittel and Terzidis' Entrepreneurial Competence Frameworks, whose lists of competencies are specific to technology entrepreneurship, include competencies related to product development. These are not in the other frameworks and may be unique to the context of technology entrepreneurship.

One criticism of entrepreneurial competency frameworks is that a focus on lower-level skills dominates over the meta-cognitive lens. The primacy of skills may be due to the relative ease of teaching and assessing them (Lackéus, 2015). However, most experts agree that competencies development benefits when higher-order meta-level competencies such as entrepreneurial mindset are also present. While skills are about what a person can do, their mindset is concerned with how they think and perceive the world around them.

Consequently, researchers and entrepreneurship educators have sought to understand the entrepreneurial mindset and how it may enhance the effectiveness of skill-based entrepreneurial competencies. Some researchers and practitioners describe an entrepreneurial mindset as a "necessary competency" (Lynch & Corbett, 2021, p. 1). Others, such as Larsen (2022), see it as a meta-cognition or frame of mind influencing how entrepreneurial competencies are applied. While more complex and less easy to define and identify, most experts believe an entrepreneurial mindset is developable. For example, Mawson et al. (2022, p. 3) describe an entrepreneurial mindset as "a set of learnable cognitive and emotional competencies conducive to developing and enacting behaviours to support value creation activity." Consequently, most programmes to develop entrepreneurial competencies also aim to foster an entrepreneurial mindset.

3.5 Measuring Entrepreneurial Competencies

It is essential to the development of entrepreneurial competencies that they can be measured. Measurement provides insight into the efficacy of educational offerings and experiences in developing entrepreneurial competencies. Part of the difficulty in developing tools to measure

Table 3.4. Tittel and Terzidis' (2020) entrepreneurial competence framework

Personal competence	Domain competence – opportunity	Domain competence – organisation	Domain competence – strategy and management	Relationship competence
1.1 Act ethically correct	2.1 Generate ideas	3.1 Acquire resources	4.1 Administrate	5.1 Communicate
1.2 Act in a creative way	2.2 Identify opportunities	3.2 Control	4.2 Design products and services	5.2 Cooperate and collaborate
1.3 Act with social responsibility	2.3 Scan the environment	3.3 Coordinate	4.3 Develop a finance and budget plan	5.3 Deal with social customs
1.4 Deal with complex information		3.4 Delegate tasks	4.4 Develop a marketing strategy	5.4 Exchange knowledge
1.5 Create empathy		3.5 Develop a team	4.5 Develop innovative products and services	5.5 Lead your team
1.6 Define your goals		3.6 Develop an organisational culture	4.6 Develop strategies	5.6 Manage customers
1.7 Develop a vision		3.7 Develop the organisation	4.7 Implement ideas and tasks	5.7 Motivate organisation members
1.8 Learn to learn		3.8 Organise processes	4.8 Manage human resources	5.8 Negotiate
1.9 Make appropriate decisions				
1.10 Recognise your limitations				
1.11 Seek and analyse unstructured information				
1.12 Solve problems				
1.13 Take actions to overcome risk				
1.14 Take initiative				
1.15 Take risks				
1.16 Think conceptually				
1.17 Think logically				

Table 3.5 Frequency of competencies in the four frameworks

Competencies common to all four frameworks	Competencies appearing in three of the frameworks	Competencies in two of the frameworks	Competencies unique to a single framework
• Solving problems, opportunity recognition, and assessment • Creativity • Planning and management • Dealing with ambiguity, uncertainty, and risk • Ability to form collaborations and partnerships	• Developing a conveying a vision • Value creation • Self-awareness and self-efficacy • Motivation, perseverance, resilience, and tenacity • Acquiring and mobilising resources • Developing a business model and financial plans • Build, lead, and develop a team • Experiment and learn	• Ethical, socially responsible, and sustainable thinking and action • Communication and negotiation • Taking initiative • Design and develop innovative products and services	• Think conceptually and logically • Guerrilla skills

entrepreneurial competencies is the lack of agreement discussed in previous sections about the definition and the included competencies. For a measurement tool to be effective, it must be clear on what it measures and, ideally, generally accepted.

Some researchers have developed scales to measure self-perception of entrepreneurial competency. For example, Armuña et al. (2020) developed a survey based on EntreComp, which was validated by López-Núñez et al. (2022). Schelfhout et al. (2016) developed a measure to assess competencies in secondary students undertaking entrepreneurship education. Similarly, Morris et al. (2013) created a scale to evaluate entrepreneurial competencies in tertiary students.

While easy to administer and amenable to collecting data for research, self-perception scales have numerous well-recognised limitations. These include the challenges of developing valid and reliable measures, respondent biases, lack of population norms, and possible insensitivity to incremental learning during short-term programmes or experiences. Thus, they should be used cautiously to document the acquisition of competencies or for programme evaluation. They are, however, useful reflective tools for individuals to consider their relative level of competency. There is little research on other means of assessing entrepreneurial competencies, but numerous possible alternatives exist. Bird (2019), for example, identified 17 potential ways to evaluate entrepreneurial competencies, as listed in Table 3.6.

3.6 Developing Entrepreneurial Competencies

It is well-accepted that entrepreneurial competencies are learnable (Mitchelmore & Rowley, 2010). Through entrepreneurship education and training, educators seek to develop participants' entrepreneurial competencies by having them participate as active learners in creating and assessing these competencies (e.g., Jones et al., 2014; Matlay, 2006; Miles et al., 2017; Robinson et al., 2016). In developing competencies, learners move through multiple stages,

Table 3.6 Potential methods for assessing entrepreneurial competencies

1 Self-reflective diaries
2 Retrospective reconstruction of events and behaviour
3 Observation
4 Oral histories
5 Archival data such as letters and calendars
6 Critical event interviewing
7 Managerial repertoire grid
8 Participant observation
9 Videotapes about entrepreneurs
10 Journalists' accounts of entrepreneurs
11 Observational ratings by role set (e.g., employee, suppliers, lenders, and customers)
12 Interviews of role-set members
13 Job shadowing over time
14 Simulations such as in-basket exercises
15 Entrepreneurship games
16 Thinking aloud and analysis of protocols
17 Cases and analysis of solutions

from conscious incompetence to conscious competence to unconscious competence, otherwise known as mastery. Essential to this process is a focus on reflection and self-awareness to enable progression through the competence stages (Mawson et al., 2022).

Entrepreneurship education aims to prepare students for entrepreneurial practice (Tittel & Terzidis, 2020). The history of entrepreneurship education at a tertiary level is long, tracing its roots to 1938 at Kobe University, Japan (Alberti et al., 2004), followed by Harvard Business School introducing a course in 1947 (Katz, 2003; Nabi et al., 2017). No longer the domain of tertiary institutions, in many countries, entrepreneurship education is offered throughout the school system, from preschool to secondary, and practising entrepreneurs and the wider public (Lackéus, 2015).

Recent years have seen a proliferation of entrepreneurship educational offerings, including innovation and entrepreneurship centres; curricula courses and programmes at the undergraduate, postgraduate, and executive levels; business plan competitions; student entrepreneurship clubs and societies; accelerators and incubators; boot camps and hackathons; maker spaces; workshops, seminars, and speaker series; and endowed professorships and many other interventions (Blenker et al., 2011; Charney & Libecap, 2012; Nabi et al., 2017; Pittaway & Cope, 2007; Pittaway et al., 2011).

Underlying most of these are a belief that entrepreneurial competencies are developed through hands-on experience. For example, Lackéus (2015) encourages teachers to have students work on projects for external organisations where they have to create innovative solutions. Such experiences require students to engage with the external world and "trigger uncertainty, ambiguity, and confusion," resulting in deep learning (p. 27).

The most well-known and widely spread framework for technology entrepreneurship education is KEEN. Their mission is "to reach all of their undergraduate engineering students with an entrepreneurial mindset so they can create personal, economic, and societal value through a lifetime of meaningful work" (*What Is KEEN? | Engineering Unleashed*, n.d.). KEEN works with engineering faculty to embed entrepreneurship in undergraduate engineering courses or create new courses. Although not explicitly focused on developing entrepreneurial competencies, the National Science Foundation's Innovation Corps is another significant example of how scientists and engineers can develop the competencies needed to move their research towards commercialisation.

Most universities provide some level of entrepreneurship education and support to students and alums through the curricula, extra-curricular activities, support services, or a combination. Students in engineering and science can develop their entrepreneurial competencies during their studies by taking courses in entrepreneurship or innovation, which often cover the process of bringing new products or services to market. Another way is to get involved in extra-curricular activities, such as hackathons or startup incubators, allowing them to work on real-world projects and learn from experienced entrepreneurs. Internships or co-op positions, especially with startups or small businesses, can provide hands-on experience in entrepreneurship. Finally, students can network with entrepreneurs and professionals through events, clubs, or online communities to gain insights and advice.

3.7 Conclusion

Developing entrepreneurial competencies, the skills, knowledge, and attitudes underlying successful entrepreneurial actions, is essential because of the benefits of entrepreneurship for many endeavours beyond founding companies (Mitchelmore & Rowley, 2010). Entrepreneurial competencies are critical for engineers and scientists aspiring to be technology entrepreneurs. They help them understand the market, identify potential customers and stakeholders, develop strategies for bringing their ideas to fruition, and increase their understanding of the business context and how to communicate and collaborate with others effectively. These competencies can be learned and developed through various entrepreneurship education programmes (Bird, 2019).

Following Gianesini et al.'s approach (2018), this chapter summarised and compared four popular taxonomies. The competencies common to these taxonomies are solving problems, opportunity recognition and assessment, creativity, planning and management, dealing with ambiguity, uncertainty, and risk, and the ability to form collaborations and partnerships. KEEN and the Entrepreneurial Competence Framework include additional competencies related to product development, which are unique to the context of technology entrepreneurship.

Measuring entrepreneurial competencies is vital for understanding the efficacy of educational offerings and experiences. Researchers have developed self-report scales to measure self-perception of entrepreneurial competency. Still, scales have limitations, including difficulty developing valid and reliable measures, respondent biases, lack of population norms, and potential insensitivity to incremental learning. While there is little research on alternative methods of assessing entrepreneurial competencies, researchers such as Bird (2019) have pointed out many possible alternatives.

Finally, entrepreneurial competencies can be learned through entrepreneurship education, which often involves active learning and focusing on reflection and self-awareness (Mitchelmore & Rowley, 2010). Entrepreneurship education has a long history and is now offered at various levels, from preschool to tertiary and to practising entrepreneurs. Most universities provide entrepreneurship education through the curriculum, extra-curricular activities, and support services. Engineering and science students can develop entrepreneurial competencies through these means, such as seeking internships or co-op positions and networking.

References

Alberti, F., Sciascia, S., & Poli, A. (2004). *Entrepreneurship education: Notes on an ongoing debate.* 14th Annual IntEnt Conference, University of Napoli Federico II (Italy). https://www.researchgate.net/publication/228971736

Armuña, C., Ramos, S., Juan, J., Feijóo, C., & Arenal, A. (2020). From stand-up to startup: Exploring entrepreneurship competencies and STEM women's intention. *International Entrepreneurship and Management Journal, 16*(1), 69–92. https://doi.org/10.1007/s11365-019-00627-z

Bacigalupo, M., Kampylis, P., Punie, Y., & Van den Brande, G. (2016). *EntreComp: The entrepreneurship competence framework.* (EUR 27939). Publication Office of the European Union. https://data.europa.eu/doi/10.2791/593884

Bird, B. (1995). Towards a theory of entrepreneurial competency. *Advances in Entrepreneurship, Firm Emergence and Growth, 2*(1), 51–72.

Bird, B. (2019). Toward a Theory of Entrepreneurial Competency. In J. A. Katz & A. C. Corbet (Eds.), *Seminal Ideas for the Next Twenty-Five Years of Advances* (Vol. 21, pp. 115–131). Emerald Publishing Limited. https://doi.org/10.1108/S1074-754020190000021011

Blenker, P., Korsgaard, S., Neergaard, H., & Thrane, C. (2011). The questions we care about: Paradigms and progression in entrepreneurship education. *Industry and Higher Education, 25*(6), 417–427. https://doi.org/10.5367/ihe.2011.0065

Charney, A., & Libecap, G. D. (2012). *The impact of entrepreneurship education: An evaluation of the Berger entrepreneurship program at the University of Arizona, 1985–1999.* Kauffman Center for Entrepreneurial Leadership. https://papers.ssrn.com/sol3/papers.cfm?abstract_id=1262343

Gianesini, G., Cubico, S., Favretto, G., & Leitão, J. (2018). Entrepreneurial Competences: Comparing and Contrasting Models and Taxonomies. In S. Cubico, G. Favretto, J. Leitão, & U. Cantner (Eds.), *Entrepreneurship and the Industry Life Cycle: The Changing Role of Human Capital and Competences* (pp. 13–32). Springer International Publishing. https://doi.org/10.1007/978-3-319-89336-5_2

Jones, P., Penaluna, A., & Pittaway, L. (2014). Entrepreneurship education: A recipe for change? *The International Journal of Management Education, 12*(3), 304–306. https://doi.org/10.1016/j.ijme.2014.09.004

Katz, J. A. (2003). The chronology and intellectual trajectory of American entrepreneurship education. *Journal of Business Venturing, 18*(2), 283–300. https://doi.org/10.1016/S0883-9026(02)00098-8

KEEN. (2022). *KEEN Framework: A guide for entrepreneurial mindset.* Engineering Unleashed. https://orchard-prod.azurewebsites.net/media/Framework/KEEN_Framework_v5.pdf

Komarkova, I., Gagliardi, D., Conrads, J., & Collado, A. (2015). *Entrepreneurship competence: An overview of existing concepts, policies and initiatives* (M. Bacigalupo, P. Kampylis, & Y. Punie, Eds.). European Commission. Joint Research Centre. Institute for Prospective Technological Studies. https://data.europa.eu/doi/10.2791/067979

Lackéus, M. (2015). *Entrepreneurship in education. What, why, when, how.* (Entrepreneurship360 Initiative of the Organisation for Economic Co-Operation and Development (LEED Programme) and the European Commission (DG Education and Culture).). OECD. https://www.oecd.org/cfe/leed/BGP_Entrepreneurship-in-Education.pdf

Larsen, I. B. (2022). Fostering an entrepreneurial mindset: A typology for aligning instructional strategies with three dominant entrepreneurial mindset conceptualisations. *Industry & Higher Education, 36*(3), 236–251. International Bibliography of the Social Sciences (IBSS). https://doi.org/10.1177/09504222211038212

Le Deist, F. D., & Winterton, J. (2005). What is competence? *Human Resource Development International, 8*(1), 27–46. https://doi.org/10.1080/1367886042000338227

López-Núñez, M. I., Rubio-Valdehita, S., Armuña, C., & Pérez-Urria, E. (2022). EntreComp questionnaire: A self-assessment tool for entrepreneurship competencies. *Sustainability, 14*(5), 2983. https://doi.org/10.3390/su14052983

Lynch, M. P., & Corbett, A. C. (2021). Entrepreneurial mindset shift and the role of cycles of learning. *Journal of Small Business Management, 61*(1), 80–101. https://doi-org/10.1080/00472778.2021.1924381

Man, T. W. Y., Lau, T., & Chan, K. F. (2002). The competitiveness of small and medium enterprises: A conceptualisation with focus on entrepreneurial competencies. *Journal of Business Venturing, 17*(2), 123–142. https://doi.org/10.1016/S0883-9026(00)00058-6

Markman, G. D., Balkin, D. B., & Baron, R. A. (2002). Inventors and new venture formation: The effects of general self-efficacy and regretful thinking. *Entrepreneurship Theory and Practice, 27*(2), 149–165. https://doi.org/10.1111/1540-8520.00004

Matlay, H. (2006). Researching entrepreneurship and education: Part 2: What is entrepreneurship education and does it matter? *Education & Training; London, 48*(8/9), 704–718. https://doi.org/10.1108/00400910610710119

Mawson, S., Casulli, L., & Simmons, E. L. (2022). A competence development approach for entrepreneurial mindset in entrepreneurship education. *Entrepreneurship Education and Pedagogy, 6*(3), 481–501. https://doi.org/10.1177/25151274221143146

McCallum, E., Weicht, R., McMullan, L., & Price, A. (2018, March 2). *EntreComp into Action - Get inspired, make it happen: A user guide to the European Entrepreneurship Competence Framework.* JRC Publications Repository. https://doi.org/10.2760/574864

Miles, M. P., de Vries, H., Harrison, G., Bliemel, M., de Klerk, S., & Kasouf, C. J. (2017). Accelerators as authentic training experiences for nascent entrepreneurs. *Education + Training, 59*(7/8), 811–824. https://doi.org/10.1108/ET-01-2017-0007

Mitchelmore, S., & Rowley, J. (2010). Entrepreneurial competencies: A literature review and development agenda. *International Journal of Entrepreneurial Behavior & Research, 16*(2), 92–111. https://doi.org/10.1108/13552551011026995

Morris, M. H., Webb, J. W., Fu, J., & Singhal, S. (2013). A competency-based perspective on entrepreneurship education: Conceptual and empirical insights. *Journal of Small Business Management, 51*(3), 352–369.

Nabi, G., Liñán, F., Fayolle, A., Krueger, N. F., & Walmsley, A. (2017). The impact of entrepreneurship education in higher education: A systematic review and research agenda. *Academy of Management Learning & Education, 16*(2), 277–299. https://doi.org/10.5465/amle.2015.0026

Orser, B., & Riding, A. (2003). *Management Competencies and SME Performance Criteria: A Pilot Study* [Small Business Policy Branch, Industry Canada]. https://sites.telfer.uottawa.ca/womensenterprise/files/2014/06/Management-Competencies-and-SME-Performance-2003_Eng.pdf

Pennetta, S., Anglani, F., & Mathews, S. (2023). Navigating through entrepreneurial skills, competencies and capabilities: A systematic literature review and the development of the entrepreneurial ability model. *Journal of Entrepreneurship in Emerging Economies, 16*(4), 1144–1182. https://doi.org/10.1108/JEEE-09-2022-0257

Pittaway, L., & Cope, J. (2007). Entrepreneurship education a systematic review of the evidence. *International Small Business Journal, 25*(5), 479–510. https://doi.org/10.1177/0266242607080656

Pittaway, L., Rodriguez-Falcon, E., Aiyegbayo, O., & King, A. (2011). The role of entrepreneurship clubs and societies in entrepreneurial learning. *International Small Business Journal, 29*(1), 37–57. https://doi.org/10.1177/0266242610369876

Rasmussen, E., Mosey, S., & Wright, M. (2011). The evolution of entrepreneurial competencies: A longitudinal study of university spin-off venture emergence: The evolution of entrepreneurial competencies. *Journal of Management Studies, 48*(6), 1314–1345. https://doi.org/10.1111/j.1467-6486.2010.00995.x

Robinson, S., Neergaard, H., Tanggaard, L., & Krueger, N. F. (2016). New horizons in entrepreneurship: From teacher-led to student-centered learning. *Education & Training, 58*(7/8), 661–683. Engineering Collection; Health Research Premium Collection; Materials Science Collection; ProQuest Central. https://doi.org/10.1108/ET-03-2016-0048

Schelfhout, W., Bruggeman, K., & De Maeyer, S. (2016). Evaluation of entrepreneurial competence through scaled behavioural indicators: Validation of an instrument. *Studies in Educational Evaluation, 51*, 29–41. https://doi.org/10.1016/j.stueduc.2016.09.001

The European Parliament and Council. (2006). Recommendation of the European Parliament and of the Council of 18 December 2006 on key competences for lifelong learning. *Official Journal of the European Union, 2006*(962). https://eur-lex.europa.eu/LexUriServ/LexUriServ.do?uri=OJ:L:2006:394:0010:0018:en:PDF

The European Parliament and Council. (2018). Council Recommendation of 22 May 2018 on key competences for lifelong learning Text with EEA relevance. *Official Journal of the European Union, 2018*, 13.

Tittel, A., & Terzidis, O. (2020). Entrepreneurial competences revised: Developing a consolidated and categorised list of entrepreneurial competences. *Entrepreneurship Education, 3*(1), 1–35. https://doi.org/10.1007/s41959-019-00021-4

Vestergaard, L., Moberg, K., & Jørgensen, C. (2012). *Impact of Entrepreneurship Education in Denmark—2011*. The Danish Foundation for Entrepreneurship – Young Enterprise. https://eng.ffe-ye.dk/media/202248/impact_of_entrepreneurship_education_in_denmark_2011.pdf

What Is KEEN? | Engineering Unleashed. (n.d.). Retrieved August 10, 2020, from https://engineering unleashed.com/what-is-keen

Winterton, J. (2002). *Entrepreneurship: Towards a competence framework for developing SME managers*. In *United States Association for Small Business and Entrepreneurship Conference Proceedings* (pp. 1–9).

Part II

From Technology to Value

4   IP Institutions and Strategic Implications for New Ventures with a Global Orientation

Yue Xu and Yumao Wang

4.1 Introduction: The Evolution of IP Protection Institutions

Intellectual property (IP) is typically classified into two principal categories: the traditional IP and the non-traditional IP (Ryder & Madhavan, 2016). Traditional IP forms such as patents, copyrights, and trademarks are well-established and form the bedrock of IP protection. They serve to incentivize innovation and creativity, ensuring that creators and inventors can reap the benefits of their work. Non-traditional IP, on the other hand, addresses the complexities of contemporary innovation such as industrial designs, domain names, circuit layout designs, confidential business information, plant breeders' rights, and trade secrets. As we move forward in the digital age, the scope of IP protection is likely to continue expanding, reflecting the broader array of innovative activities in the global economy.

Since IP rights include various categories, there is no unified origin time or a single IP protection system. IP rights sprouted in the Renaissance of Italy in the 15th century. In 1474, the world's first patent law, the "Venetian Patent Statute",[1] was promulgated by the Most Serene Republic of Venice, which has been widely accepted as the start of the modern patent system in the world. From the 16th to the 18th century, IP has received increasing attention in European countries with the perception that only by protecting inventors' rights can more innovations be stimulated, and competitiveness be enhanced. In the UK, the "Statute of Anne"[2] in 1710 marked the first copyright law to protect authors' rights directly by the government and courts. In 1886, the "Berne Convention for the Protection of Literary and Artistic Works"[3] (or the Berne Convention) was formed. The advancement of IP protection till then provided the legal foundation upon which the Industrial Revolution emerged and flourished in today's developed economies.

The 19th century witnessed a fast growth of international trade in Europe. Numerous inventions, designs, and concepts continued to emerge. At the same time, malicious competition such as technology theft and product imitation appeared, resulting in huge losses suffered by inventing countries. In 1857, France formulated the "Manufacture and Goods Mark Act",[4] which became the earliest unified trademark law in the world. In 1883, the "Paris Convention for the Protection of Industrial Property"[5] (or the Paris Convention) was formed in Geneva. The Paris Convention is regarded as the first major step to ensure IP protection across countries. This is followed by the "Madrid Agreement Concerning the International Registration of Marks"[6] (or the Madrid Agreement) formed in 1891.

The 20th century has seen more IP protection institutions established. For example, the World Intellectual Property Organization (WIPO) was established based on the "WIPO Convention"[7] in 1976. Today, WIPO has 193 member states under its protection governance. Also, in 1994, the "Trademark Law Treaty"[8] was concluded, which further unified and simplified the procedures for national and regional trademark registration. Also in 1994, the "Agreement on

DOI: 10.4324/9781003341284-6

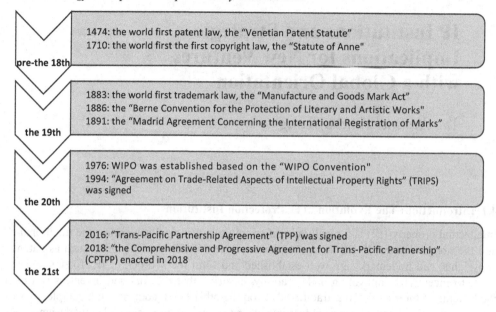

Figure 4.1 Key milestones of the emergence of IP protection institutions.

Source: Compiled by the author based on various official websites.

Trade-Related Aspects of Intellectual Property Rights"[9] was signed, which became the legal basis for bringing IP protection into the World Trade Organization. In 1996, the WIPO Copyright Treaty[10] was concluded under the "Berne Convention" which involves the protection of works and authors in the digital environment. In the 21st century, the "Trans-Pacific Partnership Agreement" was signed in 2016 followed by "the Comprehensive and Progressive Agreement for Trans-Pacific Partnership"[11] enacted in 2018. Both agreements aim to further strengthen regional IP protection. Figure 4.1 summarizes key milestones of the emergence of IP protection institutions.

4.2 Country Differences in Global IP Protection Systems

4.2.1 Patent Protection

A patent "is a right granted to an individual who has invented something" as defined by Ryder and Madhavan (2016: 8). WIPO further elaborates that a patent is an exclusive right awarded for an invention, which could be a product or a process offering a new method of doing something or presenting a new technical solution to a problem. Patents include utility patents and design patents. Holding a patent enables a person or company to prohibit others from manufacturing, using, or selling the protected invention during the protection term. To be eligible for a patent, the invention must be new (novel), useful, and non-obvious to someone skilled in the relevant field. The inventor also needs to disclose how the technology functions and its potential applications. Typically, a patent is valid for up to 20 years, during which the patent holder must pay certain fees to maintain the patent's validity. If the patent holder assesses that the technology has limited commercial value, they may choose to abandon the patent, allowing the technology to enter the public domain and become freely accessible to the public.

The differences in patent laws across countries like the U.S., China, and Japan reflecting their distinct approaches to balancing innovation promotion with public interest and economic strategies. The U.S. patent system is known for its broad protection scope, which encourages a wide range of inventions and creations by granting them legal protection. This extensive protection is designed to stimulate innovation, attract investment, and ensure that inventors can reap the financial benefits of their creations, thereby fuelling further innovation. In contrast, China's patent law,[12] at the beginning, delineates specific categories that are not eligible for patent protection indicating China's strategic approach to ensure that certain types of knowledge and methods remain in the public domain, accessible to all. In comparison, Japan's patent law includes protections for a broader array of inventions than China's system but is still more selective than the U.S. system. This reflects Japan's own nuanced balance between encouraging innovation and maintaining public access to certain types of knowledge and techniques.

Obviously, country differences in patent law can significantly impact the type of innovations that emerge in each country, and the extent to which these innovations are shared or commercialized, as well as the global flow of technological and scientific knowledge. In addition, country difference in patent law influences where companies choose to conduct research and development and how they strategize about their IP globally. Contrasting with national patent systems, the Patent Cooperation Treaty (PCT)[13] provides a robust international framework that facilitates the acquisition of patent protection for innovative technologies across multiple countries. As of 2023, the PCT has garnered the participation of 157 contracting nations. Notably, it boasts physical offices in five strategic locations: China, the U.S., Europe, Japan, and South Korea. These offices are collectively known as the "IP5 Offices", signifying their critical role in the global IP landscape. Figure 4.2 highlights the importance of each IP5 Offices based on the total number of patent applications to them from 2017 to 2021. The PCT system streamlines the patent application process, enabling inventors to protect their innovations in various authorities through a singular, consolidated procedure.

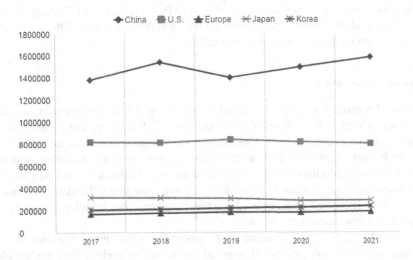

Figure 4.2 The development of patents applied to the IP5 Offices (2017–2021).

Source: Compiled by the author based on WIPO IP Statistics Data Centre.

4.2.2 Copyright Protection

According to the WIPO official website, copyrights (or author's rights) is "the rights that creators have over their literary and artistic works". Copyright covers a wide range of IP rights regarding natural sciences, social sciences, literature, music, drama, painting, sculpture, photography, and film, as well as composition of photography and other aspects of the work. Two types of benefits can be derived from owning copyright: the economic rights and the moral rights (WIPO, 2016). The economic rights are vital because they allow creators to monetize their works. By holding these rights, creators can control and receive compensation for various uses of their works, such as reproduction, distribution, public performance, and adaptation. These rights are crucial for ensuring that creators are rewarded for their efforts and can continue to contribute to culture and knowledge. The moral rights refer to the rights to prevent any distortion of the original work. Even if the economic rights are sold or licensed to others, moral rights typically remain with the creator. They ensure that the work is not altered or presented in a context that harms the creator's reputation or intent. This aspect of copyright is particularly significant in preserving the integrity and original expression of the work.

Copyright system is hugely different in common law countries and civil law countries. In common law countries, copyright law has traditionally been more focused on the economic rights of creators, emphasizing the right of reproduction. This means the main concern is with the unauthorized duplication and distribution of works. Common law systems rely heavily on judicial precedents and case law to interpret statutes. In contrast, civil law countries place a significant emphasis on the moral rights of creators alongside economic rights. Moral rights allow authors to control the context and way their works are used, ensuring their personal connection to the work is respected. Civil law systems are more codified, with detailed legal codes that cover comprehensive aspects of law.

The digital era has introduced new complexities in copyright protection. The ease of copying and distributing content online has heightened the focus on neighbouring rights, which are rights related to, but distinct from, copyright. These include rights of performers, producers of phonograms, and broadcasting organizations, among others. The provisions on neighbouring rights and the term of protection can vary significantly between countries. While international agreements like the Berne Convention and the WIPO Performances and Phonograms Treaty[14] provide certain level of standardization, national laws can differ in terms of the scope of rights, duration of protection, and enforcement mechanisms.

4.2.3 Trademark Protection

WIPO's official website notes that a trademark is "a sign capable of distinguishing the goods or services of one enterprise from those of other enterprises". Here, a sign can be any that can distinguish the goods of a natural person, legal person, or an organization from the goods of others. The sign can be text, graphics, letters, numbers, three-dimensional signs, colour combinations, sounds, as well as the combination of the above elements. A trademark is not only a sign of an identity but also the source of goods or services, in a way guarantees the quality or function of goods or services. Therefore, it can be used as a tool for advertising, bringing economic benefits and competitive advantages to its owner.

Before the Madrid System's establishment, registering a trademark internationally was a cumbersome and inefficient process. It required businesses to register their trademark separately adhering to the specific legal requirements and procedures of each country. The Madrid System helps to resolve the problem. An applicant using the Madrid System needs first to have a national trademark application or registration (known as the "basic mark") in their home country's IP office, also referred to as the "Office of Origin". The applicant can then extend the protection of their basic mark to other countries (contracting parties to the Madrid Union) by filing a single international application through the Madrid System.

While the Madrid System now facilitates the application process, the actual protection of the trademark in each designated country is governed by that country's domestic trademark laws. Each member country retains the right to examine the trademark according to its laws and decide on its registrability. After receiving an international application through the Madrid System, each designated country will conduct its own substantive examination. They will decide whether to grant protection to the trademark within their jurisdiction based on their legal standards and procedures. The ultimate decision on whether a trademark can be registered in a designated country or region lies with the IP office of that country or region. They will notify WIPO of their decision, which in turn informs the applicant. In addition, if a trademark in the country of origin is no longer protected due to reasons such as abandonment, cancellation, or invalidation, the relevant international registration will also become invalid. To make up for the deficiencies of the "Madrid Agreement", the "Protocols Relating to the Madrid Agreement on the International Registration of Marks" (also called the "Protocol")[15] was concluded in 1989. The Protocol makes it possible to protect a mark in a large number of countries more efficiently.

4.3 IP Strategies: Incumbent Multinationals vs. International New Ventures

4.3.1 Key Factors Influence IP Strategies

Ryder and Madhavan (2016: xi) stated, "IP is nothing without law because without legal protection, the value of an intangible asset is minimal, but equally important is the fact that IP is nothing without proper management". Vast examples demonstrated that IP management has a determining impact on competitive advantages of firms. Durand and Milberg (2020) address that the essence of gaining IP rights is to create intellectual monopoly in the global value chain. However, this argument is found not directly suitable for international new ventures (INVs) which are typically constrained by resources especially financial resources (Symeonidou et al., 2017).

In discussion IP strategies of firms with global orientation, it is essential to outline the context and specific aspects of their IP approaches. As summarized by Table 4.1, the formation of IP strategies of incumbent multinationals and INV are influenced by multiple factors. For example, in terms of resource conditions, the resource-rich environment of incumbent multinationals allows for a comprehensive IP strategy, unlike INVs that might adopt a more minimalist and strategic approach to IP due to resource constraints. Therefore, in terms of scale and scope of geographical coverage, incumbents have a broader and more defensive approach to IP, whereas INVs are more focused and agile, often prioritizing quick market entry and innovation. Overall, we may argue that while established multinationals may use IP to defend and expand their global presence, INVs can use IP strategically to carve out niches and rapidly scale in international markets.

4.3.2 Navigate IP Market: Implications for International New Ventures

- **Patent-based commercialization**

    Early-stage startups often rely on signals to demonstrate their commercial value to facilitate the patent-based commercialization. For example, Islam et al. (2018) found that

Table 4.1 Key factors that influence IP strategies comparing incumbent multinationals and INVs

Factors influencing IP strategies	Incumbent multinationals	International new ventures
Resources for IP	With rich resources to commit to IP development	With limited resources to commit to IP development
IP Portfolio & strategic orientation	Often possess extensive IP portfolio; tend to adopt defensive IP strategies	Concentrate on focused IP asset; tend to adopt flexible and responsive IP strategies
Global reach	Tailor IP strategy to each market; file IP in multiple countries to ensure comprehensive protection	Target global niche market; attend IP in specific, often underserved international market
IP risk	Face varied IP risks due to broader market presence; with high cost of monitoring and defending IP rights globally	Lean towards open, faster, less resource-intensive innovation; with low cost of monitoring and defending IP rights globally
IP acquisition	Frequently engaged IP transactions, using IP as strategic assets in global competition	May strategically engage in IP transactions to overcome entry barriers accelerating market entry in global competition

Created by the author.

in emerging industries the U.S. startups with government grants were 12% more likely to acquire subsequent venture capital (VC) funding. However, the value of this signalling is greater for startups that have fewer patents, which means signalling strategies do not just provide additional advantage to new ventures but have the potential to redistribute benefits. Given governments around the world, especially those from emerging economies are establishing larger pools of fund to accelerate innovative efforts and support early-stage startups, the signalling strategy can be crucial for new ventures to acquire subsequent VC and/or to commercialize their IP assets.

We note two types of high-tech–based firms: those with disruptive technologies and those with iterative technologies. For example, in the field of 5G patent technologies, Huawei, an established Chinese multinational, owns the largest number of patents, leading to the U.S. losing in the 5G technology competition and thus having to develop 6G technology ahead of schedule. In comparison, for INVs with disruptive technologies, since patents are the only core asset, smooth commercialization is crucial for them. For instance, Juno Therapeutics, which owns cell therapy technologies, has an exclusive product in its CAR-T therapy and owns the patent. In 2019, Juno Therapeutics was acquired by BMS for $74 billion and achieved a successful commercialization.

For firms with iterative technologies most foundational patents may have expired, they often apply for a series of improvement patents around iterative technologies. Take LEGO, the world's largest toy multinational as an example. After the patent for its interlocking bricks expired in 1988, LEGO must rely on continuous innovation around iterative product development. With the development of digital technology, LEGO expanded into more software products, such as LEGO Builder, thus achieving diversified development. In this line, INV with iterative technologies needs to shape the patent portfolio strategically. For example, nobody knows Crown ElectroKinetics, a firm established in 2015, focusing on glass material. However, through acquiring patents from HP and IBM, it created a robust patent portfolio. In 2021, the company successfully went public in the U.S.

- *Licensing and cross-licensing*

Licensing offers an effective tool for firms to maximize their IP value without losing the control of IP rights. Take Boeing as an example, as the leader of the global aviation aircraft industry, Boeing only licensing its related technologies to its non-competitive counterpart in the value chain to ensure the value of its IP is maximized. Grindley and Teece (1997) also recorded how IBM maximized IP value through licensing strategy. In the early 1990s, IBM suffered from serious loses due to severe competition. IBM realized that it must find a strategic solution to turn around. It decided to license its IP to other companies and collect royalties. Within a decade, a huge earning from royalty helped IBM to gain free cash flow and revive from its financial crunch.

Cross-licensing enables firms to grant reciprocal access to IP or patent. Cohen, Nelson, and Walsh (2000: 29) reported, "firms are reluctant to sell their technology but are willing to trade it only to firms that have valuable technology (intellectual property) to use as currency", the so-called IP-for-IP strategy as addressed by (Herbst & Jahn, 2017). The case of AT&T in the U.S. provides a classic example of using cross-licensing to create its success since the 1940s (Grindley & Teece, 1997). AT&T has monopolized the long-distance and local telephone markets in the U.S. for a long time. It has the world-known laboratory—Bell Labs. Most inventions in the early stage of the semiconductor industry came from this laboratory. Giving its competitors such as General Electric, Marconi, and Westinghouse held cumulative patents, AT&T and these companies licensed each other's at the lowest cost, strategically more in favour of its own development. In the end, AT&T's technologies become more diffused in the industry, sustaining its monopoly position effectively.

Part of licensing strategies aims to build strong corporate and product brands. A good example is the Walt Disney Company (hereinafter referred as Disney), the world leading cartoon producer. Hennessey (2020: 26) recorded that Walt, the founder, knew that it was important to always make sure that he owned the rights to the cartoon characters that he and his company created. Disney is now the world's leading licensor with brands that include Lucasfilm, Marvel, ABC, ESPN, DisneyPixar, and Walt Disney Studios and a total of $56.6bn in licensed merchandize sold in 2016.[16] It is noted that Disney has been criticized for its notoriously strict protection of its IP especially when it comes to Mickey Mouse (Greener, 2015). Still, the success of Disney shows that by forming strong corporate and product trademarks large multinationals can cultivate well-known brands and keep their monopoly position worldwide.

In the same line, licensing and cross-licensing strategies can be applied by INVs. For startups, such as in the internet sector, maximizing the benefits of IP licensing is crucial. For example, Microsoft's early success was partly due to its strategy of freely licensing other companies to use its MS-DOS operating system, which quickly led to market dominance. Similarly, Google's Android operating system succeeded because it was open-sourced, allowing various companies and developers to use its source code, thus creating a participatory ecosystem. In the pharmaceutical industry, patent licensing models are common among startups. For example, MacroGenics, a biopharmaceutical company founded in 2000 in the U.S., discovered and developed antibody-based therapies for cancer treatment. In 2021, MacroGenics licensed Zai Lab to develop four immuno-oncology molecules for $1.4 billion. It exemplifies how startups, through strategic licensing of their patents, can generate significant revenue and partnerships, facilitating growth and further innovation in their respective fields.

• *Location strategy*

Seeking IP protection in the global market is not straightforward due to institutional differences remaining in different countries (Athreye, Piscitello, & Shadlen, 2020). Statistics show that the U.S., Europe, and Japan, or the Triad, share a more integrated and mutually inclusive IP institutional environment. According to the "IP5 Statistics Report 2021 Edition" (The IP5 Offices, 2022),[17] there are a total of 2.9 million patent applications worldwide. The distribution of these applications shows a clear regional pattern. For inventions applied in China, the key sources of applications are China which accounts for 90% followed by the U.S. (3%), Europe (3%), Japan (3%), and South Korea (1%). In the U.S., the key sources of applicants are the U.S. which accounts for 48% followed by Europe (15%), Japan (13%), China (8%), and South Korea (6%). In Europe, the key sources of applicants are Europe which accounts for 44% followed by the U.S. (25%), Japan (11%), China (9%), and South Korea (5%). Apparently, developing countries such as China are still in the process of integrating with the Triad IP markets.

Notably, the catching-up of innovation in developing regions especially in emerging markets (EMs) has been dramatic in recent years. Take China as an example, China's overseas patents continue to rise in recent years. In 2000, the total number of patents applied through China PCT was only 781,[18] this equals to 2% of a total of 38,013 patents applied through the U.S. PCT. By contrast, in 2021, the total number of patents applied through China PCT reached 69,540. These dramatically increased applications are 119% of the total of 58,477 patents applied through the U.S. PCT (WIPO, 2021). Figure 4.4 shows patents granted by IP5 Offices and China is in the leading position over the past few years. Take 2021 as an example, the total number of patents granted to China represents almost half of the total number of patents granted by the IP5 Offices. The second largest country is the U.S. with an increasing trend followed by the other three markets: Europe, Japan, and Korea.

However, securing IP protections in EMs can be problematic due to weak IP enforcement (e.g., Keupp, Friesike, & von Zedtwitz, 2012; Nguyen, 2020). Recently, Papageorgiadis,

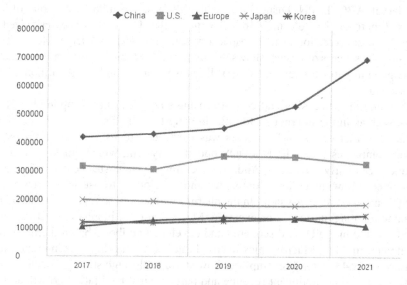

Figure 4.3 The development of patents granted by the IP5 Offices (2017–2021).

Source: Compiled by the author according to the statistics of IP5 Office.

Xu, and Alexiou (2019) found EM multinationals are more attracted by countries with either a much higher or a much lower level of IP enforcement than that of their home institutions, which indicates firms' motives in seeking various IP institutional advantages overseas. Sutherland, Anderson, and Hu (2020) also put forward that EM multinationals have a comparatively stronger patent but weaker trademark-seeking orientation than multinationals from developed countries, indicating the former prefers seeking IP assets with less location boundness.

With the advent of economic globalization, new ventures need to operate not only in local markets but also expand into major global markets. One of the biggest challenges for new ventures in their initial stages is funding. To apply for patents more effectively, it's crucial to fully utilize the PCT route and the Paris Convention route for simultaneous patent protection in major countries. This approach not only saves costs but also allows startups to make full use of the system's provisions, giving them time to decide whether to apply for a patent while the technology is being further perfected. Currently, major countries have launched the Patent Prosecution Highway programme,[19] which accelerates the patent examination process. New ventures can leverage this programme to obtain authorized patents faster in the countries where they need to establish their presence.

- ***Standard-setting strategy***

Ranganathan, Ghosh, and Rosenkopf (2018) address that today's business ecosystem is characterized by technological interdependence between firms. Accordingly, a firm's technological choices are not just based on competition but also on necessary collaboration, coordination, and integration with other firms that possess complementary technologies. Typically, standard-setting organizations (SSOs) provide collaborative arrangements to bring representative firms together to derive the technical rules. Therefore, how leading new ventures of an industry impose their influence on standard setting can be strategically important.

Standard-setting strategies had been long adopted by established multinationals. A good example is Standard Oil Company founded by John D. Rockefeller, who controlled 95% of the refining capacity in the U.S. in the early 20th century (Soeder, 2020). With the monopoly position, Standard Oil had a chance to set up important standards of the petroleum industry. For example, the grade standard of petroleum No. 92, No. 95, and No. 98 are the standards even followed today. The company also set up the gasoline engine oil standards, such as the API standard system, the ILSAC standard system, and the ACEA standard system. Controlling standards help large oil companies such as Exxon Mobil, Chevron, Shell, and British Petroleum to stabilize their IP value and market positions.

Standard-setting strategies show dynamism in high-tech industries such as the telecommunication industry. In the past, leading firms such as Qualcomm, Intel, Microsoft, and IBM occupied a high market share based on their strong IP assets. These firms are also key influencers in the formulation of international communication standards. The platforms for imposing their influence are the International Telecommunication Union, the Third Generation Partnership Project, and the European Telecommunications Standards Institute. Moving to the 5G era, multinationals from EMs intend to deploy their standard-setting strategies. For example, Huawei from China, which possesses most 5G technology patents, shows its strong IP capacity to influence the formulation of 5G communication standards today.

With the advent of the Internet of Things, Radio Frequency Identification (RFID) technology or wireless communication has become a fast-developing technology to witness standard-setting strategies. It is forecasted that soon the standardization of RFID technology will profoundly affect many other sectors such as logistics, transportation, identification, and asset management. Controlling RFID standards make leading firms so powerful that they potentially can control all RFID-related industries and even challenge national security. IDTechEx[20] notes that the global RFID market is worth $11.6 billion in 2019, rising to $13 billion in 2022, and is expected to grow to US$15.23 billion in 2024. RFID standards will solve technical problems such as coding, communication, air interface, and data sharing. Therefore, companies that master the RFID standard gain huge opportunities to commercialize IP value.

Figure 4.4 presents a step-by-step roadmap for new ventures to both compete and cooperate with established multinationals. Four areas of strategic implications are drawn for new ventures in terms of patenting, licensing, location, and standard setting in forming global IP strategy. At the first stage, the startup stage, a new venture needs to manage several types of patents. These include core technologies that the firm needs to control the ownership, the core-related technologies, the improved technologies, and rival technologies. As the firm becomes more internationalized, it may start to form a clear licensing strategy to manage IP assets. The key method includes simple licence, sole license, sub-license, and cross-license. At this stage, INVs can rely on international IP and legal systems to protect their IP properties based on location strategy. Moving to the final stage, INVs integrate its IP strategy with leading multinationals of specific industry by setting industry standards and technology standards. We address that the four steps do not stay separately but interactively. For new ventures to succeed, they must keep a close eye on large enterprises, especially those that set standards. On one hand, this involves identifying potential IP loopholes in large companies; and on the other hand, it involves discovering gaps in existing technologies and positioning new IP proactively. By participating in or even integrating into SSOs, startups can increase their chances of success.

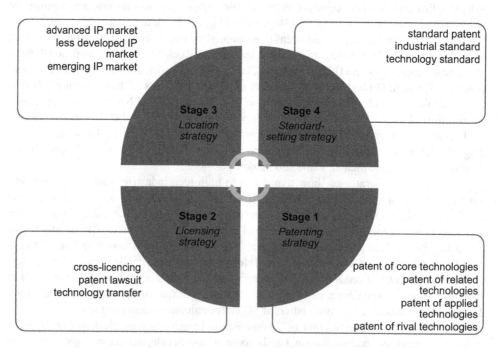

Figure 4.4 A roadmap of forming global IP strategy by new ventures with global orientation.

Source: By the author.

4.4 Conclusion

Firms' innovation is inseparable from the incentives and guidance of the IP protection system. Yet existing IP protection systems are still raising challenges for new ventures to pursue IP protection globally. The chapter focuses on IP protection intuitions which are most relevant to firms with global orientations. We also used examples from established multinationals to draw strategic and practical implications for new ventures with global orientation. We argue that IP protection is highly related to large multinationals' intentions of creating a monopoly. However, for new ventures, after its initial development, it is more likely to end up in one of three scenarios. The first is to monopolize technological advantages, possessing core competitiveness primarily through IP advantages, establishing a firm foothold in the market which continues to expand, and eventually growing into a large multinational, or being acquired at a premium by a large multinational. The second scenario is having core competitiveness, but insufficient IP advantages, making it easy to be imitated or replaced and falling into fierce competition; the best outcome in this scenario is acquisition by a larger company. The third scenario is that the core competitiveness becomes obsolete, the advantages of IP no longer exist, leading to failure due to competitive elimination. We offer a road map of IP strategy for them. For the next, we suggest future studies investigate furthermore on the role of new ventures in building a more globally integrated IP protection system.

Notes

1 More background can be referred to the "Italian Code of Industrial Property", publicly available at https://www.wipo.int/wipolex/es/text/477643, accessed on January 21, 2023.
2 More background can be referred to "The Case of Authors' Rights: A View from Within", publicly available at https://www.wipo.int/wipo_magazine/en/2014/02/article_0004.html, accessed on January 21, 2023.
3 The background can be referred to "Berne Convention for the Protection of Literary and Artistic Works", publicly available at https://www.wipo.int/treaties/en/ip/berne/, accessed on January 21, 2023.
4 The background can be referred to "WIPOD – International Trademark System Talks: Transcript of Episode 5", publicly available at https://www.wipo.int/podcasts/en/madrid/transcripts/international_trademark_system_talk_05.html, accessed on January 21, 2023.
5 The background can be referred to the "Paris Convention for the Protection of Industrial Property", publicly available at https://www.wipo.int/treaties/en/ip/paris/, accessed on January 23, 2023.
6 The background can be referred to "Madrid Agreement Concerning the International Registration of Marks", publicly available at https://www.wipo.int/treaties/en/registration/madrid/, accessed on January 21, 2023.
7 The background can be referred to "World Intellectual Property Organization (WIPO)TRT/CONVENTION/001", publicly available at https://www.wipo.int/wipolex/en/text/283854, accessed on January 21, 2023.
8 The background can be referred to "Trademark Law Treaty (TLT)", publicly available at https://www.wipo.int/treaties/en/ip/tlt/index.html, accessed on January 21, 2023.
9 The background can be referred to "Agreement on Trade-Related Aspects of Intellectual Property Rights", publicly available at https://www.wto.org/english/docs_e/legal_e/27-trips_01_e.htm, accessed on January 21, 2023.
10 The background can be referred to "WIPO Copyright Treaty (WCT)", publicly available at https://www.wipo.int/treaties/en/ip/wct/, accessed on January 21, 2023.
11 The background can be referred to "Comprehensive and Progressive Agreement for Trans-Pacific Partnership Amendment Act 2018 Commencement Order 2018", publicly available at https://www.wipo.int/wipolex/fr/text/531853, accessed on January 21, 2023.
12 The background can be referred to "Patent Law of the People's Republic of China", publicly available at https://english.www.gov.cn/archive/laws_regulations/2014/08/23/content_281474983043612.htm, accessed on April 16, 2023.

13 The background can be referred to "PCT – The International Patent System", publicly available at https://www.wipo.int/pct/en/, accessed on January 23, 2023.
14 The background can be referred to "WIPO Performances and Phonograms Treaty", publicly available at https://www.wipo.int/treaties/en/ip/wppt/, accessed on April 15, 2023.
15 The background of the Protocol can be referred to "Protocol Relating to the Madrid Agreement Concerning the International Registration of Marks", publicly available at https://www.wipo.int/treaties/en/registration/madrid_protocol/, accessed on January 23, 2023.
16 The background of Disney's licensing performance can be found from "Walt Disney Company world's is leading licensor with $56.6bn in licensed products in 2016", publicly available at https://www.thedrum.com/news/2017/04/17/walt-disney-company-worlds-leading-licensor-with-566bn-licensed-products-2016, accessed on January 25, 2023.
17 The detail of the "IP5 Statistics Report 2021 Edition" is publicly available at https://www.five ipoffices.org/node/9151, accessed on January 24, 2023.
18 The figure is from China's statistics and the actual approved application can be even lower. The IP5 Statistics Report in 2000 did not include China.
19 The background can be referred to "PCT-Patent Prosecution Highway Program (PCT-PPH and Global PPH)", publicly available at https://www.wipo.int/pct/en/filing/pct_pph.html, accessed on April 15, 2024.
20 The background can be referred to "RFID Forecasts, Players and Opportunities 2019–2029", publicly available at https://www.idtechex.com/en/research-report/rfid-forecasts-players-and-opportunities-2019–2029/700, accessed on April 16, 2024.

References

Athreye, S., Piscitello, L., & Shadlen, K. C. 2020. Twenty-five years since TRIPS: Patent policy and international business. *Journal of International Business Policy*, 3(4): 315–328.

Cohen, W. M., Nelson, R. R., & Walsh, J. P. 2000. *Protecting their intellectual assets: Appropriability conditions and why U.S. manufacturing firms patent (or not): 7552.* Cambridge: National Bureau of Economic Research, Inc.

Durand, C., & Milberg, W. 2020. Intellectual monopoly in global value chains. *Review of International Political Economy: RIPE*, 27(2): 404–429.

Greener, J. 2015. If you give a mouse a trademark: Disney's monopoly on trademarks in the entertainment industry. *Wake Forest Journal of Business and Intellectual Property Law*, 15(4): 598.

Grindley, P. C., & Teece, D. J. 1997. Managing intellectual capital: Licensing and cross-licensing in semiconductors and electronics. *California Management Review*, 39(2): 8–41.

Hennessey, K. 2020. Intellectual property – Mickey Mouse's intellectual property adventure: What Disney's war on copyrights has to do with trademarks and patents. *Western New England Law Review*, 42(1): 25.

Herbst, P., & Jahn, E. 2017. IP-for-IP or cash-for-IP? R&D competition and the market for technology. *Review of Industrial Organization*, 51(1): 75–101.

Islam, M., Fremeth, A., & Marcus, A. 2018. Signalling by early stage startup: US government research grants and venture capital funding, *Journal of Business Venturing*, 33(1): 35–51.

Keupp, M. M., Friesike, S., & von Zedtwitz, M. 2012. How do foreign firms patent in emerging economies with weak appropriability regimes? Archetypes and motives. *Research Policy*, 41(8): 1422–1439.

Nguyen, A. L. T. 2020. FDI inflows and intellectual property rights for MNEs in emerging markets: An alternative approach through the lens of trademarks in Vietnam (1986–2016). *Multinational Business Review*, 28(4): 483–519.

Papageorgiadis, N., Xu, Y., & Alexiou, C. 2019. The effect of European intellectual property institutions on Chinese outward foreign direct investment. *Management and Organization Review*, 15(1): 81–110.

Ranganathan, R., Ghosh, A., & Rosenkopf, L. 2018. Competition–cooperation interplay during multifirm technology coordination: The effect of firm heterogeneity on conflict and consensus in a technology standards organization. *Strategic Management Journal*, 39(12): 3193–3221.

Ryder, R. D., & Madhavan, A. 2016. *Intellectual property and business: The power of intangible assets.* New Delhi: Sage.

Soeder, D. J. 2020. *The history of oil & gas development in the U.S: 37–61*. Cham: Springer International Publishing.

Sutherland, D., Anderson, J., & Hu, Z. 2020. A comparative analysis of location and non-location-bounded strategic asset seeking in emerging and developed market MNEs: An application of new internalization theory. *International Business Review*, 29(2): 101635.

Symeonidou, N., Bruneel, J., & Autio, E. 2017. Commercialization strategy and internationalization outcomes in technology-based new ventures. *Journal of Business Venturing*, 32: 302–317.

The IP5 Offices. 2022. *IP5 statistics report 2021 edition*. Edited by the EPO: Jointly produced by the EPO, JPO, KIPO, CNIPA, and USPTO.

WIPO. 2016. *Understanding copyright and related rights*. Geneva: World Intellectual Property Organization.

5 From Technology Idea to Value Proposition

Sarah Manthey and Dilek Cetindamar Konazoglu

5.1 Introduction

New technologies have the potential to transform industries, change the way we live and work, and solve some of the world's most pressing problems. Some examples of emerging technologies include artificial intelligence, blockchain, virtual and augmented reality, and the Internet of Things. One of the critical advantages of emerging technologies is their ability to drive innovation and change. For instance, wearable technology refers to electronic devices worn on the body, such as smartwatches and fitness trackers (Shahrubudin and Ramlan, 2019). These devices can transform healthcare, sports, and entertainment by providing real-time data about an individual's health and performance. However, new technologies are typically created without a predefined scope and are driven by scientific curiosity rather than commercial interests. Exploring new technologies' value is essential in fostering technological innovations and commercialization, but many entrepreneurs and managers fail to do so (Manthey et al., 2022).

In this chapter, we shed light on identifying new applications based on novel technical knowledge and making their value relevant to customers. We introduce significant approaches in developing value propositions that consist of statements summarizing why a customer would choose your product or service.

The chapter is organized into five sections. After the introduction, Section 5.2 overviews the technology push (TP) innovation strategy instrumental in utilizing new technologies. Section 5.3 discusses technology value, followed by two sections, each introducing a tool to help new technologies reach their maximum value by transforming ideas into value propositions. While Section 5.4 discusses the Technology Application Selection (TAS) framework, Section 5.5 summarizes the Business Model approach. The chapter ends with concluding remarks.

5.2 Exploring the Technology Value through the Technology Push Innovation Strategy Lens

Following the concept of technology entrepreneurship, which describes the transformation of new technologies into products and services (Bailetti, 2012), the TP innovation strategy can be applied to leverage them. TP is about identifying a technology with potential and developing it further to create value (Maier et al., 2016). It is based on discovering innovative products, driven by finding exceptional applications for new or existing technologies, and literally thrusting technologies into the market (Brem and Voigt, 2009). Generally, it is initiated by technology and ends up with an application for this technology (Henkel and Jung, 2009). Especially regarding the future, TP-based innovations can result in a positive impact on the environment, international relations, industrial structures, and, last but not least, economic growth (Utterback, 1971).

DOI: 10.4324/9781003341284-7

R&D, science, and technology investments significantly generate commercial success (Berkhout et al., 2010). The investment process may involve further research and development, prototyping, testing, and commercialization (Henkel and Jung, 2009). TP is a complex process involving many activities, ranging from basic research to market adoption. It is characterized by significant uncertainty and high risk since the technologies in question are often new. Still, the potential of the benefits is substantial, which explains the ongoing research in this area. Further, customer needs evolve more slowly and change less rapidly compared to the improvement rates of designers of new technologies (Christensen, 1997).

In contrast, Market Pull (MP) innovation strategy starts the other way around by developing products for existing market demand (Maier et al., 2016). For example, market research identifies unsatisfied customer needs or problems that require a solution (Dixon, 2001). Both concepts are essential in effectively managing ideas, trends, or technologies. The coexistence of both approaches (TP and MP) was vigorously debated in past literature, whereby the focus kept shifting from one concept to the other. As a result, over many years, no consensus about which of the two is more promising manifested itself (Maier et al., 2016). Today, the conclusion prevails that neither strategies lead to higher success rates but that the two concepts work hand in hand (Di Stefano et al., 2012). A seamless transition and connection of both strategies are recommended, starting with TP and moving to MP when the idea is sufficiently mature.

Indeed, TP projects tend to have a more radical or disruptive character and promise longer-term, more sustainable, and tremendous success (Roth, 2022), while incremental innovations or improvements are superficially user-centric (Verganti, 2011). Due to their radical character, game-changing technologies can form new markets, turn underestimated market players into leaders, or draw attention to a new brand. Consequently, possible market potentials are high for TP projects, making the predicted sales from business cases superior to MP (Herstatt and Lettl, 2000). However, a comprehensive strategy for TP needs to consider both the technical feasibility of the technology and its market potential to ensure successful commercialization.

This chapter adopts the Unified Process Model of Technology Push (UPMTP) as a feasible strategy for commercializing new technologies. In contrast to several models available for TP innovation that depict different phases to support the initial stages of the innovation, the UPMTP (Terzidis and Vogel, 2018) is a consolidated model, encompassing all the necessary and outlined process steps. This model provides a structured approach consisting of four stages to managing the complex process of technological innovation, as shown in Figure 5.1. Furthermore, including the Technology Readiness Level provides a metric for assessing the maturity of the technology being developed at each stage.

According to the findings of Terzidis and Vogel (2018), the development process for TP innovations can be divided into four phases and two segments, technology advancement and supporting management activities. The foundation phase focuses on the technical side of detecting, planning, and finding, while the management side sets the project scope. In the TAS phase, a detailed understanding of the technology is required. Several applications must be identified, evaluated, and selected to verify the strategy-idea fit and set a strategy for the following process. The third phase, explorative development, aims to improve and test the technology in iterative steps to gain management approval and secure financial resources. Product introduction's final phase involves developing a market-ready product, establishing close market relationships, and achieving market penetration. The Technology Readiness Level coincides with all four phases (Terzidis and Vogel, 2018).

According to Terzidis and Vogel (2018), a critical stage in the TP process is the second stage, the TAS. The application must be discovered before a new technology can lead to successful change (Shane, 2000). Hence, supporting approaches for identifying application fields are

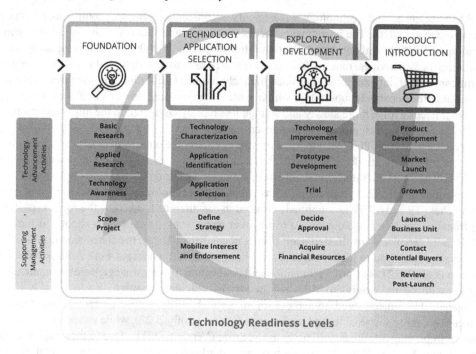

Figure 5.1 The unified model of the technology push process, adapted from Terzidis and Vogel (2018).

sparse (Henkel and Jung, 2009). Many delays in technology commercialization are justified by a poor match between the solution and the customer's needs (Jolly, 1997). Research shows that the decisions in the early phase of the front-end innovation, particularly during application identification and selection, determine the later success of companies (Koen et al., 2001). Although numerous patented technologies can potentially create TP innovations, most remain untouched (Manthey et al., 2022). The reason for this seems to be the lack of practical approaches for the technology application in an innovation process. Many methods and tools exist for user-centric MP innovations, such as design thinking. However, TP innovations are perceived as complex and challenging (Bishop and Magleby, 2004). By modifying a generic MP model, Larsen (2001) developed a general model for the technology integration step, indicating a linear flow from technology development to technology integration and product development (Larsen, 2001).

This modification led to the first generic TP model, which was further developed by Terzidis and Vogel (2018), who focused on facilitating the second phase of the TP process. They developed a workshop design aimed at reducing the hurdles encountered during this phase and facilitating progress through this phase. The resulting model, the TAS framework, is designed for workshop application and incorporates selected methods and tools from the literature to support technology advancement activities. It also forms the basis for the work of Manthey et al. (2022), whose TAS framework is further explored in the following section.

5.3 From Idea to Value Proposition: TAS Framework

The TAS framework focuses on the technology advancement activities in the second phase of the UPMTP (Terzidis and Vogel, 2018) and was further developed by Manthey et al. (2022). It is designed as a workshop in several contexts and aims at several target groups

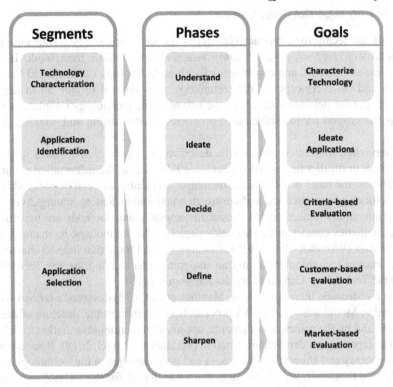

Figure 5.2 Three segments and five phases of the TAS framework, own illustration.

of different institutions, tech-based companies, educators, and many more. It includes three phases: technology characterization, application identification, and application selection process. The segments comprise the five phases shown in Figure 5.2, each supported by several methods. The following paragraphs describe the individual phases in more detail by presenting their objectives and the methods included.

The segments comprise five phases, each aiming to achieve different goals. The first phase, "Understand," seeks to gain a fundamental and deep understanding of the underlying technology, which should be achieved through a technology characterization. The second phase, "Ideate," aims to explore potential applications for the underlying technology with the support of different ideation anchors. Furthermore, duplicates should be eliminated and clustered thematically by sorting the ideas. In the third phase, "Decide," the focus lies on the primary evaluation of the identified applications with the support of pre-defined evaluation criteria. An assessment with experts from different fields complements this. Experts elaborate on the most promising idea in detail at the end of this phase. The fourth phase, "Define," aims to understand customers and their needs using different methods. Finally, critical hypotheses need to be determined and scored out of quantified risks and impacts to test and compare the basic assumptions aligning with the development of the idea. The last phase, "Sharpen," intends to identify competitors and compare the developed idea based on relevant dimensions with those. Subsequently, the value proposition, a customer value created by products or services (Clark et al., 2012), is to be determined and defined. Consequently, the outcome of the TAS process is a validated value proposition based on technology.

5.3.1 Risks in Early Stage Technology Ventures

The phase of the technology characterization is the first technology advancement activity in the second step, *technology application selection*, of the TAS framework. It aligns the characteristics, advantages, and challenges of a given technology (Terzidis and Vogel, 2018). All features and basic concepts of the technology are analyzed to gain an in-depth understanding and transfer detailed facts about the nature of the technology (Winken et al., 2010). It serves as the ground for the subsequent processes by structuring and aligning the present concepts.

Technology characterization can also be described as a process that refers to solutions to solve a problem or fulfill a functionality (Taylor, 1978). Due to the information about the technical capabilities, the basic principles are mediated, and ambiguity can be reduced. The intention is to facilitate communication and ensure an equal understanding among diverse types of engineers (Galvan and Malak, 2015). Standard templates and methods are used to describe different technologies consistently, with fields depicting the technology, its maturity level, and performance data (Warschat et al., 2015). Commonly used tools that help to characterize and intensively analyze technologies to gain an in-depth understanding are the Technology Fact Sheets and the Technology Canvas (Terzidis and Vogel, 2018).

Based on a systematic literature review, Manthey et al. (2023) designed a refined Technology Characterization Model used in the TAS process. It is inspired by the structure of the business model canvas and by the principles of patents, specifying essential information to define a new invention and capturing all detailed information (Terzidis and Vogel, 2018). It accounts for clarity and transparency and shows the advantages and disadvantages of the technology (Lipsmeier et al., 2018). On this basis, numerous ideas can be collected for the technology's application during the following step, the *application identification* (Henkel and Jung, 2009).

5.3.2 Application Identification

The application identification represents the second phase in the *Technology Application Selection* stage of the TAS framework (Terzidis and Vogel, 2018). After the technology is characterized, diverse application possibilities must be generated (Danneels and Frattini, 2018). An application is "a way in which something can be used for a particular purpose" (Cambridge Dictionary, 2022) – analogous to searching for the proper use case. Ordinarily, the outcome of this phase is not just a single use case but many different possible applications (Kornish and Hutchison-Krupat, 2016). Other researchers use the synonym opportunity identification or idea generation to describe this process (Ardichvili et al., 2003) – while these terms are often found in entrepreneurship literature (Arts, 2012).

The identification process depends strongly on knowledge and further cognitive aspects (Ucbasaran et al., 2009). Above all, creativity and divergent thinking are crucial aspects during this phase that can be triggered by various external or internal stimuli (Salvi and Bowden, 2016). Examples of such incentives are discussions, communication exchange (Gemmell et al., 2012), technological or industry trend screenings (Schallmo, 2018), or patent mapping (Cooper, 2008). The latter looks at existing patents to identify new, unavailable application areas for technologies through comparisons to draw up new opportunities (Cooper, 2008). Many well-known creativity techniques, e.g., brainstorming, the 5W+H method, role playing, social listening, brain sketching, 6-3-5, or mind mapping, support this process (Osborne, 2019). The present technology must be understood entirely since, without a clear understanding, no good use cases can be identified (Gallersdörfer and Matthes, 2020).

In the ideation phase, the user is supposed to explore ideation anchors for which three different anchors are available as inspiration. One is the Gartner Hype Cycle, a graphical representation of emerging technologies and applications, including their potential relevance to solving real business problems and seizing new business opportunities, which is supposed to separate trends from actual drivers. Also included as inspiration is the ISIC (International Standard Industrial Classification), a standard United Nations Statistics Division classification of economic activities arranged so entities can be classified according to their activities. In addition, the Sustainable Development Goals are available, comprising the 17 goals written by the United Nations to serve sustainable economic, ecological, and social development. After exploring the ideation anchors, multiple ideas should be identified and sorted so that duplicates are eliminated before the ideas are supposed to be clustered. For example, the ideas can be sorted in a How-Wow-Now-Ciao Matrix that categorizes the ideas to what extent they are feasible and original. In sum, ideas must be rigorously reviewed and cultivated to result in profitable opportunities.

5.3.3 Application Selection

Evaluating and selecting ideas is one of the most critical steps in the new product development process, can provide immense business value, and coins the future shape of the company's success (Cooper, 2008). Finding the most promising opportunity for technology can be called idea selection in innovation management (Danneels and Frattini, 2018). During the process, vague ideas are transformed into promising concepts worth entering the subsequent development stages. It is about uncovering hidden opportunities or novel application areas for new or existing technologies, thereby creating central value for users (Magistretti et al., 2020). After the ideas have been generated, the selection of the most worthwhile ideas to invest in follows (Koen et al., 2001). The stage aims to filter out the most promising ideas (Divakaran, 2016).

Application Selection compromises three phases: Decide, Define, and Sharpen. In Decide, the focus is initially on the common understanding of the evaluation criteria, such as the technical feasibility or profitability, before the identified ideas are evaluated in a decision matrix. In the decision matrix, the ideas are rated on a five-point scale. With the network of experts that the users have built up, the ideas are re-evaluated. In the process, users may encounter surprising findings. Finally, the most promising ideas should be determined and can be visually sketched for a better idea description.

The purpose of the Define phase is primarily to understand the customers and their needs. Methods, such as the Persona, can be used to determine potential customers. Furthermore, users are supposed to define the core functional job. With the support of the job map, opportunities can be identified, whereafter desired outcomes are to be monitored. Then, critical hypotheses should be determined, and scores out of quantified risks and impacts should be generated to test and compare the essential assumptions.

Competitors will be identified starting the TAS framework's final phase (Sharpen). The most important factors of the user's solution should be evaluated and compared to the competitors in a Value Profile. Subsequently, the value proposition, a customer value created by products or services (Clark et al., 2012), is to be determined and defined. The outcome of this final phase is the assessment of the critical value for the customer, represented in a value proposition statement.

5.4 From Idea to Value Proposition: Business Model Approach

In recent years, technology entrepreneurship has been undergoing a significant transformation, as digitalization has had a tremendous impact on technological innovations and the TP innovation strategy (Giones and Brem, 2017). Typically, TP processes were triggered by new advancements in materials, manufacturing processes, or design that led to new products. Nowadays, digitalization and the integration of digital technologies into all aspects of the economy and society have created new opportunities and challenges for technology entrepreneurs, as the digitization of the "technology" not only changes its properties but also impacts the overall technology entrepreneurship process (Nambisan, 2016). Moreover, digitalization has enabled the adoption of technology to push innovation strategy. This strategy involves identifying emerging technologies and developing new products and services that leverage those technologies. The rapid pace of technological change in the digital age means entrepreneurs must constantly scan the horizon for emerging technologies and trends. Giones and Brem (2017), therefore, constitute the concept of digital technology entrepreneurship, which combines elements of technology and digital entrepreneurship, proposing an extension of the existing definition of technology entrepreneurship (Bailetti, 2012): digital technology entrepreneurship is focused on the identification and exploitation of opportunities based on scientific or technological knowledge through the creation of digital artifacts. Digital technology entrepreneurs build firms based on technologies on the one hand and services on the other hand.

Technology-based ventures deal with high uncertainties. Hence, digital entrepreneurs find themselves managing open innovation initiatives such as digital platforms. An open innovation-based process refers to a process where ideas and projects can be transferred as inputs to a company at any innovation stage. Still, similarly, they might turn into outputs transferred to external organizations. In particular, monitoring how partners or customers utilize technology innovations is critical for technology entrepreneurs to succeed in commercialization (Earle et al., 2019). A digital platform such as the Uber taxi application is a set of core resources and technology standards that support value co-creation through digital technologies with stakeholders such as customers and suppliers (Cetindamar and Phaal, 2021).

Open innovation works well for digital entrepreneurs, who exploit market opportunities across boundaries by constantly designing value propositions rather than merely innovating (Antonopoulou and Begkos, 2020). This is because digital entrepreneurs rely on digital innovations. These digital innovations have the potential to be modular, resulting in many entrepreneurial ways of combining digital components, platforms, and infrastructure (Si et al., 2022). Digital components refer to the applications or media contents with specific functions and values embedded in digital products or services, such as mobile phone applications. A digital platform is a set of shared, common services and architectures, such as extensible operating systems like Android. Finally, digital infrastructure refers to digital technology tools and systems that provide communication, collaboration, or computing capabilities and support resource aggregation, such as network platforms that provide computing, communication, and resource aggregation channels (Marion and Fixson, 2021).

The overview of digital technologies clearly shows the complexity digital startups are facing. In addition, like any technology, digital entrepreneurs face a crucial problem any other technology entrepreneur faces: the "Valley of Death." In other words, a given technology fails to market because many startups fail to translate their research into successful products/services (Auerswald and Branscombe, 2003).

Ghezzi and Cavallo (2020) underline that the difficulties in the early stages of a technology-focused venture come from two primary sources. First, when technology moves from the laboratory to the market, it necessitates several experiments and adjustments to the product/service offerings. These adjustments are known as pivoting. Second, digital startups have to cope with environmental dynamism that either forces them to adapt their business model to the volatile environment or offers them the chance to innovate their business model.

Technology entrepreneurs constantly think of value offerings that are the heart of any business model. Teece (2010) defines a business model as "how the enterprise creates and delivers value to customers and then converts payments received to profits." Chesbrough (2010) highlights which startup has the highest success potential by claiming, "A mediocre technology pursued within a great business model may be more valuable than a great technology exploited via a mediocre business model." In a nutshell, the business model could be seen as a constellation of the three critical activities shown in Figure 5.3: value proposition, generation, and capture.

The core of the business model is the definition of a value proposition to communicate the most evident benefit customers receive by giving you their business. Every value proposition should speak to a customer's challenge and make a case for your company as the problem-solver. In other words, value proposition describes the benefit that a firm creates for its (potential) customers or partners. It explains in-depth which product/service will be offered to customers and in which configuration. Thus, it entails defining the critical market, including its key segments (segmentation of everyday customer needs). A great value proposition may highlight what differentiates you from competitors, but it should always focus on how customers define your value.

Digitization has profoundly reshaped the way business opportunities are discovered and exploited. In particular, business digitization calls for firms to adopt a system-based, value-creation–centric perspective for designing and organizing their resource configurations (Amit

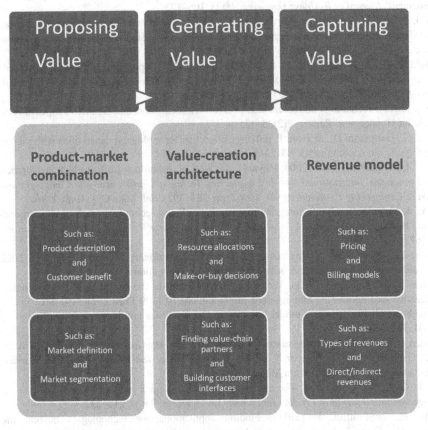

Figure 5.3 Business Model, own illustration adapted from Stähler (2001).

and Han, 2017). This process necessitates resource configuration prototypes, value-creation sources, and the underlying resource configuration processes enabled by digitization. Digitization expands the scope of resources a firm could utilize while requiring firms to take a holistic approach in considering the resources and addressing the needs of all customers and partners (e.g., resource providers). Hence, it is essential to highlight the importance of a holistic approach to enhancing the value creation potential in the digital age for entrepreneurs and managers.

5.5 Concluding Remarks

This chapter aims to clarify how technology entrepreneurs could identify and develop applications based on novel technical knowledge and how they could create a compelling value proposition that drives success in the marketplace. We suggested two key tools: the TAS framework and business model approaches in tackling the transition from idea to product or service.

References

Amit, R., & Han, X. (2017). Value creation through novel resource configurations in a digitally enabled world. *Strategic Entrepreneurship Journal, 11*(3): 228–242.

Antonopoulou, K., & Begkos, C. (2020). Strategizing for digital innovations: Value propositions for transcending market boundaries. *Technological Forecasting and Social Change, 156,* 120042

Ardichvili, A., Cardozo, R., & Ray, S. (2003). A theory of entrepreneurial opportunity identification and development. *Journal of Business Venturing, 18*(1), 105–123.

Arts, B. J. M. (2012). *New business development at ASML: Towards a framework for identifying, selecting, and developing new business opportunities* [Master Thesis, Eindhoven University of Technology]. Elsevier.

Auerswald, P. E., & Branscombe, L. M. (2003). Start-ups and spin-offs. Collective entrepreneurship between invention and innovation. In D. M. Hart (Ed.) *The Emergence of Entrepreneurship Policy* (pp. 61–91). Cambridge: Cambridge University Press.

Bailetti, T. (2012). Technology entrepreneurship: Overview, definition, and distinctive aspects. *Technology Innovation Management Review, 2*(2), 5–12.

Berkhout, G., Hartmann, D., & Trott, P. (2010). Connecting technological capabilities with market needs using a cyclic innovation model. *R&d Management, 40*(5), 474–490.

Bishop, G. L., & Magleby, S. P. (2004, January). A review of technology push product development models and processes. *International Design Engineering Technical Conferences and Computers and Information in Engineering Conference* (Vol. 46962, pp. 383–392). Salt Lake City, Utah, USA.

Brem, A., & Voigt, K. I. (2009). Integration of market pull and technology push in the corporate front end and innovation management—Insights from the German software industry. *Technovation, 29*(5), 351–367.

Cambridge Dictionary. (2022). Application. In *Cambridge Dictionary*. Retrieved March 2, 2022, from https://dictionary.cambridge.org/de/worterbuch/englisch/application

Cetindamar, D., & Phaal, R. (2021). Technology management in the age of digital technologies. *IEEE Transactions on Engineering Management.* https://doi.org/10.1109/TEM.2021.3101196

Chesbrough, H. (2010). Business model innovation: Opportunities and barriers. *Long Range Planning, 43*(2–3), 354–363.

Christensen, C. M. (1997). Marketing strategy: Learning by doing. *Harvard Business Review, 75*(6), 141–151.

Clark, T., Osterwalder, A., & Pigneur, Y. (2012). *Business Model You: Dein Leben-Deine Karriere-Dein Spiel.* Campus Verlag, Frankfurt am Main, Germany.

Cooper, R. G. (2008). Perspective: The Stage-Gate ® idea-to-launch process – Update, what's new, and NexGen systems. *Journal of Product Innovation Management, 25*(3), 213–232.

Danneels, E., & Frattini, F. (2018). Finding applications for technologies beyond the core business. *MIT Sloan Management Review.* https://sloanreview.mit.edu/article/finding-applications-for-technologies-beyond-the-core-business/

Divakaran, P. K. P. (2016). When users offer up ideas: How to evaluate them. *Journal of Business Strategy*, *37*(5), 32–38.

Di Stefano, G., Gambardella, A., & Verona, G. (2012). Technology push and demand pull perspectives in innovation studies: Current findings and future research directions. *Research Policy*, *41*(8), 1283–1295.

Dixon, J. (2001). The market pull versus technology push continuum of engineering education. *2001 Annual Conference Proceedings* (pp. 6–1027). Albuquerque, New Mexico, USA.

Earle, A. G., Merenda, M. J., & Davis, J. M. (2019). Strategy-as-Process in a technology venture: A case study of pivots, pauses, partners, and progress. *Technology Innovation Management Review*, *9*(1), 9–19.

Gallersdörfer, U., & Matthes, F. (2020). Towards valid use cases: Requirements and supporting characteristics of proper blockchain applications. *Seventh International Conference on Software Defined Systems (SDS)* (pp. 202–207). IEEE.

Galvan, E., & Malak, R. J. (2015). P3GA: An algorithm for technology characterization. *Journal of Mechanical Design*, *137*(1), 011401.

Gemmell, R. M., Boland, R. J., & Kolb, D. A. (2012). The socio–cognitive dynamics of entrepreneurial ideation. *Entrepreneurship Theory and Practice*, *36*(5), 1053–1073.

Ghezzi, A., & Cavallo, A. (2020). Agile business model innovation in digital entrepreneurship: Lean startup approaches. *Journal of Business Research*, *110*, 519–537.

Giones, F., & Brem, A. (2017). Digital technology entrepreneurship: A definition and research agenda. *Technology Innovation Management Review*, *7*(5), 44–51.

Henkel, J., & Jung, S. (2009). The technology-push lead user concept: A new tool for application identification. Working Paper. https://research.wu.ac.at/en/publications/technology-push-lead-user-concept-a-new-tool-for-application-iden-5.

Herstatt, C., & Lettl, C. (2000). *Management of "technology push" development projects* [Working paper, TU Hamburg-Harburg]. https://tore.tuhh.de/handle/11420/106

Jolly, V. K. (1997). *Commercializing new technologies: Getting from mind to market*. Boston: Harvard Business Press.

Koen, P., Ajamian, G., Burkart, R., Clamen, A., Davidson, J., D'Amore, R., ... & Wagner, K. (2001). Providing clarity and a common language to the "fuzzy front end". *Research-Technology Management*, *44*(2), 46–55.

Kornish, L. J., & Hutchison-Krupat, J. (2016). Research on idea generation and selection: Implications for management of technology. *Production and Operations Management*, *26*(4), 633–651.

Larsen, J. B. (2001). *An engineering approach for matching technology to product applications*. Department of Mechanical Engineering, Brigham Young University.

Lipsmeier, A., Bansmann, M., Roeltgen, D., & Kuerpick, C. (2018). Framework for the identification and demand-orientated classification of digital technologies. In *2018 IEEE International Conference on Technology Management, Operations and Decisions (ICTMOD)*, 31–36. Marrakech, Morocco

Magistretti, S., Dell'Era, C., & Verganti, R. (2020). Look for new opportunities in existing technologies: Leveraging temporal and spatial dimensions to power discovery. *Research-Technology Management*, *63*(1), 39–48.

Maier, M. A., Hofmann, M., & Brem, A. (2016). Technology and trend management at the interface of technology push and market pull. *International Journal of Technology Management*, *72*(4), 310–332.

Manthey, S., Eckerle, C., & Terzidis, O. (2022, September). Tackling the critical hurdles: Revising technology-based ideation processes. In *European Conference on Innovation and Entrepreneurship* (Vol. 17, No. 1, pp. 327–335).

Manthey, S. I., Scholtysik, M., and Terzidis, O. (2023). Exploring the Role of Application Identification and Selection in Technology Push Models: A Comprehensive Analysis IEEE International Conference on Technology Management, Operations and Decisions (ICTMOD).

Marion, T. J. & Fixson, S. K., (2021). The transformation of the innovation process: How digital tools are changing work, collaboration, and organizations in new product development. *Journal of Production and Innovation Management*, *38*(1), 192–215.

Osborne, J. (2019). *7 Creative idea generation methods*. StartUs Magazine. Retrieved May 19, 2022, from https://magazine.startus.cc/7-creative-idea-generation-methods/

Roth, M. (2022). 'Wie die Lemminge' – Technologie Push vs. Technologie Pull. Dos und Dont's bei Technologie Push Projekten. *MoreThanDigital*. Retrieved March 3, 2022, from https://morethandigital. info/wie-die-lemminge-technologie-push-vs-technologie-pull/

Salvi, C., & Bowden, E. M. (2016). Looking for creativity: Where do we look when we look for new ideas? *Frontiers in Psychology*, *7*(161), 1–12.

Schallmo, D. R. A. (2018). Techniken der Geschäftsmodell-Visions-Entwicklung. In D. R. A. Schallmo, *Geschäftsmodelle erfolgreich entwickeln und implementieren* (pp. 125–149). Berlin, Heidelberg: Springer.

Shahrubudin, N., Lee, T. C., & Ramlan, R. J. P. M. (2019). An overview on 3D printing technology: Technological, materials, and applications. *Procedia Manufacturing*, *35*, 1286–1296.

Shane, S. (2000). Prior knowledge and the discovery of entrepreneurial opportunities. *Organization Science*, *11*(4), 448–469.

Si, S., Hall, J., Suddaby, R., Ahlstrom, D., & Wei, J. (2022). Technology, entrepreneurship, innovation and social change in digital economics. *Technovation*, 139. https://doi.org/10.1016/j.technovation.2022.102484

Stähler, P. (2001). *Geschäftsmodellen in der digitalen Ökonomie: Merkmale, Strategien und Auswirkungen*. Lohmar, Köln: Josef Eul Verlag.

Taylor, G. C. (1978). *Methodologies for characterizing technologies*. Palo Alto, CA: Electric Power Research Inst.

Teece, D. J. (2010). Business Models, Business Strategy and Innovation. *Long Range Planning*, 43(2–3), 172–194.

Terzidis, O., & Vogel, L. (2018). A unified model of the technology push process and its application in a workshop setting. In A. Presse & O. Terzidis (Eds.). *Technology Entrepreneurship. FGF Studies in Small Business and Entrepreneurship*. Springer, Cham. https://doi.org/10.1007/978-3-319-73509-2_6.

Ucbasaran, D., Westhead, P., & Wright, M. (2009). The extent and nature of opportunity identification by experienced entrepreneurs. *Journal of Business Venturing*, *24*(2), 99–115.

Utterback, J. M. (1971). The process of innovation: A study of the origination and development of ideas for new scientific instruments. *IEEE Transactions on Engineering Management*, *18*(4), 124–131. https://doi.org/10.1109/TEM.1971.6448350

Verganti, R. (2011). Radical design and technology epiphanies: A new focus for research on design management. *Journal of Product Innovation Management*, *28*(3), 384–388.

Warschat, J., Schimpf, S., & Korell, M. (2015). *Technologien frühzeitig erkennen*. Stuttgart: Frauenhofer Verlag.

Winken, M., Boße, S., Bross, B., Helle, P., Hinz, T., Kirchhoffer, H., Lakshman, H., Marpe, D., Oudin, S., & Preiß, M. (2010). Description of video coding technology proposal by Fraunhofer HHI. In *Joint Collaborative Team on Video Coding (JCT-VC) of ITU-T SG16 WP3 and ISO/IEC JTC1/SC29/WG11 1st Meeting, Dresden, DE*.

6 Product Development

Saadeddine Shehab, Rachel Switzky, and Keilin Jahnke

6.1 Introduction

Firms of all sizes engage in technology entrepreneurship through new product development. Both large organizations and small start-ups benefit from the development of new products and processes, although the context in which they function – including organizational structure, budgetary constraints, and space and laboratory access – is varied. In general, large organizations can dedicate research and development resources and funding to innovative product development with relatively low risk while start-ups work in a climate that makes innovation a potentially high-risk endeavor. Regardless of organization size, product development is a key element of technology entrepreneurship and intrapreneurship. The purpose of this chapter is to first describe how organizations that engage in technological entrepreneurship can develop products by implementing a Human-Centered Design (HCD) approach and then discuss the implications of using this approach on the product development process.

Organizations need a product, service, or process for its customers and can use techniques and strategies to develop innovative offerings or systems (Keeley et al., 2013). As described in the previous chapter, successful entrepreneurs understand how to systematically develop products, services, and processes that deliver on the organization's defined value proposition and meet a need for particular stakeholders. In some enterprises, this understanding of the stakeholder and their needs comes first before the development of a product. In this case, a customer or client is identified and products are designed and iterated specifically for this group and their context. In other cases, products are designed without a specific application or market in mind. This process of innovation is utilized in many organizations, including in research laboratories, and concludes in the development of interesting, novel, and often complex or highly technical outputs. If technology commercialization subsequently becomes a goal, then the individual or team must then determine how to strategically develop a robust understanding of the market, identify a specific customer segment, and make modifications to the product as necessary to more successfully meet the requirements of the customer. Furthermore, Cropley distinguishes between *bottom-up* and *top-down design* in engineering in which bottom-up design seeks to determine what needs might be addressed with a particular, already developed object whereas top-down asks what objects might be designed to satisfy a particular need (2015). For all inventions designated for commercialization, regardless of origination path, entrepreneurs benefit from having a framework that entails a toolbox of techniques and processes to facilitate deep understanding and framing of a design challenge, innovative ideation, and successful implementation of a proposed solution to the challenge.

One such framework is HCD. HCD places an emphasis on needs-based design and understanding the constraints and desires of the stakeholders (Brown, 2008). HCD processes aid

DOI: 10.4324/9781003341284-8

designers in understanding the context in which they are designing and the stakeholder for whom they are developing a product or service. A comprehensive design approach, HCD offers strategies in problem definition, ideation, rapid prototyping, and implementation. This is a useful and beneficial process for organizations with a variety of value propositions and financial, time, and resource constraints. HCD processes can be used in conjunction with any primary constraints and technical requirements to help technology entrepreneurs answer this question: *Given the constraints and requirements of our organization, how might we develop a product that will be both (1) initially useful to and (2) continued to be used by our customer/client and other stakeholders?*

Subsequently, this question leads to a process of defining who the customer/client and stakeholders are, defining what qualifies as "useful" to this customer/client, identifying organization constraints and technical requirements and standards, and then embarking on product ideation, prototyping, and implementation. This can also be described as first taking a desirability perspective and then incorporating viability and feasibility constraints.

This chapter seeks to aid practitioners in understanding this HCD framework and how it can be directly applicable to technology entrepreneurship and provide tools to enhance the likelihood of success. We begin by defining HCD, its processes, and mindsets, then we discuss the implications of HCD on product development. In this chapter, the terms "user", "client", and "customer" are used interchangeably to represent the group for which a new product is directly being developed (i.e., the market). This is the organization or individuals that will directly interact with the new product. The term "stakeholder" is used to more broadly define all of the actors within the problem space and who have a stake in the commercialization process of the specific technology.

6.2 Human-Centered Design Processes and Mindsets

Design thinking can be described as (1) the development of a toolbox of specific divergent and convergent thinking methods, (2) a process for design, and (3) a mindset to test assumptions and seek novelty in ideation (de Paula et al., 2022). HCD is a creative problem-solving approach where designers implement design thinking methods and tools to understand the unmet needs of a population in order to collaboratively and iteratively develop relevant and meaningful solutions (Brown, 2008). HCD provides technology entrepreneurs with a set of design tools to develop innovative ideas, an agile process for product development, and structure to test hypotheses. The commercialization of technology – making a product available on the market – is typically done after a product has been developed and tested. HCD provides a framework for product development to make commercialization the primary objective of the entire development process.

HCD relies on empathy and iteration (Brown, 2008). It emphasizes the human elements in the design processes such as the designers, the team members in the project, and all other possible stakeholders. When using HCD, designers collaborate with individuals from different disciplines and backgrounds to understand stakeholders' needs, explore topics, observe relevant sites, and reflect on their assumptions and biases (Brown & Katz, 2011; Dorst, 2011; Zhang & Dong, 2008). They identify problems and gaps and synthesize design opportunities. Then, they collaborate with the stakeholders to generate design ideas and prototype these ideas. As certain designs and concepts start to emerge, designers need to consider factors that may influence or are influenced by the implementation in the market.

Building on existing design thinking models (e.g., IDEO, 2015), Lawrence et al. (2024) devised a three-tiered model that outlines the complex mechanisms of the HCD approach.

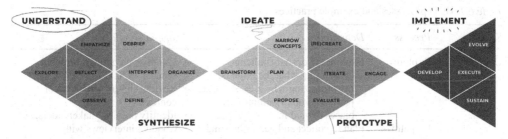

Figure 6.1 Human-Centered Design framework.

Within the model, the three tiers are (1) spaces, (2) processes, and (3) practices. The model consists of five spaces: *Understand, Synthesize, Ideate, Prototype*, and *Implement* (Figure 6.1). Each design space is a unique, stand-alone component where individuals engage with four different processes of HCD to create and make choices. While there is a general sense of linearity to this representation, it was designed intentionally to be flexible, wherein the triangles can be rearranged and duplicated to illustrate the reality of the emergent approach (Boling & Smith, 2010; Teal, 2010). It is also important to note that the triangular segments that make up each space have equal sizes indicating that equal weight is placed on each HCD process in the framework. Exploring the problem or need context in the Understand space, for instance, is as important as evaluating different ideas in the Prototype space. This does not, however, necessitate that equal amounts of time or duration is spent in each space or process. Design teams can determine a timeframe that is appropriate for their specific context.

Table 6.1 presents the definition of the 20 HCD processes that are shown in Figure 6.1. It also provides brief descriptions of example practices that designers implement when executing each process.

The presented HCD framework can be used to systematically develop a technological product for commercialization. The framework consists of processes and practices that allow product developers to develop a contextualized understanding of the market, highlight potential opportunities that address user needs within this market, and create novel solutions using their science and engineering knowledge to make effective decisions throughout the design process. The following are key concepts that science and engineers can employ during product development in technological entrepreneurship per each space of the presented framework.

6.2.1 Understand

The Understand space processes seek to help product developers discern the context in which they are working and empathize with the stakeholders for whom they are designing. Let us imagine a scenario where a team of scientists and engineers are working on developing a technological product within an established technological firm. Before generating a wealth of technical ideas and building prototypes of the product, the team should first spend an adequate amount of time implementing the processes of the Understand space. For example, the team can start by exploring the possible capacities, limitations, and impacts of the targeted technology on stakeholders, society, environment, and economy. The team can also explore their strengths and weaknesses, build a joint understanding of the project at hand, and set up communication channels so team members can stay informed about what others are doing. Later, the team can compile a list of possible stakeholders and conduct in-depth interviews with the different stakeholders in order to immerse themselves in their experiences and understand their needs.

Table 6.1 HCD processes and example practices

Space	Process	Definition	Example practices
Understand	Explore	Explore the design challenge by defining what the issue is, hypothesizing why it exists, and realizing your assumptions and biases toward it.	• Establish a common problem space. • Review current landscape or context. • Identify possible stakeholders.
	Empathize	Plan to collect and gather existing information or experiences from stakeholders.	• Conduct interviews with stakeholders. • Identify extreme users. • Use empathic modeling.
	Observe	Plan to collect and gather existing observations of a space or immersion with environments relevant to your design challenge.	• Conduct observations in a certain setting. • Immerse oneself within an environment.
	Reflect	Reflect on the goals and context and plan to make progress on the design challenge.	• Revisit project context. • Find gaps. • Modify research plans. • Identify and clarify stakeholders. • Document assumptions, biases, and predictions.
Synthesize	Debrief	Share collected data with stakeholders or team members.	• Establish shared understanding of the problem space. • Review current landscape or context accuracy. • Clarify and record your team biases and predictions.
	Organize	Develop themes by drawing comparisons across ideas to generate patterns and insights.	• Collapse content from debrief. • Find themes and patterns. • Document insights from data.
	Define	Identify design opportunities through creating a "how might we" (HMW) question.	• Identify solution opportunities. • Develop HMW questions. • Prioritize your users' needs.
	Interpret	Using the themes, insights, opportunities, and HMWs to identify how to move the project forward and what the next steps are.	• Find gaps: What do we still need to know? • Clarify parameters of the project. • Simplify and focus the HMWs to inspire. • Understand constraints and project scope.
Ideate	Brainstorm	Generate ideas to seize design opportunities by answering the HMW questions.	• Go for quantity. • Defer judgment. • Exhaust possibilities.
	Propose	Communicate the proposed ideas to stakeholders to collect and integrate feedback.	• Communicate suggested ideas. • Iterate your ideas based on new feedback received. • Think of alternative ideas to share again.
	Narrow Concepts	Identify which concepts are the most viable to move forward with the project.	• Revisit stakeholders' needs. • Examine available resources. • Make decisions on most viable concepts.

(Continued)

Table 6.1 (Continued)

Space	Process	Definition	Example practices
	Plan	Using the developed concepts, plan for the next steps, including what and how to prototype and implement a concept.	• Prepare for prototyping your idea. • Develop a plan for prototyping. • Determine the level of fidelity for your prototypes and who will give feedback.
Prototype	Create	Construct low and high-fidelity prototypes of the proposed physical, digital, or experiential concept (e.g., physical model and sketch).	• Determine the best way to show and share proposed solutions. • Create different versions of the proposed idea.
	Engage	Communicate the created prototype to users, stakeholders, or team members.	• Share prototypes with users, stakeholders, or team members for feedback • Iterate based on the new feedback received. • Think of alternative ideas to share again.
	Evaluate	Evaluate the engagement process and outcomes.	• Observe users', stakeholders', or team members' responses to and uses of the prototypes through interviews, testing, practice, and documentation.
	Iterate	Explore multiple variations of your concept.	• Use feedback from users, stakeholders, or team members to revise prototypes to build more effective, viable, and desirable solutions. • Repeat evaluation cycle as needed.
Implement	Develop	Develop a plan to make the design a reality.	• Present prototyped solution. • Prepare marketing materials to attract investment. • Plan for a launch within an organization.
	Evolve	Plan for, collect, and implement stakeholders' feedback to ensure successful implementation and evolution.	• Continue to resolve issues with solutions based on user feedback, presentation, and team discussions. • Document changes and save ideas for future iterations or versions of the solution.
	Sustain	Monitor and evaluate social, economical, and environmental factors that are associated with the design.	• Plan for sustainability (e.g., environmental, societal, business practices).
	Execute	Execute functional versions of the design.	• Create materials to support the functional problem solution (e.g., instructions, feedback forms, schedules, and back-end management).

6.2.2 Synthesize

The Synthesize space is characterized by using the collected data, information, and perspectives from a variety of stakeholders and sources and synthesizing them into meaningful insights that then directly impact design. This entails the use of frameworks that can help the design teams identify design opportunities and ask "how might we?" questions that are informed by insights and can prompt ideation.

6.2.3 Ideate

The Ideate space exists for designers to practice divergent thinking and develop a large quantity of ideas before converging and selecting one to move forward for more detailed evaluation, building, and possible implementation. Increasing the duration of the ideation process (i.e., providing dedicated sessions and time for coming up with a quantity of ideas) increases the likelihood that novel, innovative ideas are developed (Karni & Shalev, 2004). To facilitate ideation, product development teams can engage in dedicated brainstorming sessions – both independently and in groups – in which they defer judgment and go for a quantity of ideas. It is worth noting that ideation need not last an extensive amount of time. Additionally, product development teams can also ask "how might we?" questions to promote ideation. Reinig and Briggs (2008) identified that, often, the relationship between the number of generated ideas and the number of good ideas is curvilinear with a decreasing slope. This is helpful information to product developers working in entrepreneurship; while it is beneficial to formally dedicate explicit time to come up with interesting, innovative, and new product ideas and modifications, this time can be constrained in a way that does not prohibit novel idea generation. Technology entrepreneurs often need to work at a fast and concentrated pace in order to minimize the amount of resources that are utilized before a new product is launched in the market.

6.2.4 Prototype

The Prototype space provides tools for evaluating and iterating on product designs. Prototyping is often described as a means to develop a whole product using limited resources and a low budget. To generate greater impact from prototypes (i.e., to gather deeper insights from prototypes that provide insight into necessary product modifications and pivots), it is helpful to think of prototypes from the lens of testing assumptions and hypotheses. Constable and Rimalovski (2018) frame this method of prototyping as understanding a business's riskiest assumptions, testing them through prototypes and feedback, and then iterating (p. 31). From this perspective, prototyping becomes a quick and efficient way to test specific aspects of a product design, obtain qualitative and quantitative data from relevant stakeholders, and then turn this data into insights that are used to iterate on the product.

Examples of prototypes can be a select grouping of wireframes, physical models or representations, mock-ups of specific technical components, and renderings. The key outcome of prototyping is to generate iterative feedback and provide lean methods of testing before extensive resources are utilized.

6.2.5 Implement

The Implement space provides specific techniques for bringing a new product idea to fruition so that it is ready for commercialization. Continuing to collect stakeholder feedback is crucial even as a product is being brought to market to ensure that the social, economical, and environmental factors that are associated with the design are regularly monitored and evaluated.

Table 6.2 Mindsets in HCD

Mindset	Definition
Human-centeredness	Is characterized by a central focus on empathy for others and putting oneself in others' shoes.
Experimental	Is characterized by a realization that everything may be considered a prototype that can be evaluated and modified accordingly.
Collaborative	Is characterized by a belief that working with others (i.e., learning from a diverse set of perspectives and building on the ideas of others) is a key component of problem-solving.
Metacognitive	Is characterized by an awareness of one's own thinking and learning processes, and the ability to intentionally and purposefully change them in order to successfully complete a task.
Communicative	Is characterized by an ability to exchange ideas and thoughts through conversations, presentations, and writings.
Creative	Is characterized by an ability to think of new and original ideas.

Eventually, engaging in the presented HCD spaces, processes, and practices can lead to the development of six important mindsets over time (Goldman et al., 2012; Royalty, 2018). These mindsets are beneficial and critical for scientists and engineers in both new product and business development. Table 6.2 presents these mindsets.

In technological entrepreneurship, implementing the HCD processes and mindsets that are entailed by the presented framework allow scientists and engineers to focus on the teams and stakeholders involved in the development of a technological product rather than the product or the technology itself. The HCD processes and mindsets will also inform the decision making processes before, during, and after developing a technological product.

6.3 Implications for Product Development

The HCD framework, when applied to new product development, provides entrepreneurial practitioners with tools and mindsets to increase the likelihood of success in designing and commercializing a product that fits the overarching business value proposition and meets the needs or expectations of the customers, clients, or users. Using HCD, technology entrepreneurs will:

- Strive to maximize creativity, innovation, and collaboration when developing a product through engaging in the process of divergent and convergent thinking, which leads to greater novelty of ideas.
- Identify their assumptions and biases and evaluate them in order to validate or invalidate and subsequently iterate on the design.
- Ideate, prototype, and iterate while involving direct and indirect stakeholders in these processes.
- Effectively communicate with multiple stakeholders throughout the product development process.
- Consider the sustainability and evolution of their products during the development process and during market implementation.

It is worth noting that an implicit bias may exist against creative (i.e., novel) ideas within organizations and those who make product development and implementation decisions (Mueller et. al., 2012). Knowing that there might be a bias against the selection of innovative products due to their inherent uncertainty, firms must be diligent in not only encouraging the development of innovative ideas but also in creating an environment that is positioned and incentivized to commonly and consistently select and consider implementation of these ideas that fit within fixed constraints.

6.4 Conclusion

The presented model offers a comprehensive, human-centered approach to technology entrepreneurship and product development. The presented model simplifies HCD processes and practices and makes it possible for any individual to embrace the HCD mindsets and utilize the Understand, Synthesize, Ideate, Prototype, and Implement spaces during product development. By using HCD, technology entrepreneurs will take a desirability perspective to embark on the product design process and gain understanding of the design context and user perspective before quickly incorporating viability and feasibility constraints to modify and refine the design.

References

Boling, E., & Smith, K. M. (2010). *Intensive Studio Experience in a Non-Studio Masters Program: Student Activities and Thinking across Levels of Design*. Design and Complexity: Design Research Society Conference 2010. Montreal, QC, Canada: School of Industrial Design.

Brown, T. (2008). Design Thinking. *Harvard Business Review, 86*(6), 1–9.

Brown, T., & Katz, B. (2011). Change by Design. *Journal of Product Innovation Management, 28*(3), 381–383. https://doi.org/10.1111/j.1540-5885.2011.00806.x

Constable, G., & Rimalovski, F. (2018). *Testing with Humans: How to Use Experiments to Make Faster, More Informed Decision Making*. Giff Constable.

Cropley, D. H. (2015). *Creativity in Engineering: Novel Solutions to Complex Problems*. Academic Press. London, England.

Dorst, K. (2011). The Core of 'Design Thinking' and Its Application. *Design Studies, 32*(6), 521–532. https://doi.org/10.1016/j.destud.2011.07.006

Goldman, S., Carroll, M. P., Kabayadondo, Z., Cavagnaro, L. B., Royalty, A. W., Roth, B., Roth, B., Kwek, S. H., & Kim, J. (2012). Assessing d.learning: Capturing the Journey of Becoming a Design Thinker. In H. Plattner, C. Meinel, & L. Leifer (Eds.), *Design Thinking Research* (pp. 13–33). Berlin Heidelberg: Springer. https://doi.org/10.1007/978-3-642-31991-4_2

IDEO (Firm). (2015). *The Field Guide to Human-Centered Design: Design Kit*. IDEO.

Karni, R., and Shalev, S. (2004). Fostering Innovation in Conceptual Product Design through Ideation. *Information Knowledge Systems Management, 4*(1), 15–33.

Keeley, L., Pikkel, R., Quinn, B., & Walters, H. (2013). *Ten Types of Innovation: The Discipline of Building Breakthroughs*. Wiley. Hoboken, N.J.

Lawrence, L., Shehab, S., & Tissenbaum, M. (2024). Understanding non-designers' practices and processes in a human-centered design course. *International Journal of Innovation in Education, 9*(5), 1–27.

Mueller, J. S., Melwani, S., & Goncalo, J. A. (2012). The Bias against Creativity: Why People Desire but Reject Creative Ideas. *Psychological Science, 23*(1), 13–17.

de Paula, D., Cormican, K., & Dobrigkeit, F. (2022). From Acquaintances to Partners in Innovation: An Analysis of 20 Years of Design Thinking's Contribution to New Product Development. *IEEE Transactions on Engineering Management, Engineering Management, IEEE Transactions on, IEEE Trans. Eng. Manage, 69*(4), 1664–1677.

Reinig, B. A., & Briggs, R. O. (2008). On the Relationship between Idea-Quantity and Idea-Quality during Ideation. *Group Decision & Negotiation, 17*(5), 403–420.

Royalty, A. (2018). Design-based Pedagogy: Investigating an Emerging Approach to Teaching Design to Non-Designers. *Mechanism and Machine Theory, 125*, 137–145.

Teal, R. (2010). Developing a (Non-linear) Practice of Design Thinking. *International Journal of Art & Design Education, 29*(3), 294–302.

Zhang, T., & Dong, H. (2008). Human-Centered Design: An Emergent Conceptual Model. In *Proceedings of Include2009*, Royal College of Art, London, April 8–10, 2009. https://bura.brunel.ac.uk/bitstream/2438/3472/1/Fulltext.pdf

Part III
Strategy and Business Model

7 Personal Values, Core Competencies, Entrepreneurial Vision, and Mission

Panagiotis Kyriakopoulos and Alexander Tittel

7.1 Introduction

Starting a new venture is an intense and challenging endeavor. At the same time, it can be a fulfilling, and rewarding, mission, providing an opportunity to realize the entrepreneur's aspirations, and achieve personal and professional goals in life. In theory and practice, the core of entrepreneurial action involves recognizing, assessing, and exploiting business opportunities to develop innovative products and solutions (Venkataraman, 1997; York, and Venkataraman, 2010). However, as Sarasvathy et al. (2003, p. 143) pointed out, "the opportunity has no meaning unless the actor(s) actually act upon the real world within which the opportunity eventually has to take shape". It is, therefore, critical to shed light on the following questions:

- What are the decisive factors for the perceived attractiveness of a business opportunity?
- What is needed to create a strong resonance between the entrepreneur and the business opportunity?

A profound resonance and a deep connection between the entrepreneur and the business vision can enhance the persistence and resilience of the entrepreneur during the entrepreneurial journey and serve as a solid foundation for a meaningful company mission. Entrepreneurship theory discusses the fit between the entrepreneurial individual and the external business opportunity as the entrepreneur-opportunity nexus (Shane and Venkataraman, 2000; Shane, 2012). It describes a coherent fit and a vibrant resonance between entrepreneurial individuals on the one hand and the nature of the business opportunity discovered or created by the entrepreneur on the other. On the individual level, the personal values and core competencies of the entrepreneur and the entrepreneurial team play a critical role. They are not only essential factors for achieving competitive advantage and increasing the firm's survival after the first years of creation (Reese et al., 2021). They also can serve as the solid foundation for the company's strong and inspiring vision (Vyakarnam et al., 1999) and foster the entrepreneur's motivation, perseverance, and resilience when reflected in the enterprise's mission, and vision, its value proposition, future products, and services.

7.2 Personal Values

The concept and theory of fundamental human values proposed by Schwartz (1992) have been extensively studied and confirmed through intercultural research across numerous countries globally. Personal values are defined as "trans-situational goals that vary in importance and serve as guiding principles in the life of a person or a group" (Schwartz, 2007, p. 712). Additionally, it

DOI: 10.4324/9781003341284-10

is posited that personal values play a crucial role in shaping human decision-making and career preferences (Dietz et al., 2005; Schwartz, 1992). Liñán and Fayolle (2015) delve into the impact of personal values on an individual's willingness to pursue entrepreneurial ventures, highlighting a clear connection to and noteworthy significance of personal values in the process of opportunity recognition. Thus, the entrepreneur's values can and should be reflected in the new firms' strategy, backgrounds, and leadership styles (Klotz et al., 2014). Literature on social psychology indicates that individuals who establish new firms tend to share similar values (Shah et al., 2019). However, the entrepreneurial team must be diverse to compete in modern and highly dynamic economies. Having interdisciplinary and intercultural competencies to cope with the immense variety of tasks and critical challenges can foster entrepreneurial success. At the same time, Chowdhury (2005, p. 728) discovered that the diversity of the team composition "is not as important as team commitment, and the process of cognitive comprehensiveness that utilizes diverse decision criteria". Thus, shared team values can contribute to a strong common business vision, harmonious decision-making processes, and effective team collaboration. Clarity about personal and team core values may also support the entrepreneurial team in formulating strategic goals (Shah et al., 2019) and overall affect firm performance (Shepherd et al., 2021).

In addition to the individual level, the national and the local culture of the ecosystem play a significant role. Culture includes a set of norms, values, and beliefs that may affect entrepreneurial behavior (Baron and Shane, 2007). Noticeably, cultural values reflect the degree to which a society considers entrepreneurial behaviors desirable or not (Kyriakopoulos et al., 2024; Stephan and Pathak, 2016).

7.3 Core Competencies

Building on the profound overview of entrepreneurial competencies presented and discussed in Chapter 3, competence can be defined as "the disposition to generate adequate actions to responsibly solve problems in variable situations" (Tittel and Terzidis, 2020, p. 19). Its main components on the individual level include critical knowledge, skills, and attitudes as defined by the European Parliament and Council (EU, 2006). Next to personal values, core competencies play an important role in developing the entrepreneur-opportunity nexus. They encompass more than just the entrepreneurial competencies discussed in Chapter 3. It refers to the core ability and readiness to overcome obstacles and solve problems in various situations. This ability and readiness can be operationalized and measured using psychometric constructs in established behavioral models. The theory of planned behavior (TPB) is a well-established framework that aims to explain and predict human behavior, particularly in relation to intentional actions. A closer look reveals that it includes the above-mentioned components of competence (attitude) and reflects the personal values influenced by the national culture (subjective norms). Developed by Ajzen (1991), the TPB suggests that three main factors influence behavioral intentions:

1 Attitude: The individual's positive or negative evaluation of the behavior and their beliefs about its outcomes.
2 Subjective Norms: The perceived social pressure, and expectations from others regarding the behavior.
3 Perceived Behavioral Control: The individual's perception of their ability to perform the behavior and overcome any potential obstacles.

According to the TPB, these factors collectively shape an individual's intention to engage in a specific behavior, leading to actual behavior enactment. The theory has been widely applied in various fields, such as psychology, marketing, and organizational behavior, to understand and modify behaviors through targeted interventions. In that model, the Perceived Behavioral Control specifically reflects on the individual's competencies to solve problems (perform the behavior) in variable situations. Similar concepts are self-efficacy (Bandura, 1982) and perceived feasibility. Perceived feasibility is "the degree to which one feels personally capable of starting a business" (Krueger et al., 2000, p. 419). In Liñán (2004, p. 4), it is defined "as the degree to which people consider themselves personally able to carry out that behavior".

In summary, personal and cultural values and core competencies are critical individual factors in fostering the entrepreneur-opportunity nexus. The team's core competencies can serve as a solid basis to develop a strong vision of the new venture (Abatecola and Uli, 2016). In addition, it can foster team building, identify the right human resources, and hone their problem-solving competence in line with the firm's values (Shah et al., 2019).

7.4 Entrepreneurial Vision

Positive visioning has been recognized for guiding future behavior in various domains, including sports psychology, medical treatment, musical performance, and academic performance (Boyatzis and Soler, 2012). According to Neff (2011), when examining the elements contributing to the sustained financial success of family businesses, it was revealed that having a shared vision between the family and management played a pivotal role. Alongside factors such as trust, confidence in management, and cultivating a network for learning, the presence of a shared vision emerged as the most influential predictor. "Ironically, leaders, and managers often know the importance of a shared vision, yet they often do not take the time to articulate its formulation" (Boyatzis and Soler, 2012, p. 27). These factors often lead individuals to experience a sense of aimlessness and a lack of purpose, or they may become impassive to their potential aspirations (Boyatzis and Soler, 2012, p. 27).

Creating a business idea is a cognitive act that involves analytical and creative processes formulating a vision of future conditions and circumstances. A vision as a concept has been the focus of many studies in entrepreneurship, organizational management, and leadership. It is defined as "a mental perception of the kind of environment an individual, or an organization, aspires to create within a broad time horizon, and the underlying conditions for the actualization of the perception" (El-Namaki, 1992, p. 25). Ruvio et al. (2010, p. 145) define entrepreneurial vision as a "future-oriented image of the new venture, intended to motivate both the entrepreneurs and their followers (investors, future employees) toward this desirable future".

In their study, Ruvio et al. (2010) explored the consequences and effects of entrepreneurial vision on entrepreneurial strategy and new venture performance. The authors discovered that entrepreneurs' actions are highly affected by their visions. Moreover, having a clear entrepreneurial vision is critical for acquiring resources for the new venture. Next to entrepreneurial competencies, professional experience, leadership, and strategic capabilities, providing a clear company vision to the team is one of the decision criteria for early investors and business angels (Jain and Tabak, 2008). The entrepreneurial vision includes a set of goals for the entrepreneur or the entrepreneurial team for the next 5–10 years. It is a concept that drives a new venture and its members to achieve collective goals (Abell, 2006). By having a clear vision, the entrepreneur can effectively exploit opportunities, be best prepared for future events, and have a competitive advantage in the market (Güzel et al., 2021). A solid vision may also increase communication among the team members, employees, and stakeholders, providing explicit directions and motivation, and is positively associated with innovation (Strese et al., 2018). The following conditions for a sound vision are presented by El-Namaki (1992, p. 27):

- Be realistic, feasible, simple, and clear
- Provide a challenge for the whole organization
- Mirror the goals and aspirations of the constituents
- Far but close in terms of time span and organizational commitment
- Able to focus attention with respect to scope and time
- Translatable into goals and strategies
- Endorsed and frequently articulated by top management
- Derived from a sense of direction

In summary, powerful visions make a significant impact on customer, and employee satisfaction and should possess certain characteristics: conciseness, clarity, abstractness, challenge, future orientation, stability, and desirability or the ability to inspire (Kantabutra and Avery, 2010). According to Kantabutra and Avery (2010, p. 40), "effective visions contain between 11 and 22 words, rendering them easy to communicate and remember". Existing literature has presented findings supporting the idea that a company characterized by a strong shared vision promotes the cultivation of common values among its employees. Additionally, a company with a higher degree of shared vision ensures that all its members collectively embrace goals aimed at attaining a competitive advantage (Tsai and Ghoshal, 1998).

7.5 Mission

The mission includes the personal motivation of the founding team members and refers to what the entrepreneurs do, for whom, and why (Abell, 2006). It is the purpose for which a firm exists, and a mission statement can be significant for stakeholders when they make decisions (Spear et al., 2009). The firm's mission can also establish goals and provide future directions as it grows (Blank and Carmeli, 2021). A meaningful mission statement often encompasses the core goals that an entrepreneur aims to achieve, capturing the firm's purpose and values (Tsai and Ghoshal, 1998).

The mission is also crucial for opportunity identification, as it acts as a filter for entrepreneurs to choose the most suitable opportunities that align with the firm's core goals and strategy (Shane and Venkataraman, 2000). Moreover, when the mission aligns with the firm's overall direction, it enhances decision-making effectiveness. A well-designed mission can also assist entrepreneurs in resource allocation, including money and time (Barney and Clark, 2007). For example, a mission can prioritize the actions required to meet firms' goals, while it can also facilitate the reallocation of resources in the face of uncertainty, such as changes in market demand (Pfeffer and Salancik, 1978).

In addition, the mission can be related to shareholders' needs, such as considerations about society, and the environment (Bart and Hupfer, 2004). This means that entrepreneurs also include concerns such as sustainability, ethics, and contribution to the community and society in their mission statements, driven by institutional pressures (Bartkus and Glassman, 2008). However, this can sometimes lead to unrealistic goals for the firm to effectively address and meet shareholders' needs (Wright, 2002). Proper alignment of the mission with shareholders' needs can enhance the firm's credibility and reputation, thus contributing to the firm's success (Mahon and Wartick, 2003). Therefore, realistic and short-term mission statements can lead to effective shareholder management (Bartkus and Glassman, 2008).

All in all, a powerful and well-communicated mission statement can help entrepreneurs not only to formulate and implement effective goals but also to build long-term relationships with stakeholders. Notably, when the firm's mission drives entrepreneurs, they are more likely to demonstrate specific behaviors that align with the firm's mission (Bartkus and Glassman, 2008). In addition, the social context can shape the expectations of shareholders and, therefore, influence the mission of the firm (Meyer and Rowan, 1977). Thus, we can see that the mission plays a crucial role in the formulation and implementation of what entrepreneurs decide to do, and the reasons behind their actions.

7.6 Conclusion

To sum up, personal values, core competencies, entrepreneurial vision, and mission are interconnected and play a crucial role not only in achieving competitive advantage and firm success but also in its future growth (Reese et al., 2021). Evaluating emerging opportunities in line with the firm's vision, mission, and core competencies is essential to effectively exploit them. However, entrepreneurs must carefully integrate these elements to ensure alignment with the overall goals of the firm. Coherent decision-making can also be achieved when these elements are in harmony, thereby increasing the firm's credibility and facilitating effective communication among different stakeholders.

References

Abatecola, G., and Uli, V. (2016). Entrepreneurial competences, liability of newness, and infant survival: Evidence from the service industry. *Journal of Management Development*, 35(9):1082–1097.

Abell, D. F. (2006). The future of strategy is leadership. *Journal of Business Research*, 59(3):310–314.

Ajzen, I. (1991). The theory of planned behavior. *Organizational Behavior, and Human Decision Processes*, 50(2):179–211.

Bandura, A. (1982). Self-efficacy mechanism in human agency. *American Psychologist*, 37(2):122.

Barney, J. B., and Clark, D. N. (2007). *Resource-based theory: Creating, and sustaining competitive advantage*. Oxford: Oxford University Press.

Baron, R.A., and Shane, S.A. (2007). *Entrepreneurship: A process perspective*. Mason, OH: South-Western.

Bart, C. K., and Hupfer, M. (2004). Mission statements in Canadian hospitals. *Journal of Health Organization, and Management*, 18(2):92–110.

Bartkus, B. R., and Glassman, M. (2008). Do firms practice what they preach? The relationship between mission statements, and stakeholder management. *Journal of Business Ethics*, 83(2):207–216.

Blank, T. H., and Carmeli, A. (2021). Does founding team composition influence external investment? The role of founding team prior experience, and founder CEO. *The Journal of Technology Transfer*, 46:1869–1888.

Boyatzis, R. E., and Soler, C. (2012). Vision, leadership, and emotional intelligence transforming family business. *Journal of Family Business Management*, 2(1), 23–30.

Chowdhury, S. (2005). Demographic diversity for building an effective entrepreneurial team: Is it important? *Journal of Business Venturing*, 20(6):727–746.

Dietz, T., Fitzgerald, A., and Shwom, R. (2005). Environmental values. *Annual Review of Environment, and Resources*, 30:335–372.

El-Namaki, M. (1992). Creating a corporate vision. *Long Range Planning*, 25(6):25–29.

EU (2006). Recommendation of the European parliament, and the council of 18 December 2006 on key competencies for lifelong learning. (2006/962/EC) 12, European Parliament.

Güzel, Ö., Ehtiyar, R., and Ryan, C. (2021). The success factors of wine tourism entrepreneurship for rural area: A thematic biographical narrative analysis in Turkey. *Journal of Rural Studies*, 84:230–239.

Jain, B. A., and Tabak, F. (2008). Factors influencing the choice between founder versus non-founder CEO for IPO firms. *Journal of Business Venturing*, 23(1):21–45.

Kantabutra, S., and Avery, G. C. (2010). The power of vision: statements that resonate. *Journal of Business Strategy*, 31(1):37–45.

Klotz, A. C., Hmieleski, K. M., Bradley, B. H., and Busenitz, L. W. (2014). New venture teams: A review of the literature, and roadmap for future research. *Journal of Management*, 40(1):226–255.

Krueger Jr, N. F., Reilly, M. D., and Carsrud, A. L. (2000). Competing models of entrepreneurial intentions. *Journal of Business Venturing*, 15(5–6):411–432.

Kyriakopoulos, P., Herbert, K. & Piperopoulos, P. (2024). I am passionate therefore I am: The interplay between entrepreneurial passion, gender, culture and intentions. *Journal of Business Research*, 172, 114409.

Liñán, F. (2004). Intention-based models of entrepreneurship education. *Piccolla Impresa/Small Business*, 3(1):11–35.

Liñán, F., and Fayolle, A. (2015). A systematic literature review on entrepreneurial intentions: Citation, thematic analyses, and research agenda. *International Entrepreneurship, and Management Journal*, 11(4):907–933.

Mahon, J. F., and Wartick, S. L. (2003). Dealing with stakeholders: How reputation, credibility, and framing influence the game. *Corporate Reputation Review*, 6(1), 19–33.

Meyer, J. W., and Rowan, B. (1977). Institutionalized organizations: Formal structure as myth, and ceremony. *American Journal of Sociology*, 83(2):340–363.

Neff, J. (2011). *Non-financial indicators of family firm performance: A portfolio model approach*. Cleveland, OH: Case Western Reserve University.

Pfeffer, J., and Salancik, G. R. (1978). *The External Control of Organizations, a Resource Dependence Perspective*. New York: Harper, and Row.

Reese, D., Rieger, V., and Engelen, A. (2021). Should competencies be broadly shared in new ventures' founding teams? *Strategic Entrepreneurship Journal*, 15(4):568–589.

Ruvio, A., Rosenblatt, Z., and Hertz-Lazarowitz, R. (2010). Entrepreneurial leadership vision in nonprofit vs. for-profit organizations. *The Leadership Quarterly*, 21(1):144–158.

Sarasvathy, S. D., Dew, N., Velamuri, S. R., and Venkataraman, S. (2003). Three views of entrepreneurial opportunity. In *Handbook of Entrepreneurship Research* (International Handbook Series on Entrepreneurship). New York: Springer-Verlag, 141–160.

Schwartz, S. H. (1992). Universals in the content, and structure of values: Theoretical advances, and empirical tests in 20 countries. In Zanna, M.P. (ed.) *Advances in Experimental Social Psychology*. (Vol. 25, pp. 1–65). New York: Academic Press.

Schwartz, S. H. (2007). Universalism values, and the inclusiveness of our moral universe. *Journal of Cross-cultural Psychology*, 38(6):711–728.

Shah, S. K., Agarwal, R., and Echambadi, R. (2019). Jewels in the crown: Exploring the motivations, and team building processes of employee entrepreneurs. *Strategic Management Journal*, 40(9):1417–1452.

Shane, S. (2012). Reflections on the 2010 AMR decade award: Delivering on the promise of entrepreneurship as a field of research. *Academy of Management Review*, 37(1):10–20.

Shane, S., and Venkataraman, S. (2000). The promise of entrepreneurship as a field of research. *Academy of Management Review*, 25(1):217–226.

Shepherd, D. A., Souitaris, V., and Gruber, M. (2021). Creating new ventures: A review, and research agenda. *Journal of Management*, 47(1):11–42.

Spear, R., Cornforth, C., and Aiken, M. (2009). The governance challenges of social enterprises: Evidence from a UK empirical study. *Annals of Public, and Cooperative Economics*, 80(2):247–273.

Stephan, U., and Pathak, S. (2016). Beyond cultural values? Cultural leadership ideals, and entrepreneurship. *Journal of Business Venturing*, 31(5):505–523.

Strese, S., Keller, M., Flatten, T. C., and Brettel, M. (2018). CEOs' passion for inventing, and radical innovations in smes: The moderating effect of shared vision. *Journal of Small Business Management*, 56(3):435–452.

Tittel, A., and Terzidis, O. (2020). Entrepreneurial competences revised: Developing a consolidated, and categorized list of entrepreneurial competences. *Entrepreneurship Education*, 3: 1–35.

Tsai, W., and Ghoshal, S. (1998). Social capital, and value creation: The role of intrafirm networks. *Academy of Management Journal*, 41(4):464–476.

Venkataraman, S. (1997). *The distinctive domain of entrepreneurship research*, volume 3. Bingley: Emerald Publishing Limited.

Vyakarnam, S., Jacobs, R., and Handelberg, J. (1999). Exploring the formation of entrepreneurial teams: The key to rapid growth business? *Journal of Small Business, and Enterprise Development*, 6(2):153–165.

Wright, J. N. (2002). Mission, and reality, and why not? *Journal of Change Management*, 3(1):30–44.

York, J. G., and Venkataraman, S. (2010). The entrepreneur – Environment nexus: Uncertainty, innovation, and allocation. *Journal of Business Venturing*, 25(5):449–463.

8 Designing the Business Model

Lorena Berrón Cadenas and June Y. Lee

8.1 Introduction

A business model is a process in which firms create, deliver, and capture value (Budler et al., 2021; Lee & Patel, 2020). The theoretical foundation of business model research was established in the early 2000s in the fields of strategic management and entrepreneurship (Teece, 2010; Zott et al., 2011). In these early days, business model research was studied as a way in which firms assembled and accumulated values in a linear value chain setting (Porter, 1985). This was applicable and valuable in a traditional industrial environment that emphasized the development of competitive advantages and resources.

With the development of technology, availability of data, and accelerated growth of digital firms, prior understanding of business models needs to be revisited to highlight and incorporate more recent emerging trends (Haaker et al., 2021; Haftor & Costa, 2023). More specifically, the Internet of Things and digitally transformed industry exhibit unique characteristics in which users are often part of value creation and delivery. This changes the traditional, transactional relationship between buyers and sellers. According to 22 firms studied by Haftor and Costa (2023), there are five dimensions of a business model innovation: (1) exchangeable, which refers to tangibles and intangible outputs created by activity within a business model; (2) activities that refer to interrelated actions that provide meanings to a business model; (3) actors that have capabilities to execute certain activities; (4) transaction mechanisms that can serve as a source of innovation; and (5) governance set up that controls the execution of business model activities by actors (Haftor & Costa, 2023). When one of these dimensions is altered, innovation can occur.

This chapter aims to reframe how business model research has been addressed in entrepreneurship and strategic management. This chapter is organized as follows. First, we discuss the business model and address specific characteristics of business models from high technology and engineering perspectives and introduce a few examples from different subindustries within high technology and engineering. Then, we introduce a business model canvas (BMC) as a design tool to understand the business model concept better and review related previous literature on business model research. Next, we discuss how business models innovate and the rise of business experiments regarding business model research. We conclude by summarizing the different considerations or inputs for business model design and innovation.

8.2 Business Model Characteristics from High Technology and Engineering Perspectives

Bailetti (2012) defines a business model as "an investment in a project that assembles and deploys specialized individuals and heterogeneous assets that are intricately related to advances

DOI: 10.4324/9781003341284-11

in scientific and technological knowledge for the purpose of creating and capturing value for a firm" (Bailetti, 2012: 9). This definition is fused with digital technology entrepreneurship but, conceptually, must still be differentiated by how said value depends on or implements technology within the businesses' key activities. Giones and Brem (2017) categorize types of technology and digital business ventures into (1) technology entrepreneurship when technology is new and identifies key activities of this model to be the technology's proof of concept (e.g., Fractus, Oryzon Genomics, Rust Patrol) and the first customer validation; (2) digital technology entrepreneurship, in which activities are implementation of existing technologies and market validation (e.g., Go Pro, Fitbit, Tesla); and (3) digital entrepreneurship, in which activities such as staying ahead of competitors and achieving high growth rely on technology as an input factor or key resource (e.g., Airbnb, Just Eat, Dropbox, Giones & Brem, 2017).

Data is an important element of a business model that deserves more focus and study, even though all types of businesses that generate or consume data – knowingly or unknowingly – are central to digital and technological ventures. In the literature, data-driven business models incorporate data, and data sources are two critical components (Hartmann et al., 2016; Mathis & Kobler, 2016; Kühne & Bohmann, 2018). More specifically, Hartmann et al. (2016) classify data sources as internal and external. Internal sources include (1) existing data and (2) self-generated data, which can be either crowd-sourced or tracked, generated, and others. External data sources cover (3) acquired data, (4) customer-provided data, and (5) free available data, which includes open data, social media data, and web-crawled data (Hartmann et al., 2016). At the same time, through their analysis of data-driven business model literature, Kühne and Bohmann (2018) identify that these data sources are mostly considered part of the traditional BMC block, key resources.

In practice, firms generally have access to internal and external data but may choose to incorporate them as part of the business model. Key activities in which data is a key resource are data generation, acquisition, processing, aggregation, management, visualization, distribution, and analytics (Hartmann et al., 2016; Kühne & Bohman, 2018). Again, firms may implement one or more of these activities and incorporate them as part of their value proposition as data, as a product or service, or as a value-added component of the offer. Finally, in the measure that this data is unique or valuable, it is incorporated into the business model as revenue streams. Examples include usage fees, subscription fees, licensing, lending, renting or leasing, asset sale, or advertising or multi-sided revenue streams (i.e., gain-sharing, buy-and-sell data, and pay-with-data), which require combining one or more data-based activities, resources, or revenue streams (Shüritz et al., 2017; Kühne & Bohmann, 2018).

8.3 Business Model Canvas as a Design Tool

A business model can succinctly and effectively communicate what values firms create and users buy into. To support this purpose, many researchers and practitioners turn to a visual framework or canvas, which depicts a condensed map of how each element of the business will participate in the value creation, delivery, and capture. If we assume the business model as the business equivalent to the scientific method in testing hypotheses (Magretta, 2002), a BMC is a very high-level block diagram showing how all the pieces work together. In this chapter, we highlight the importance of embedding continuous testing mechanisms into the business model that can help validate and iterate the individual elements of a venture, as well as the elements as part of a whole.

One of the most widely known methodologies is the BMC (Osterwalder & Pigneur, 2010), a blank canvas divided into nine sections. These building blocks classify the model into three main categories of risk that should be assessed: (1) desirability, focusing on market risk (i.e., customer segments, channels, value proposition, customer relationships); (2) feasibility, focusing on infrastructure risk (i.e., key activities, key resources, and key partners), and (3) viability, regarding financial risk (i.e., revenue streams, cost structure; Bland & Osterwalder, 2019). The scholars also suggest mapping the various assumptions in these nine blocks in a matrix, prioritizing them in order of importance to the business versus the amount of supporting evidence for each, to further reduce risk by testing according to prioritization.

Another visual framework is based on the lean startup methodology, which also emphasizes the importance of implementing continuous experimentation and measurement throughout the business model in several cycles (Ries, 2011). Through these iterations, assumptions are validated each time, incorporating the new observations and gradual adjustments according to market, product, and financial feedback, taking a "build-measure-learn" approach. In order to implement this process correctly, certain measurable goals or metrics must first be defined for the startup for each iteration to be scientifically evaluated as a variable in the experiment. With this methodology in mind, Maurya (2012) expanded on the BMC to create the lean canvas, also employs nine blocks to depict the components of the business model but emphasizes the importance of focusing on a customer's problem to bring about the solution, as well as identifying key metrics of success and a competitive advantage right from the business model definition. Another particularity of this model is that the said nine sections must be defined in a specific order, again to bring the focus to the customer and their problems before thinking of a solution or any other details.

From both a theoretical and practical standpoint, the holistic nature of the BMC allows for applicability to all industries, products, and services. It is also characteristically flexible to adapt and expand to particular scenarios (Antunes & Tate, 2022) by modifying, dividing, reordering, adding, or linking the aforementioned blocks, as well as determining hierarchical processes to develop the canvas, such as layered canvases for different levels of detail (Kühne & Bohmann, 2018). Consequently, several adaptations, and extensions of the canvas, such as the said Lean Canvas, Service BMC (Zolnowski et al., 2015), Service Logic BMC (Ojasalo & Ojasalo, 2015), and Strategic BMC (Ionescu, 2015) have been raised to suit specific applications of business models.

Particularly in technology and digital entrepreneurship, BMC expansions and entirely new frameworks that aim to target the technological dependencies of the business model or incorporate new factors, such as data and big data, have surfaced in recent years (Allen, 2019; Hartmann et al., 2016; Kühne & Bohmann, 2018; Schüritz et al., 2017). These extend the canvas or the business model design by incorporating elements that should exist at the core of any digitally reliant business model to date. Allen (2019) states that a digital business design revolves around the "Acquisition-Behavior-Conversion" process, which covers the stages of *acquiring* new visitors online, expecting a *behavior* resulting from an invitation to a visitor to perform an action or interaction with the digital presence of the business, thus *converting* those visitors into customers. Other elements of this framework can be considered similar or in the same way as traditional business model sections, including revenue streams and advantage over competitors, although these sections also orient entrepreneurs toward defining the digital matters of the business, such as keyword optimization, social media presence, content planning, and setting goals and metrics for each step (Allen, 2019).

8.4 Business Model Innovation and Business Experimentation

Firms that fail to innovate their business models suffer from detrimental consequences, including losing market shares to their competitors or seeing a decrease in their financial performance (Bhatti et al., 2021). Recent studies on business model innovation highlight the importance of business experiments and testing, particularly for digital firms. Due to the amount of available data and the dynamic power of computing, firms can run large-scale experiments regularly to test their hypotheses and business model assumptions, including how values are created and delivered (Ghezzi & Cavallo, 2020; Keiningham et al., 2020; Mostaghel et al., 2022).

Business experiments are an attractive way for firms to scale up and innovate, particularly in a contemporary digital context. This experiment- and data-informed approach is embedded and iterated in decision-making processes within firms. The benefits of business experiments are clear. For instance, Camuffo et al. (2020) study two groups of entrepreneurs who follow intuition versus rigorous testing of hypotheses during the decision-making process. They find that the group that conducted experiments not only performs better but is also less likely to drop in the early stages of startups and pivot to a greater extent to pursue a different idea based on findings from experiments. These findings are consistent with other studies that demonstrated faster learning and reduced errors (Thomke, 2020).

This well-established business experiment approach is commonly practiced at startups and high-growth firms, but it is rather understudied and lacks clear theoretical constructs in strategy, innovation, and entrepreneurship. Leatherbee and Katila (2020) claim two methods by which firms probe business ideas: learning by thinking and learning by doing (Gans et al., 2019; Ott et al., 2017). More specifically, learning by doing has three main approaches: trial and error, bricolage, and business experiment. Business experiments include hypothesis development, casual propositions, and controlled variation of activities with somewhat controlled circumstances for testing them (Aghion et al., 1991; Camuffo et al., 2019). Additionally, business experiments are often used in highly uncertain environments (Contigiani and Levinthal, 2018; Kerr et al., 2014). This method is referred to as the agile learning process (Alamäki et al., 2021).

Oftentimes, firms have multiple hypotheses about various aspects of the business. For startups, this can require implementing a series of consecutive experiments; for larger firms, simultaneous large-scale experimentation is vital for collecting data for decision-making. In the same study, Camuffo et al. (2019) train startup firms to implement an experimental process through which they "(1) identify the problem, (2) articulate theories, (3) define clear hypotheses, (4) conduct rigorous tests to prove or disprove them, (5) measure the results of the tests, and (6) make decisions based on these tools". In one particular case, Inkdome (i.e., a startup creating a search engine of tattoo artists), the experimentation involved four tests including a BMC, customer interviews, defining a minimum viable product, and creating a prototype (would be Concierge in the case of a service).

On a large scale, tech firms have turned experimentation into an integral part of their operations and business innovation practices. Facebook runs thousands of versions of the app to test several iterations of features and new feature releases simultaneously. Their large number of widely diverse users allows them to accurately conduct A/B testing that can systematically provide evidence for decision-making. During proof-of-concept stages, stage startups often opt for one-on-one customer interviews or other tests to empirically collect and gather feedback, but as the organizational processes and operations grow, implementation of systematic data collection and analytics becomes a need for the experimentation process. For large companies, implementing data collection infrastructure that allows them to statistically analyze the performance of each experiment becomes a key activity of the business model (and data from experiments a key resource).

In the case of Alibaba, this kind of infrastructure has become a natural part of their business processes, as they automate operating decisions based on the predictions their algorithms provide. They attribute the growth of Taobao, their domestic retailing website to the four-step process of their smart business: (1) "datafying" their customer interactions by collecting data at every touch point, (2) "software" every activity by implementing software that will substitute human-decision-making based on the collected data at step 1, (3) getting data flow from every direction by connecting to internal and external parties that are involved in their operations through API integrations, and (4) implementing algorithms that can provide accurate predictions through machine-learning and AI-powered tools.

Having a team of data scientists and engineers allows Alibaba to develop these tools and algorithms from scratch. However, for earlier-stage firms and small businesses, off-the-market applications such as Amplitude, Google Analytics, Google Data Studio, or even Microsoft Excel can be integrated into your processes and products to provide initial insights into smaller scale experiments.

Another important aspect when validating a technology and digital venture business model is defining clear metrics and thresholds of success for each hypothesis that is being validated through the experiment. When it comes to data-based experiments, quantitative metrics can be easily implemented and automated to meet specific conversion rates, click-through rates, or any precise business goals. One example is Netflix as any changes made to the product impact retention rates, which correlates to engagement (i.e., time spent by the users in the app), but it takes significant changes to the product to observe a 0.1% difference in their retention rate. Thus, the results from the A/B tests that they run are analyzed from a statistical perspective compared to the control group (Gomez-Uribe & Hunt, 2015). In the case of Inkdome, an early stage startup conducting proof-of-concept tests, the metric defined for hypothesis confirmation was 60% of customer interviews providing corroborating evidence, which resulted in three out of four hypotheses being discarded. Camuffo et al mention that startups can benefit from this scientific approach by being able to identify when projects exhibit low or high returns or when it is more profitable to pivot (Camuffo et al., 2019).

8.5 Conclusion and Contributions

In this chapter, we provide an overview of the multiple elements that should be considered by the entrepreneur of a technology and digital venture during the process of business model design and stress the importance of being clear from the beginning on how each of these components plays a role in the business model. We summarize these inputs to the business model design process in Table 8.1.

We also discussed the BMC by Osterwalder (Osterwalder & Pigneur, 2010), and its variations ranging from iterations and extensions of the BMC to frameworks with specific purposes, which sprouted the creation of science and technology business models. We encourage the readers to implement Table 8.1 as a means to think through the business model design process, identifying which of these elements should be incorporated into their BMC of choice, and how each will play a role in the business model, either by becoming a part of key activities, key resources, value proposition, etc. As mentioned throughout this chapter, designing a business model is an iterative process, which can be improved through planned experimentation for hypothesis validation. It is important to remain with an objective view and open to questioning every component through testing in order to arrive at the ideal combination of elements, until the next iteration.

Table 8.1 Inputs for the business model design process

Inputs for technology & digital venture business model design			

Type of technology and digital venture
(Giones & Brem, 2017)

Technology entrepreneurship	Digital technology entrepreneurship	Digital entrepreneurship
Proof of concept of new technologies Key activities: Proof of concept and first customer validation	Implementation of existing technologies Key activities: Market validation	Existing technologies as a resource or input Key activities: Stay ahead of competition or achieve growth

Type of data usage
(Hartmann et al., 2016; Shüritz et al., 2017; Kühne & Bohman, 2018)

As resources	As activities	As value	As revenue stream
Internal: - Existing data - Self-generated data External: - Acquired data - Customer-provided data - Free-available Data	- Generation - Acquisition - Processing - Aggregation - Management - Visualization - Distribution - Analytics	- Data as value proposition - Data as product or service - Data as value-add component	- Usage fees - Subscription fees - Licensing - Lending - Renting or leasing - Asset sale - Advertising - Multi-sided revenue streams

Type of innovation
(Haftor & Costa, 2023)

Innovative exchangeables (Product or service)	Innovative activities	Innovative actors	Innovative transaction mechanisms	Innovative governance set up

Type of iterations (learning by doing)
(Leatherbee & Katila, 2020)

Trial and error	Bricolage	Business experiments
Trying new ideas until one works	Recombination of existing solutions	Hypothesis validation through controlled variations

References

Allen, J. P. 2019. *Digital Entrepreneurship*. New York: Routledge.

Antunes, P., & Tate, M. 2022. Examining the canvas as a domain-independent artifact. *Information Systems and e-Business Management*, 20, 495–514. https://doi.org/10.1007/s10257-022-00556-5.

Bailetti, T. 2012. Technology entrepreneurship: Overview, definition, and distinctive aspects. *Technology Innovation Management Review*, 2(2), 5–12.

Bland, D. J., & Osterwalder, A. 2019. *Testing Business Ideas: A Field Guide for Rapid Experimentation*. Hoboken: John Wiley & Sons.

Budler, M., Župič, I., & Trkman, P. 2021. The development of business model research: A bibliometric review. *Journal of Business Research*, 135, 480–495.

Camuffo, A., Cordova, A., Gambardella, A., & Spina, C. 2020. A scientific approach to entrepreneurial decision making: Evidence from a randomized control trial. *Management Science*, 66(2), 564–586.

Gans, J. S., Stern, S., & Wu, J. 2019. Foundations of entrepreneurial strategy. *Strategic Management Journal*, 40(5), 736–756.

Ghezzi, A., & Cavallo, A. 2020. Agile business model innovation in digital entrepreneurship: Lean startup approaches. *Journal of Business Research*, 110, 519–537.

Giones, F., & Brem, A. 2017. Digital technology entrepreneurship: A definition and research agenda. *Technology Innovation Management Review*, 7(5), 44–51.

Gomez-Uribe, C. A., & Hunt, N., 2015. The netflix recommender system: Algorithms, business value, and innovation. *ACM Transactions on Management Information Systems (TMIS)*, 6(4), 1–19.

Haftor, D. M., & Costa, R. C. 2023. Five dimensions of business model innovation: A multi-case exploration of industrial incumbent firm's business model transformations. *Journal of Business Research*, 154, 113352.

Hartmann, P. M., Zaki, M., Feldmann, N., & Neely, A. 2016. Capturing value from big data – a taxonomy of data-driven business models used by start-up firms. *International Journal of Operations & Production Management*, 36(10), 1382–1406.

Keiningham, T., Aksoy, L., Bruce, H. L., Cadet, F., Clennell, N., Hodgkinson, I. R., & Kearney, T. 2020. Customer experience driven business model innovation. *Journal of Business Research*, 116, 431–440.

Kühne, B., & Böhmann, T. 2018. *Requirements for representing data-driven business models - towards extending the business model canvas*. [Paper presentation] The Americas Conference on Information Systems 2018: Digital Disruption, AMCIS 2018. Retrieved from www.scopus.com

Leatherbee, M., & Katila, R. 2020. The lean startup method: Early-stage teams and hypothesis-based probing of business ideas. *Strategic Entrepreneurship Journal*, 14(4), 570–593.

Lee, J. Y., & Patel, S. J. 2020. An innovating business model for the higher education sector: A platform-based approach to university career services. *Industry and Higher Education*, 34(2), 91–99.

Magretta, J. 2002. Why business models matter. *Harvard Business Review*, 80(5): 86–92.

Mathis, K., & Köbler, F. 2016. Data-need fit – Towards data-driven business model innovation. *Service Design Geographies. Proceedings of the ServDes.2016 Conference*, 125, 458–467.

Maurya, A. 2012. Why lean canvas vs business model canvas?, Love the Problem [blog], February 27. Available at: https://medium.com/lean-stack/why-lean-canvas-vs-business-model-canvas-af62c0f250f0 (Accessed November 5, 2024).

Mostaghel, R., Oghazi, P., Parida, V., & Sohrabpour, V. 2022. Digitalization driven retail business model innovation: Evaluation of past and avenues for future research trends. *Journal of Business Research*, 146, 134–145.

Ojasalo, K. & Ojasalo, J. 2015. Adapting Business Model Thinking to Service Logic: An Empirical Study on Developing a Service Design Tool. In Johanna Gummerus & Catharina von Koskull (Eds.) *The Nordic School - Service Marketing and Management for the Future*. Helsinki: Hanken School of Economics, 309–333. https://www.theseus.fi/bitstream/handle/10024/511152/Ojasalo_Ojasalo.pdf?sequence=2

Osterwalder, A., & Pigneur, Y. 2010. *Business Model Generation: A Handbook for Visionaries, Game Changers, and Challengers*. New York: John Wiley & Sons.

Ott, T. E., Eisenhardt, K. M., & Bingham, C. B. 2017. Strategy formation in entrepreneurial settings: Past insights and future directions. *Strategic Entrepreneurship Journal*, 11(3), 306–325.

Porter, M.E. 1985. *Competitive Advantage*. New York: Free Press.

Ries, E. 2011. *The Lean Startup: How Today's Entrepreneurs Use Continuous Innovation to Create Radically Successful Businesses*. United States: Currency.

Schüritz, R., Seebacher, S., & Dorner, R. 2017. Capturing value from data: Revenue models for data-driven services. *Proceedings of the 50th Hawaii International Conference on System Sciences*, Hilton Waikoloa Village, Hawaii.

Teece, D.J., 2010. Business models, business strategy and innovation. *Long Range Planning*, 43(2-3), 172–194

Thomke, S. H. 2020. *Experimentation Works: The Surprising Power of Business Experiments*. Cambridge: Harvard Business Press.

Zolnowski, A. 2015. Analysis and design of service business models (Doctoral dissertation, University of Hamburg).

Zott, C., Amit, R., & Massa, L. 2011. The business model: Recent developments and future research. *Journal of Management*, 37(4), 1019–1042.

9 Challenges in Entrepreneurial Decision-Making under Uncertain Business Environments

Marcos Hashimoto

9.1 Introduction

Picture the following scenario: You and your team spent the last few weeks working hard in collecting as much data as you can to prepare a well-detailed strategic plan for your company. You are very confident that the plan will work perfectly and you are about to make an executive presentation of your strategy to the board of directors. Now, while you are rehearsing your pitch in your mind, a few hours before the meeting, a staff member comes to you with a completely new piece of information that poses a new opportunity that you know the company doesn't want to miss, but pursuing that opportunity means that all your planning efforts are gone, now everything changed and you have to make new assessments to take a turn to a completely new strategic direction. You were not prepared for that and you feel confused and insecure about how to conduct the meeting. A decision that was easy to be taken earlier now becomes the pivot that will determine the future of the company. What should you do? Should you just forget this amazing new opportunity and go with your original plan or take two steps back in your strategy so you don't miss this chance?

Making decisions is one of the human acts that we do several times in a day, most of the time without even realizing it. From waking up or sleeping a little bit more in the morning to going to bed or watching that movie on TV at the end of the day, we are making decisions all the time. Most of the time, the consequences of a bad decision are trivial and have little repercussions, but sometimes, like the story that opens this chapter, it can mean the entire future of a corporation.

As an entrepreneur, together with all the benefits of being the owner of your own business, you also have to deal with the stress of making meaningful and relevant decisions that may affect the lives of hundreds of people, whatever they are employees, customers, suppliers, competitors, stockholders, partners and many others. Living with the consequences of these decisions is a weight many people are not prepared to bear.

Fortunately, the academia has been very diligent in conducting meaningful research to improve the knowledge in decision-making processes in organizations. From early applied research by Scholz & Scholz (1983), March (1994), and Jennings & Wattam (1998) to the development of practical tools and methods that help leaders and entrepreneurs to make better decisions (Shapira, 1996; Byrnes, 1998; Triantaphyllou, 2000), research in decision-making in businesses is far from being exhausted.

In entrepreneurship, the decision-making process has been investigated from a wide variety of perspectives, Wickham (2001), for example, examined how entrepreneurs make decisions when formulating their business strategies, and Catalani and Clerico (1996) investigated the process taken by entrepreneurs when making decisions under uncertainty. The human aspect of the decision-making process was well explored under the entrepreneurial motivation aspect

DOI: 10.4324/9781003341284-12

(Shane et al., 2003) and the influence of entrepreneurial self-efficacy on the decision-making process (Forbes, 2005). Practical tools for entrepreneurs also have been suggested, like the form of decision implications framework by Camuffo et al. (2020).

Nevertheless, in this chapter, we want to focus on one of the most recently academically accepted concepts in entrepreneurship studies, effectuation (Sarasvathy, 2001), a concept that challenges most part of the existing planning models in place during the last century.

9.2 Causation vs Effectuation

The process of developing a business plan is one of the several hands-on learning experiences provided by business schools in most parts of the world. A business plan is a written document that describes a long-term vision of the company and its environment (Burns, 1996). It is mostly used to set objectives and a tool to monitor a business performance. Learning how to write a business plan became one of the key requirements for a candidate to get a degree in business (Jones & Penaluna, 2013).

The problem with this approach is that students who have never worked on the industry apply pricing techniques to determine the prices of products or services they never seen before. They conduct interviews with potential customers to determine the best communication strategies to reach that market segment. They need to prepare five-year pro-forma sales and revenues forecast without any real-life experience. They have to determine the best ways to beat competitors they never heard about. They have to estimate salaries of employees they don't even know their roles or positions. Can anybody trust on any of the projections described in the business plans written by these students? Probably not.

Even experienced professionals, with years working in the industry, when writing business plans they have to take some assumptions. Their sales projections are based on assumptions about the target market. Their revenue projections are based on assumptions about pricing. Their growth projections are based on assumptions about the competitors. Their wages costs assume the current labor legislation. Their supply chain costs assume a specific foreign exchange rate. Their packaging costs assume specific traffic and storage conditions. Each one of these assumptions can either be proven wrong or can be challenged at any time in the near future with the dynamism of the industry.

Several of these assumptions are only possible to prove after the business starts its operations. This is when real contracts are signed, real estimates are made and deals are negotiated. Once the first assumption falls down in the first weeks of operation of the business, some or many parts of the original business plan may, and will, change, forcing the entrepreneur to review all their projections and spend some valuable time modifying the plan to accommodate the new proved assumptions. Situations in which new circumstances change the entire plan are more and more common in the business world. It can be a new fact that challenges existing assumptions, a new opportunity that emerged out of nothing or an unexpected occurrence that has never been considered when the original plan was written. No matter how detailed is the risk assessment section or how many different scenarios were projected, no business plan can predict all the things that can happen.

Sarasvathy (2001) refers to this traditional line of thinking, defended by consultants and academics and massively taught in business schools as causation logic, a predictive way of thinking, in which the elements required for decision-making are known and controlled and, therefore, can be predicted, which supports the traditional process of planning. Entrepreneurs, she defends, do not follow this process in the real life for the simple reason that they don't own or control the resources they need to establish and grow their businesses.

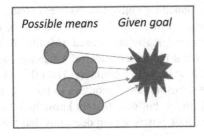 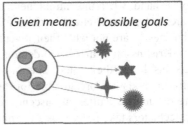

Figure 9.1 Contrasting causation and effectuation.

Instead, entrepreneurs use the effectuation logic, the opposite to causation. Rather than acquiring the resources they need to accomplish the expected goal and objectives, entrepreneurs use the resources they currently have and find out ways to make use of them in a way that can accomplish something.

Under the causation logic, the effect (objective) is fixed and the process involves selecting the means to create that effect. Under the effectuation logic, the collection of given means (resources) is driven towards possible effects that can be achieved through those means (Figure 9.1).

A causation logic entrepreneur would ignore new raising opportunities because they would be a distraction to accomplish the objectives already proposed in its strategic plan. An effectual logic entrepreneur would take the business to a new course of action, making the proper adaptations to the original plan in order to pursue the opportunity, even if the final results end up being different from the original plan, and that would be OK because achieving different results, but better results, is the ultimate goal of effectual entrepreneurs.

Effectual entrepreneurs tend to change routes constantly, considering emerging new circumstances, like barriers or opportunities. When these circumstances are unexpected, it is common that a certain level of uncertainty presents to the business. In these cases, entrepreneurs imagine possible scenarios these new circumstances may offer and they make small-scale trials and experiments to test the assumptions they have about these scenarios. These assumptions can either be proven right or wrong. When they are wrong, entrepreneurs can try new scenarios without having spent too much effort, resources or time, because those were just experiments. If the assumptions are proven right, then they move forward with that scenario, narrowing down the options to more concrete and stable scenarios, turning the decision-making process easier.

For effectual entrepreneurs, every time an assumption is not proved, the test fails, but this is a good fail, because it brings a lesson, it brings the realization that the business could have gone the wrong direction if an entire planning was performed in that direction. The failed experiment shows where not to go and the entrepreneur has the opportunity to pivot the business concept towards new directions or even new purposes.

9.3 Effectual Entrepreneurs and the Decision-Making Process

The decision-making process is different between the causation and the effectuation logic. Entrepreneurs using the causation logic tend to use a whole process of raising information, like industry statistics or market research. Decisions are taken after a deep analysis of given information. This process is more suitable if the new venture adopts existing business models with higher chances of proven information to consider about how to start and grow the business.

On the other hand, when the entrepreneur is launching innovative business concepts, probably there aren't many references to copy from. 'From Apple to Twitter, some of the most successful businesses are not what their inventors originally envisioned' (Mullins & Komisar, 2010, p. 12). Kristinsson et al. (2016) demonstrated the lesser effect of causation logic when making decisions during the implementation of new ideas in a business. The effectual logic of trial-and-error methods is more suitable for these businesses. According to the effectual principle, failure occurs more often in nascent industries, but effectuators know how to fail fast and early. Effectuators take failures as a learning tool, where wrong decisions don't lead to big consequences. This is the experimentation cycle mentioned above.

When talking about possible consequences of wrong decisions, it is inevitable to think about taking risks. The decision-making process is inherent to the risk-taking process. The larger the risk, the more unlikely the entrepreneur would be willing to make a wrong decision. Risk taking is directly correlated with consequences. When effectuators try new things in small scale, they are reducing the risk by reducing the negative consequences of a wrong decision. By reducing the scale of a trial, the costs of making the wrong decision are more affordable to the entrepreneur.

Another important component of risk assessment is the level of uncertainty. The higher the level of uncertainty, in other words, the less we know about a subject, the higher the chances that something unexpected happens, therefore, the higher the inherent risks are. When trying new things, like a new business model, or entering into a new industry, entrepreneurs face high levels of uncertainty, leading them to take more effectual approaches on their decisions. Being a follower in an existing industry, like opening another traditional bakery or a regular gas station, represents low risk because there are plenty of guidelines on how to start these types of businesses. Following a pre-established guideline to open a known business model, is basically following the causation logic.

This means that entrepreneurs following the causation logic are effect-dependent, as the choice of means to reach a pre-determined goal (opening a business) is driven by the characteristics of the effect the decision-maker wants to create and his or her knowledge of possible means (existing guidelines on how to start a known business).

Effectual entrepreneurs, on the other hand, are actor-dependent, because, given the specific means (the existing resources owned by the entrepreneur), the choice of effect is driven by the characteristics of the actor (entrepreneur) and his/her ability to discover and use contingencies (the trial-and-error process in low scale models) (Sarasvathy, 2001).

While causation focuses on predictable aspects of an uncertain future, effectuation focuses on the controllable aspects of an unpredictable future (Sarasvathy, 2001). This way, the decision to where do effectuators go is not determined by the scarce information source (unpredictable), but from the circumstances that raise from the combination of the entrepreneur's resources (abilities, knowledge, resources) and the results of the trial-and-error process that will give new directions on how to use these resources (controllable aspects).

Using the simple metaphor of a sailing boat, causators establish a destination and do whatever it takes to maneuver the boat under the wind conditions to get to that destination, while effectuators just let the boat go following the wind and wherever it lands it will be their destination.

Here is a hypothetical example to demonstrate these concepts: A causation entrepreneur starts a bakery business by writing a business plan, raising the resources needed for a bakery and opening the bakery in the desired spot for the desired market. Effectual entrepreneurs may start the same bakery by baking some cookies from home (low scale trials) and get an invitation from one of the customers to cater a party (new fact). After that, the entrepreneur learns that catering is the real business and starts cooking and baking for parties, until someone asks to organize the entire party, not only cater it (pivot the business), and the business ends up being a big event planning corporation, nothing to do with the original home-made cookies.

Because of the nature of their small businesses, entrepreneurs are more subjected to the inconsistencies of a continuously changing business environment, therefore they have to be more adaptative and flexible to accommodate the inevitable contingencies along the way. In this sense, existing literature about decision-making in business does not fit well to entrepreneurial decision-making (Laskovaia et al., 2019).

9.4 A Combined Approach in Decision-Making

Although these concepts and examples may lead to the conclusion that entrepreneurs are essentially effectuators and the causation logic is not fit for the entrepreneurial decision-making process, it is important to emphasize that they are not mutually exclusive (Sarasvathy, 2008). The effectuation logic is mostly used in the very early stages of the nascent business when the level of uncertainty is high and most entrepreneurs in this stage can count on their own limited resources only.

As the entrepreneur goes through the effectual process of trial and error and the pathway for the future of the business becomes clearer, the causation logic of raising information and reducing uncertainty starts to take place on the daily decision-making process of the entrepreneur (Brinckman et al., 2010). As the business grows, the entrepreneur tends to share part of his/her role and responsibilities with people hired to take care of specific areas of the business, like sales, production or administration. Shared responsibilities require more steady directions to the future of the business, giving less room for pivots, improvisation or radical change of directions, therefore, more causal thinking (Hmieleski & Corbett, 2008).

Smolka et al. (2016) created the term 'planning effectuator' to designate entrepreneurs who make decisions by balancing both approaches. In their study, they concluded that entrepreneurs take into consideration both (1) experimentation with the product offering and (2) making use of the resources in hand, together with the designing of business strategies for a new venture. While the effectual approach tends to target the product of the firm, the causal approach allows the entrepreneur to map the general direction the business is heading to.

On the other hand, Laskovaia et al. (2019) investigated small businesses' performance during the Russian economic crisis of 2015 and realized that entrepreneurs may balance causation and effectuation approaches differently when under stressful situation. According to their findings, the effectual thinking helps them to decide when and how to pivot their businesses under crisis. Once they make the decision, the causal approach helps them to diligently plan and pursue performance improvements for the new strategy the business has taken. These findings are in line with previous research driven by Delmar and Shane (2003) and Miller and Cardinal (1994) about decision-making under high uncertainty.

These studies show that not only new business models require the effectual approach, but also new circumstances, like economic crisis, challenging the success recipes from the past or demanding new ways of thinking that break the existing patterns which are not working anymore. At the same time, during economic crisis, the level of uncertainty raises the perception of risk, for existing businesses with a lot to lose; planning has been proven to reduce risks by reducing uncertainty, so the causation logic takes precedence.

This hybrid perspective is also demonstrated by Reymen et al. (2015). They investigated the antecedents of the effectual vs. causal logic by investigating tech startup entrepreneurs, and they concluded that entrepreneurs use both logics in decision-making processes simultaneously, while the dominant logic shifts over time due to specific conditions resulting in two venture scope levels, narrow or wide. Entrepreneurs narrow the scope of their business when they focus on a particular market segment and they widen the scope when they are willing to diversify their market and business.

The scope determines the preferred logic, narrowing the scope of the business calls for the causal thinking and widening the scope of the business calls for the effectual thinking. The authors got to the same conclusion of previous studies about the effect of the level of uncertainty in the environment (increased uncertainty leads to a wide scope and effectual thinking, while decreased uncertainty leads to narrow scope and causal thinking) and the perceived level of resources they control (the less available resources, the more they tend to use the effectual reasoning in their decisions).

But the real contribution of their study relies on the finding that the number of stakeholders demonstrated a direct correlation to the tendency of narrowing or widening the scope of the business (Reymen et al., 2015). Tech companies are often immersed in pressures for fast growth, as a required demand from investors, partners and other stakeholders, but these entrepreneurs are also immersed in a high dynamic business environment, where things change all the time. Few environments seem to be so appropriate to understand the hybrid nature of entrepreneurial decision-making.

The nature of the business, the unstable environment and the flexibility to quickly pivot the business concept normally favour the effectual reasoning, but when other people are directly involved in the business (stakeholders), the entrepreneur tends to use more rational reasoning, by establishing focus to the business, specific goals and a clear strategy on how to reach them, a causal approach. Investors bring all the resources the business needs, therefore, increasing the risk by increasing the potential impact in case of failure. These resources are used to reduce uncertainty, balancing the risk and forcing the entrepreneur to make decisions based on upcoming circumstances, sometimes using the effectual mode (high uncertainty) and sometimes using the causal mode (high risk, big resources).

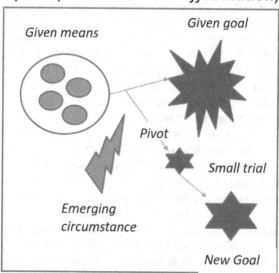

Figure 9.2 Hybrid approach combining causation and effectuation.

Back to our opening case, the executive and his team spent time and resources to conceive the 'perfect plan', maybe they could have brought some effectual approach by taking some of the assumptions with high levels of uncertainty and leave that part of the plan open enough to take decisions only when trials are made to test those assumptions and then take the proper routes to the strategy. A good strategy is made out of a balance between the effectuation and the causation logics, giving room to what the uncertainty can bring as new threats or opportunities and by taking the appropriate actions to try the possible scenarios through small-scale and low-cost experiments that can direct the business to better decisions about its future. When executing the plan, the level of uncertainty naturally reduces, giving room to the raising of new facts and circumstances. Eventually, some of them may give insights to new pathways for the business which no one had the opportunity to predict. Deciding to pivot the business under these circumstances maybe easier and maybe the right pathway to make better decisions along the entire entrepreneurial journey. As visually demonstrated in Figure 9.2.

When reaching a crossroad in a foggy road, sometimes you just have to trust your instincts and take a step forward in one direction even without seeing the end of the road. Entrepreneurs know they don't need to predict the future, because they are aware that whatever decision they make they can build the future they want.

References

Brinckmann, J., Grichnik, D., & Kapsa, D. (2010). Should Entrepreneurs Plan or Just Storm the Castle? A Meta-Analysis on Contextual Factors Impacting the Business Planning–Performance Relationship in Small Firms. *Journal of Business Venturing* 25(1): 24–40. doi:10.1016/j.jbusvent.2008.10.007

Burns, P. (1996). The business plan. In: Burns, P., and Dewhurst, J. (eds) *Small Business and Entrepreneurship*. Macmillan Small Business Series. Palgrave. https://doi.org/10.1007/978-1-349-24911-4_9

Byrnes, J. P. (1998). *The Nature and Development of Decision-Making: A Self-Regulation Model.* Taylor & Francis Group.

Camuffo, A., Cordova, A., Gambardella, A., & Spina, C. A. (2020). Scientific Approach to Entrepreneurial Decision Making: Evidence from a Randomized Control Trial. *Management Science* 66(2): 564–586. doi:10.1287/mnsc.2018.3249

Catalani, M. S., & Clerico, G. F. (1996). *Decision Making Structures: Dealing with Uncertainty Within Organizations.* Physica-Verlag, 67–167. doi:10.1007/978-3-642-50138-8

Delmar, F., & Shane, S. (2003). Does Business Planning Facilitate the Development of New Ventures? *Strategic Management Journal* 24(12): 1165–1185.

Forbes, D. P. (2005). The Effects of Strategic Decision Making on Entrepreneurial Self-Efficacy. *Entrepreneurship Theory and Practice* 29(5):599–626. doi:10.1111/j.1540-6520.2005.00100.

Hmieleski, K. M., & Corbett, A. C. (2008). The Contrasting Interaction Effects of Improvisational Behavior with Entrepreneurial Self-Efficacy on New Venture Performance and Entrepreneur Work Satisfaction. *Journal of Business Venturing* 23: 482–496.

Jones, C., & Penaluna, A. (2013). Moving beyond the Business Plan in Enterprise Education. *Education + Training* 55(8/9), 804–814. doi:10.1108/ET-06-2013-0077

Laskovaia, A., Marino, L., & Shirokova, G. (2019). Wales W. Expect the Unexpected: Examining the Shaping Role of Entrepreneurial Orientation on Causal and Effectual Decision-Making Logic during Economic Crisis. *Entrepreneurship and Regional Development* 31(5–6):456–475. doi:10.1080/08985 626.2018.1541593

Jennings, D., & Wattam, S. (1998). *Decision Making: An Integrated Approach.* 2nd ed. Financial Times Pitman Publishing.

Kristinsson, K., Candi, M., & Sæmundsson, R. J. (2016). The Relationship between Founder Team Diversity and Innovation Performance: The Moderating Role of Causation Logic. *Long Range Planning* 49(4): 464–476. doi:10.1016/j.lrp.2015.12.013

March, J. G. (1994). *Primer on Decision Making: How Decisions Happen.* Free Press

Miller, C. C., & Cardinal, L. B. (1994). Strategic Planning and Firm Performance: A Synthesis of More Than Two Decades of Research. *Academy of Management Journal* 37(6): 1649–1665.

Mullins, J., & Komisar, R. (2010). A business Plan? Or a Journey to Plan B. *MIT Sloan Management Review* 51(3): 1–5.

Reymen, I. M. M. J., Andries, P., Berends, J. J., Mauer, R., Stephan, U., & van Burg, J. C. (2015). Understanding Dynamics of Strategic Decision-Making in Venture Creation: A Process Study of Effectuation and Causation. *Strategic Entrepreneurship Journal* 9(4), 351–379. https://doi.org/10.1002/sej.1201

Sarasvathy, S. D. (2001). Causation and Effectuation: Toward a Theoretical Shift from Economic Inevitability to Entrepreneurial Contingency. *The Academy of Management Review* 26(2):243–263. doi:10.2307/259121

Sarasvathy, S. D. (2008). *Effectuation: Elements of Entrepreneurial Expertise*. United Kingdom: Edward Elgar.

Shane, S., Locke, E. A., & Collins, C. J. (2003). Entrepreneurial Motivation. *Human Resource Management Review* 13(2): 257–279. doi:10.1016/S1053-4822(03)00017-2

Shapira, Z. (1996). *Organizational Decision Making*. 1. Paperback ed. Cambridge: Cambridge University Press. doi:10.1017/CBO9780511584169

Scholz, R. W., & Scholz, R. W. (1983). *Decision Making under Uncertainty: Cognitive Decision Research, Social Interaction, Development and Epistemology*. Elsevier Science & Technology.

Smolka, K., Verheul, I., Burmeister-Lamp, K., & Heugens, P. (2016). Get It Together! Synergistic Effects of Causal and Effectual Decision-Making Logics on Venture Performance. *Entrepreneurship Theory and Practice* 42(4): 571–604. doi:10.1111/etap.12266

Triantaphyllou, E. (2000). *Multi-Criteria Decision Making Methods a Comparative Study*, 44. Springer. doi:10.1007/978-1-4757-3157-6

Wickham, P. A. (2001). *Strategic Entrepreneurship: A Decision-Making Approach to New Venture Creation and Management*. 2. ed. Financial Times Prentice Hall.

Part IV
Entrepreneurial Marketing

10 Market and Competitor Analysis

Gérard Martorell

10.1 Introduction

In published papers, there is a big discussion on whether entrepreneurs must follow their instincts when making decisions. Instead, the majority is inclined to be systematic (Bonabeau, 2003; Liviniuk, 2019) arguing that doing so is less risky. Others claim that basing your decisions on intuition may have some advantages (Huang, 2019; Malsberger, 2017). Historical data (Katz & Green, 2018) show a relationship between middle age and entrepreneurial success, and this seems to be due to those entrepreneurs having an extensive knowledge of the market they are going to be active in (Azoulay et al., 2019; Ramirez-Flores, 2021). Thus, for young or first-time entrepreneurs, the general advice is to catch up on market understanding to limit the associated risks of a new venture. However, to do that in an efficient way, new entrepreneurs should follow a method to approach their market research and analysis (Eisenmann, 2021) because that can help assess the market potential of the venture idea (Wenzel, 2012).

10.2 Key Concepts

10.2.1 Market Research Process

There are different ways to define market research. According to Twin (2022), it is "the process of determining the viability of a new service or product through research conducted directly with potential customers." The US Small Business Administration (2022) asserts that market "research blends consumer behavior and economic trends to confirm and improve your business idea." Robertson (2006) defines it as "an organized effort to gather information about target markets and customers: know about them, starting with who they are."

With a bias toward marketing, the American Marketing Association claims "Marketing research is the systematic gathering, recording, and analyzing of data about problems related to the marketing of goods and services." According to Gheethu (2019), the main difference between marketing research and market research is that the latter is "the appropriate term when marketing research is being conducted in a specific customer group in a specific geographic area."

Traditional market research is mostly based on surveys. This can lead to dramatic conclusions and incorrect decisions on what to offer to consumers. Talking about this, Steve Jobs stated (Smith, 2019),

> Some people say to give the customers what they want, but that's not my approach. Our job is to figure out what they're going to want before they do. I think Henry Ford once said, 'If I'd

DOI: 10.4324/9781003341284-14

ask customers what they wanted, they would've told me a faster horse.' People don't know what they want until you show it to them. That's why I never rely on market research. Our task is to read things that are not yet on the page.

To avoid such mismatches, a systematic approach to market research means following a consistent logic. This can be simplified as a linear process:

- Start with research about what is known about the specific market and competitors. There are many available data sets or proxies that can be found online. If your competitor is 3M, then research what 3M is proposing and doing in your aimed market.
- Explore and understand the reasoning the customers use to make decisions about products/services similar to the one the entrepreneur is planning to develop. Engaging with competitors and market customers is a great exercise in this phase.
- Elaborate a theory that explains the behavior and the needs/wishes of the customer.
- Validate this theory with a larger one. Some products may not support this phase, especially if we are talking about B2B with very few customers to sell to.
- With the available data in hand, entrepreneurs can start to create prototypes or mockups of their product/service with a fairly high probability to be right. Those prototypes need to be tested quickly with potential customers. This will be explained in Chapter 11 on Lean Startup.
- Once this is done, we get an acceptable prototype and a good idea of how successful the product/service will be. That helps to assess how big the expected sales can be (demand).
- The next step is making decisions on the business structure and value chains, but these parts must also be filtered by usable infrastructure/machines, readily available money, the entrepreneur's wishes, and involved people at their disposal.

This total linear process can be observed in Figure 10.1.

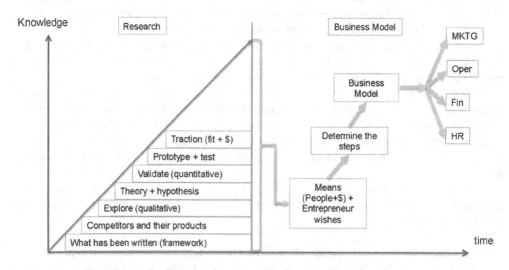

Figure 10.1 Market research process.

Table 10.1 Types of marketing research

By source	By methodology	By objectives
- Secondary - Internal - External - Primary	- Qualitative - Quantitative	- Exploratory - Descriptive - Causal or experimental

10.2.2 Types of Market Research

Figure 10.1 shows different types of research that fit under the category of market research. In fact, there are very different ways to approach market research. According to Geevarghese (2013), market research can be divided into three basic categories: by source, by methodology, and by objectives. However, there are also sub-clusters and variations within each of the categories (see Table 10.1).

The first way to categorize the research types is by their sources: primary or secondary. Hassan (2022) defines primary sources as "original and collected by the researcher to answer a specific research question." In other words, these data have not been previously published by somebody else for that same purpose. On the other hand, secondary data are data previously collected and published for purposes other than the research at hand. Also, secondary sources can have an internal origin (sales reports, Customer Relationship Manager software, etc.) or an external one (publications, other company reports, associations, government, etc.).

Market research can also be categorized by the methodology to be used. In this case, we have qualitative or quantitative types of research. According to Creswell (2013), "Qualitative research is the naturalistic study of social meanings and processes, using interviews, observations, and the analysis of texts and images." So, when there are stories to tell and not just numbers, qualitative research is the preferred way. This methodology provides an in-depth picture of what is happening, including emotions and other rich details that can help the understanding of the phenomena. According to Yin (2013), a case study, one of the qualitative research methods, is particularly suited when the research questions start with "how" or "why."

On the other hand, Creswell (2013) states that quantitative research focuses on numbers/statistics and "provides a large surface picture." This method may have, if correctly performed, the advantage of being objective and thus enables broad generalizations about the researched populations. However, both have drawbacks and are more and more seen as complementary or needed to be conducted in a sequence. This combination is called mixed-methods (Creswell, 2013).

As an example, when Isaac Newton saw an apple fall, he tried to understand why apples always fall perpendicularly to the ground. He decided that there must be an attraction between the earth and the apple to explain it. The idea of gravitation seemed to be a logical way of resolving the observation. However, at the time, he had no means to check if all types of apples were falling the same way or if pears, peaches, and rocks abided by the same law or not.

As described, Newton's theory was put forward after an observation (or a few of them) in the form of a qualitative research case study. However, to be certain that his theory was also valid for the other elements on earth, Newton needed a massive validation testing procedure. This validation phase is what quantitative research performs well. Table 10.2 shows a comparative table of advantages and disadvantages of both methods.

Table 10.2 Qualitative vs. quantitative research

	Qualitative	*Quantitative*
Type of question	Probing	Simple
Sample size	Small	Large
Information per respondent	High	Low(ish)
Questioner's skill	High	Low(ish)
Analyst's skill	High	High
Type of analysis	Subjective, interpretative	Objective, statistical
Ability to replicate	Low	High
Areas probed	Attitudes, feelings, motivations	Choices, frequency, demographics

Based on Geevarghese (2013).

Table 10.3 Market research categorization by objective

Market research categorization by objective	
Exploratory	Preliminary data is needed to develop an idea. - This applies to outline concepts, gather insights, formulate theories - Usually uses a qualitative approach - Example: What kind of features can we add to our product?
Descriptive	Describe an element of an idea with precision. - This applies to the description of target market, how big it is, what are the trends, etc. - Both qualitative and quantitative approaches are used - Example: What is the age range for our customers?
Causal	Test and validate some theory or cause-and-effect relationship. - This applies to price elasticity - Could be done using an experiment - The suitable methods are quantitative surveys and/or experiments - Example: What is the price sensitivity of our products?

Qualitative and quantitative methods can be used to address similar problems, but the focus is different. For instance, qualitative research also collects demographic data. However, the focus of those data is to complement the understanding of the customer behavior. On the other hand, demographics might be a key validating element for quantitative research.

The third way to categorize market research methods is by objectives. In this case, the methodologies are exploratory, descriptive, and causal (Geevarghese, 2013; Guyader, 2016) (Table 10.3).

This categorization has also an advantage in assessing the most suitable methodology depending on the market research required flexibility. The exploratory methods are more flexible and gather a broader scope of data. On the other hand, results are not as clear and can be fuzzy. Causal methodologies require a rigid design requiring a control group. However, they only collect what is in the questionnaires, so they might be missing some important elements that are not asked about. But results are clear and measurable.

Each market research step has its own tricks and requires some skills that are specific to that step. Thus, the global process is usually performed in teams. In Table 10.4, we can see the different steps, some comments on each, and who is usually in charge of each of the steps.

This model implies several elements that are not that obvious. For instance, that the company has the means/money to perform the market research. Thus, there are some elements to check before implementing market research (Figure 10.2). As an example, a startup with very limited resources may not have the means to launch a costly quantitative survey with

Table 10.4 Market research process

Define the problem	Check methodology	Research design	Fieldwork	Data analysis	Present report
Steps					
- What are the objectives? - Clearly state the problem	- Decide what methodology suits the defined problem	- Formulate the research design - State-raised topics/ Questionnaire	- implement the research plan - Gather data/ sampling - Usually done by third parties	- Cluster and analyze the data	- Write and present the report
Comments					
If a problem is vaguely defined, results can have little bearing	If the problem is not well defined, the chosen methodology might not be the appropriate one	The plan needs to be decided upfront but be flexible enough to incorporate changes/ iterations	This phase is the costly one and also the one that can introduce the most liable errors	The analysis method depends very much on the chosen research methodology	This phase depends on who needs the information and how he/ she wants it
Who					
Marketing manager	Market research specialist	Market research specialist + usually a fieldwork party	Most of the time performed by a third party specialized in fieldwork	Market research specialist and/or the fieldwork third party	Market research specialist and/or the fieldwork third party to Marketing Management

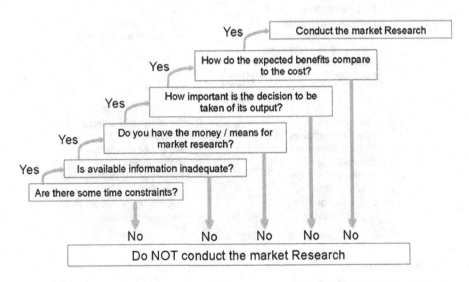

Figure 10.2 Market research decision process.

a third party. Therefore, proxy research can provide acceptable information. The output will probably not be as good as what could be accomplished with a lot of money, but a startup cannot afford it, or it is not worth the effort. This is where the Lean Methodology and Customer Discovery come in. It is not the quantity of research but the quality that is most important. We will see in Chapter 11.

Feasibility might also weigh in the balance. For a B2B business, there might not be enough customers in the world to support valid quantitative causal research. In that case, the only way is exploratory or descriptive research. Finally, real-life market research can bring up unexpected surprises. It is common to see that what were thought to be the initial customer motivations turn out to be different ones during the research process. This framing/reframing process, which will be explained in Chapter 11, should allow the entrepreneurial team to undertake a problem re-definition. That is why proceeding step by step can help in performing market research that is addressing the real problem. Figure 10.1 shows those steps.

10.2.3 Review on the Market and Competitors

The first step of market research is to define what information is looked for with this process. The second step is to assess what information is already available on the market we aim to be active in and who the active competitors are.

One practical tool to do this is the PEST analysis, which stands for political, economic, social, and technological factors. Figure 10.3 shows what it can look like.

Another practical tool to perform this analysis is the Porter Five Forces, which analyses the five competitive forces that shape each industry and helps determine an industry's weaknesses and strengths. See Figure 10.4.

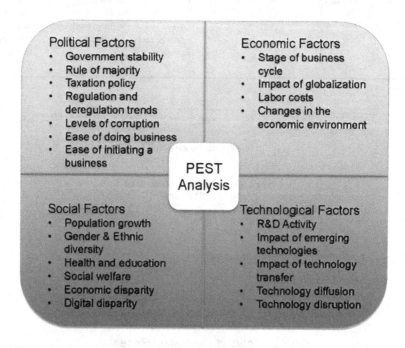

Figure 10.3 Pest analysis.

Based on https://businessfrontiersblog.files.wordpress.com/2016/03/pest.jpg.

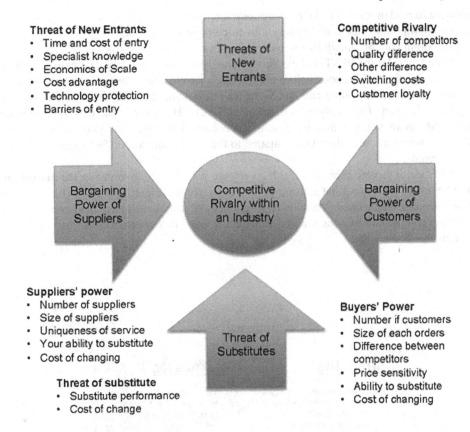

Threat of New Entrants
- Time and cost of entry
- Specialist knowledge
- Economics of Scale
- Cost advantage
- Technology protection
- Barriers of entry

Competitive Rivalry
- Number of competitors
- Quality difference
- Other difference
- Switching costs
- Customer loyalty

Threats of New Entrants

Bargaining Power of Suppliers

Competitive Rivalry within an Industry

Bargaining Power of Customers

Suppliers' power
- Number of suppliers
- Size of suppliers
- Uniqueness of service
- Your ability to substitute
- Cost of changing

Threat of Substitutes

Buyers' Power
- Number if customers
- Size of each orders
- Difference between competitors
- Price sensitivity
- Ability to substitute
- Cost of changing

Threat of substitute
- Substitute performance
- Cost of change

Figure 10.4 Porter 5 forces.

Based on https://image.slidesharecdn.com/portersfiveforcesofcompetitiveanalysiswithexamples-170327090832/95/porters-five-forces-model-of-competitive-analysis-7-1024.jpg?cb=1490606952.

However, this latter tool implies the analysis of the competitors. That is to analyze the companies that offer or can offer similar products. Competitors can be classified into three categories:

- The direct one who offers comparable or similar products.
- Indirect ones whose products cover similar needs but in a different way. For instance, bicycle or scooter producers both offer mobility to their customers.
- And could-be competitors that do not have a competing product but have the resources to move quickly into the same space. For instance, a fridge producer could start offering AC devices as the technology is relatively similar.

To help find out competitors' and customers' wishes, the Job-to-be-done (JTBD) framework theory can be very useful as it removes the focus from the product itself and places it on the customer. Here are some ways to use it (Christensen, 2016; Ulwick, 2016):

- Something a customer wants to accomplish in a specific situation or circumstance.
- A metaphor to refer to what customers want from the products they buy.
- Something functional in a customer's life, with emotional and social components.

If you want to read more on JTBD, here are some useful links:

https://www.productplan.com/glossary/jobs-to-be-done-framework/
https://builtin.com/product/jobs-to-be-done-framework

In the end, besides the PEST and the Porter Five Forces, the secondary data market analysis should end with the market opportunities and threats, which list the different important elements that make the market appealing and not. Some may also argue the company's weaknesses and strengths to this part. This analysis is then called SWOT. However, if the new venture is not active in the market yet, you may have some technological strengths, but your main weakness is not being active in the market yet compared to the other competitors. See Figure 10.5 for a SWOT example.

To conclude, it is very recommendable to engage with people involved in the market you plan to be active in. It is a great starting point for the market research process. That is talking with people in the value chain, stakeholders, suppliers, potential customers, and even competitors. However, it should be done with an aim and deployed in a systematic way to avoid being misled by unrealistic wishes.

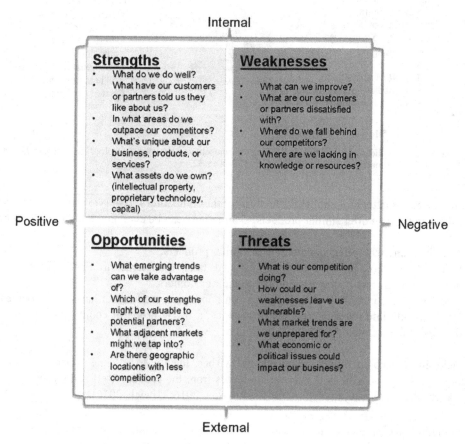

Figure 10.5 SWOT analysis.

Based on https://www.cybermedian.com/fr/how-to-do-swot-analysis/.

10.2.4 Exploratory Phase

Secondary information alone generally is necessary but not sufficient to answer your venture questions. Primary data must be collected and transformed into usable information, and it is the most important and useful of all the data gathered. As mentioned before, the first step for this is exploring the market. The objective is to discover ideas and understand the consumers' and the customers' problems by finding out the reasons behind consumers' and customers' behaviors. It is useful to build up a mental model explaining the behaviors in a particular context (Zeithaml, 2019). The most appropriate way to find it is by using exploratory methods.

There are various exploratory methods:

- In-depth interviews (IDI)
- Focus groups
- Purposed and private communities
- Ethnographic research
- Projective techniques such as word association, completion test, thematic apperception, or expression techniques
- Observation and immersion case studies
- Social media monitoring
- Listening platform (automatic and intelligent social media opinion mining)
- Netnography (ethnography applied to social media)

Exploratory techniques can be classified into three categories:

- Observation and social media monitoring consist of observing what happens and trying to understand how and why people behave the way they behave.
- Direct techniques where individuals provide information freely or answer direct questions, being aware of the research objective and why they are there. IDI and focus groups fall into this category.
- Indirect techniques where individuals provide information when responding to stimuli that divert their attention from the true objective of the research, ensuring spontaneity and sincerity. Projective techniques, experiments, and pilot studies fall into this category.

The advantages of qualitative research can be seen in the following Table 10.5.

Table 10.5 Advantages of qualitative research

Factor	Qualitative methods
Goals/objectives	Discover/identification of new ideas, thoughts, feelings; preliminary understanding of relationships; understanding of hidden psychological and social processes
Type of research	Exploratory
Type of questions	Open-ended, unstructured, probing
Time of execution	Relatively short time frame
Representativeness	Small samples, only the sampled individuals
Type of analysis	Content analysis, interpretative
Researcher skill	Interpersonal communications, observation, interpretation of text, or visual data
Generalizability	May be limited

Source: Based on Hair, J. et al. (2020).

For further reading, here is a useful link on this:
https://www.scribbr.com/methodology/exploratory-research/
https://researchmethod.net/exploratory-research/

10.2.5 Building a Theory

The aim of the exploration phase and the descriptive phase is to build up a construct that can explain what has been observed and/or described. The term *theoretical model* describes a collection of ideas that a researcher connects to explain a particular phenomenon. Using a theoretical model or hypothesis during a research process can give the researcher the ability to connect different theories to each other and form their own.

In general, the theory construction process is inductive in nature. The identification of patterns that apply to the observations helps create the new theoretical construct explaining the phenomenon. In other words, the aim is to find a logical reasoning that can explain what has been observed. If all interviewees mention this is the price consumers want to pay, maybe this is part of the model. The process can also be deductive. Researchers may set up models, settings, and scenarios with different characteristics and derive implications for the deduced model. The observed characteristics can then be linked together to form the new theory.

A way to build that model goes by splitting the product/service into different areas, such as service quality, market orientation, and consumption experience. This approach has the advantage of incorporating different aspects of the consumer experience within their specific marketing setting. This can be a practical and useful way to develop conceptual frameworks (Zeithaml, 2019). In the end, all methodologies want the researcher to revise the findings, to find common themes/ideas, and abstract commonalities to form the building blocks of the emergent theory that explains the market behavior.

10.2.6 Innovation Phase

Innovation is built on something that already exists while invention is new to the world. It is important to note that in both cases the entrepreneur must bring something new to the market that some people might be interested in purchasing. The novelty does not mean that all product features must be better than competitors' proposals. In fact, they might not be. Unless a product is outstandingly better (e.g., cure for cancer with one pill one time and no side effects), chances are that the way the company is set and how the resources are allocated (i.e., the business model) will be more important than the product itself. For instance, Apple is focused on being able to launch a competitive product every six months, not so much that their model characteristics are far better than the competitors', though Apple must also periodically raise the bar and introduce something completely new to disrupt the market.

There are many ideation techniques, but the most common one is probably design thinking, which principles are attributed to Herbert A. Simon in his 1969 book, *The Sciences of the Artificial*. The Hasso Plattner Institute of Design at Stanford proposed a model for the design thinking process. The methodology is usually deployed in five steps (Figure 10.6) that group related activities into three processes: inspiration, opportunity or ideation, and innovation or implementation (Lewrick et al., 2018).

For technology-driven projects, the idea is to gain an empathetic understanding of the problem you're trying to solve, typically through user research. Empathy allows you to set aside your own assumptions about the world and gain real insight into users and their needs. How? Exploratory methods such as observation, engagement, or immersion are the preferred ways.

Stanford d.school Design Thinking Process

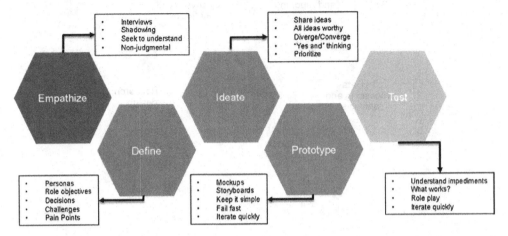

Figure 10.6 Design thinking process.

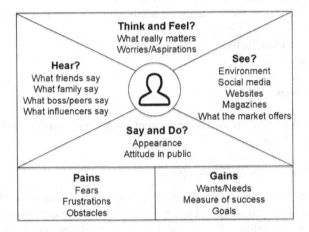

Figure 10.7 Empathy map.

The results can be visualized by using an empathy map that clusters the customer-centered observations in six blocks, each one led by specific questions (Figure 10.7). The results can help to understand the reasoning behind a purchasing process.

10.2.7 Validation of the Ideas

The last phase of market research is to validate the concept. This validation process is accomplished by asking a large number of possible customers' simple questions. Creating these surveys must follow some specific steps:

- To define the problem to assess. In other words, what elements/hypotheses do you want to validate?

Figure 10.8 Iteration process in market research.

- To sample the right people in the appropriate amount
- To measure the interest by identifying what needs to be measured and creating an acceptable scale for it.
- To design the questionnaire to fit the research objectives
- To gather the data
- To analyze the data
- To draw Conclusions

Concerning the sample, there are two basic concepts to pay attention to: the type of sample and the number of respondents.

- For this type of sample there are two options:

  • Probability-driven samples are either simple random or systematic random samples.
  • Non-probability–driven samples can be convenience, judgment, quota, or snowball samples. Most entrepreneurs use convenience samples. However, the entrepreneur must ensure that the sample is not biased.

- The number of people in the sample is linked to the Central Limit Theorem, which states that the sampling distribution of the means is normal. In general, for social sciences, each of the small sub-groups you may be interested in observing must have at least 25 members/people. The tinier the groups, the more samples are needed to take the survey.

In any case, if conclusions from the market research are not satisfactory, this process might have to be repeated. See Figure 10.8.

10.3 Conclusion

Market research is a tool to assist entrepreneurs in making decisions. It is not a replacement for good judgment. It is helpful for improvements to existing products, but less so for radical innovations. The main problem is that customers cannot properly talk about or provide feedback on what they have never seen or experienced. Also, markets are increasingly becoming micro-segmented (e.g., sports socks for wealthy ecology-conscious women to be used during their yoga or aerobic sessions). So, research on the mass market might be irrelevant or even impossible (especially for B2B). That is the reason qualitative research can be key to developing a competitive product.

Once the market understanding is clear, it is time to start building and testing the prototypes. That phase should enable the entrepreneur to assess how attractive the product/service is in the market and, thus, assess the possible demand.

References

Azoulay, P., Jones, B. F., Kim, J. D., and Miranda, J. (2019). "Age and high-growth entrepreneurship." Kellogg Northwestern University, retrieved October 5, 2022. https://www.kellogg.northwestern.edu/faculty/jones-ben/htm/Age%20and%20High%20Growth%20Entrepreneurship.pdf

Bonabeau, E. (2003). "Don't trust your guts." *HBR*. Retrieved October 5, 2022. https://hbr.org/2003/05/dont-trust-your-gut

Christensen, C. M., Hall, T., Dillon, K., Duncan, D. S. (2016). "Know your customers' jobs to be done." *Harvard Business Review*, 94(9), pp. 54–62.

Creswell, J. (2013). "Qualitative research." *Stanford Library*. Retrieved November 1, 2022. https://guides.library.stanford.edu/qualitative_research

Eisenmann, T. (2021). "Why startups fail: A new roadmap for entrepreneurial success." *Currency Random House*, ISBN 978-0-593-23939-1. https://hbr.org/2021/05/why-start-ups-fail

Geethu, J. (2019). "Marketing research." *Slideshare*. Retrieved November 1, 2022. https://www.slideshare.net/gheethumariajoy/marketing-research-152533183

Geevarghese, G. (2013). "Types of market research." *Slideshare*. Retrieved November 1, 2022. https://www.slideshare.net/geeg33/market-research-26908858

Guyader, H. (2016). "Market research methods." *Slideshare*. Retrieved November 10, 2022. https://www.slideshare.net/guyaderhugo/marketing-research-methods

Hair, J. et al. (2020). *Essentials of marketing research*" 5th Edition. Columbus, OH: McGrawHill.

Hassan, M. (2022). "Primary data – Types and methods." *ResearchMethod.net*. Retrieved November 1, 2022. https://researchmethod.net/primary-data/

Huang, L. (2019). "When it's OK to trust your gut on a big decision." *HBR*. Retrieved October 5, 2022. https://hbr.org/2019/10/when-its-ok-to-trust-your-gut-on-a-big-decision

Katz, J. A., & Green, R. P. (2018). *Entrepreneurial Small Business*, 5th Edition. Columbus, OH: McGraw-Hill. Irwin. ISBN# 978-1-259-57379-8.

Lewrick, M., Patrick, L., and Leifer, L. (2018). *The design thinking playbook. Mindful digital transformation of teams, products, services, businesses and ecosystems. With assistance of Nadia Langensand*. Hoboken, NJ: John Wiley & Sons. Available online at https://ebookcentral.proquest.com/lib/gbv/detail.action?docID=5357893

Liviniuk, T. (2019). "Your gut instinct is usually wrong." *Medium*. Retrieved October 5, 2022. https://medium.com/@tannisliviniuk/your-gut-instinct-is-usually-wrong-fd88c2e6f8bb

Malsberger, K. (2017). "Trust your gut: How instinct can lead to faster and better decisions." *Dropbox blog Work in Progress*. Retrieved October 5, 2022. https://blog.dropbox.com/topics/work-culture/trust-your-gut-instinct

Ramirez-Flores, A. (2021) "What is the average age of successful entrepreneurs?" *My San Antonio*. Retrieved October 5, 2022. https://www.mysanantonio.com/business/article/What-is-the-average-age-of-successful-16668422.php

Robertson, C. (August 1, 2006). "Nielsen brings a new marketing strategy to Broadway." *The New York Times*. https://www.nytimes.com/2006/08/01/arts/01niel.html.

Simon, H. A. (1969). *The sciences of the artificial*. Cambridge: MIT Press.

Small Business Administration (n.d.). Retrieved October 5, 2022. https://www.sba.gov/business-guide/plan-your-business/market-research-competitive-analysis

Smith, D. (2019). "What everyone gets wrong about this famous Steve Jobs quote, according to Lyft's design boss." Retrieved October 5, 2022. https://www.businessinsider.com/steve-jobs-quote-misunderstood-katie-dill-2019-4

Snyder, H. (2019). "Literature review as a research methodology: An overview and guidelines." *Journal of Business Research*, 104, November 2019, pp. 333–339. doi:10.1016/j.jbusres.2019.07.039

Twin, A. (2022). "Researching the market: How to conduct market research, types, and example." *Investopedia*. Retrieved October 5, 2022. https://www.investopedia.com/terms/m/market-research.asp

Ulwick, A. W., and Osterwalder, A. (2016). *Jobs to be done. Theory to practice*. Houston, TX: Idea Bite Press.

Wenzel, A (2012). *The entrepreneur's guide to market research*. Bloomsbury Academic, ISBN 978-0-313-39605-2.

Yin, R. K. (2013). *Case study research. Design and methods*. Thousand Oaks, CA: Sage Publications.

Zeithaml, V., Jaworski, B., Kohli, A., Tuli, K., Ulaga, W., & Zaltman, G. (2019). "A theories-in-use approach to building marketing theory." *Journal of Marketing*, 84. 002224291988847. doi:10.1177/0022242919888477.

11 Customer Discovery and the Lean Startup Method

Kathleen R. Allen

The Lean Startup Method in entrepreneurship aims to provide a scientific approach to what has been historically an uncertain, inefficient, and risk-intensive process. Lean Startup is designed to reduce risk by enabling experimentation with customers and stakeholders to create value through collective learning. Although now in widespread use, the Lean Method and the Customer Discovery Process are still being studied to learn where they add the most value and where they may not be suitable. This chapter details what is currently known about the Customer Discovery Process and the Lean Method as ways to achieve maximum value at startup.

11.1 Introduction

"Lean Startup" is an approach to launching new ventures that emerged in the mid-2000s, popularized by Eric Ries in his book, *The Lean Startup* (2011). The approach posed a stark contrast to the long-held practice of creating comprehensive written business plans based primarily on intuition and design, rather than on evidence and the scientific method. In the Lean Startup Method, entrepreneurs test their initial theories about value, customer needs, and the target market, among many other factors. They develop small hypotheses that can be quickly tested on potential customers using a minimal prototype and minimal effort in what is called a build-measure-learn (BML) feedback loop. The resulting customer feedback becomes data the entrepreneur can use to iterate on the features and benefits of the proposed solution to achieve an optimal match to customer requirements.

The source of customer feedback for the BML loop is a process known as *customer discovery* where entrepreneurs interact with potential customers through interviews, observation in their native environment, and by using an early prototype of a solution to understand customers' problems and learn whether the problem the entrepreneur has identified has a viable commercial solution. The Lean Startup Method is widely used today because it has given some structure to the earliest stages of a new venture, and we now have some validated support for its effectiveness (Leatherbee and Katila 2020). In their first-ever longitudinal study of 152 National Science Foundation (NSF)-supported I-Corps teams, Leatherbee and Katila found that teams adopting the Lean Startup Method experienced higher performance from their ventures 18 months out from launch. By contrast, teams comprised of MBAs who did not use the Lean Startup Method did not perform as well. The researchers concluded that the MBAs, who had been trained in "learning-by-thinking" methods or the traditional business plan approach, may have resisted a "learning-by-doing" approach. In other words, the MBAs were more comfortable planning and conducting secondary research than interacting with potential customers and gathering primary research.

Some of the most successful entrepreneurs, such as Elon Musk, might actually agree with the MBAs about the relative importance of thinking over doing. Entrepreneurs like Musk are often

DOI: 10.4324/9781003341284-15

able to envision a future that others cannot see. That is how they are able to develop disruptive concepts before anyone else. When you're envisioning a unique and discontinuous future, relying heavily on customer feedback can be limiting, because the more novel the product or complex the business model, the more difficult it is for the market (customers) and investors to accurately assess it (Benner and Zenger, 2016). Nevertheless, one can argue that for any potential business interaction with customers via Customer Discovery elevates most entrepreneurs' hypotheses about value from mere guesses or intuition to verifiable facts, thereby making their research more scientific and evidence-based (Blank and Dorf, 2012).

Speaking to the appropriateness of the Lean Method, some research (Felin et al., 2020) has concluded that the Lean Method might not be the proper method for ideation in the fuzzy front end (FFE) of new product development (NPD) because, as noted previously, it can limit the free-thinking process of ideation. However, the Lean Method and Customer Discovery do appear to be suitable for the design and testing of assumptions underlying a proposed value proposition and business model, because these elements generally derive from the concept or vision developed in the front end of product development. In this way, potential customers can provide the feedback needed to ensure the entrepreneur is on the right path and isn't over-committing quickly to a vision that is too far from what is possible.

11.2 Key Concepts

11.2.1 The Fuzzy Front End

The "Fuzzy Front End" (FFE) refers to all those activities that occur in the ideation phase of NPD before more formal processes, such as Customer Discovery, feasibility analysis, and building the prototype. FFE is characterized by high degrees of uncertainty, experimentation, and bootstrap funding (Koen et al., 2001). Consequently, it is no surprise that new projects fail more often in the FFE than later in the NPD process (Khurana and Rosenthal, 1997). "Fail early, fail fast" is the mantra for Lean startups. By contrast, radically new or disruptive technologies often follow a different path in the FFE, principally because these technologies do not have identified markets in the earliest stages. They are new to the world. However, that does not mean that entrepreneurs with disruptive technologies should avoid Customer Discovery. On the contrary, although a ready market may not be present at the time of discovery, market demand must be created before launch; and significant time with the right early customers may provide clues to the nature of that market and its subsequent development.

11.2.2 Customer Discovery and Development

Customer Discovery is a critical element of the Lean Startup Methodology. It involves gathering primary and secondary data to support an initial customer definition. The goal of Customer Discovery is to develop deep empathy or understanding with potential customers so that product features and benefits can be determined and refined to precisely meet customer needs. Customer Discovery is an iterative process involving observation, experimentation, feedback, and redesign.

11.2.3 Minimum Viable Product: Build, Measure, Learn

In 1987, consultant Frank Robinson coined the term *minimum viable product (MVP)* to denote an early prototype that displays enough of the functionality and value proposition or benefits to attract early adopters who then provide important feedback to the entrepreneur to assist in further refining and modifying the product features and benefits. With information from the MVP, the entrepreneur can better determine which segment of the market will contain the first purchasers and what the level of demand might be. Software-based solutions typically take advantage of a process known as *agile development,* a term that refers to iterative software development. A project is broken into short increments called *sprints.* Each sprint must deliver production quality code that includes coding, testing, and quality verification. The nature of this process is compatible with continuous customer feedback.

11.2.4 Product Lifecycle, Adoption, and Diffusion Curves

To predict when a new technology is ready for market introduction and to identify the points in the sales cycle where product sales will accelerate or slow down, it is important to understand product lifecycles, adoption patterns, and diffusion. Product lifecycles are very much like industry lifecycles with periods of introduction, growth, maturity, decline, and obsolescence. A complete product lifecycle can be as short as a few months in the case of fads or as long as decades in the case of essential products such as automobiles or refrigerators. Today lifecycles have shrunk considerably due to rapid prototyping, rapidly changing customer expectations, and competition, forcing entrepreneurs to plan for frequent new product introductions and a continuous innovation pipeline much earlier than they might have done previously.

Entrepreneurs often use the adoption/diffusion curve as a tool to understand and manage demand for their products. Developed at the Agricultural Extension Service at Iowa State College in 1957, the curve was used to monitor the adoption of new hybrid seed corn by farmers to understand which farmers tended to be early adopters versus those who were laggards and avoided new technology adoption. Geoffrey Moore modified and updated the original adoption/diffusion curve to focus on tech products in his popular book, *Crossing the Chasm* (Moore, 1999). As seen in Figure 11.1, Moore identified five adopter groups of customers: innovators, early adopters, early majority, late majority, and laggards.

Innovators: These customers are the tiny user base that serves as gatekeepers because of their technical knowledge. They tend to understand new technology faster because they are younger and regularly follow new technologies from the earliest stages of development. Moreover, they often serve as beta version testers to provide early feedback.

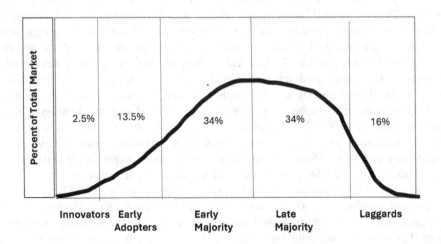

Figure 11.1 The adoption-diffusion curve.

Early Adopters: These customers are the first paying customers. They look for technologies that solve a problem and will give them a competitive advantage. They are an optimistic group that only requires that technology solve at least 80% of their problem; therefore, they are not representative of the mass market.

Early Majority: This group is very pragmatic and usually waits to purchase a technology until enough buyers have demonstrated that the product works reliably. It is in this market that the entrepreneur will see multiple applications for the technology that could amount to the critical mass needed to cross the chasm.

Late Majority: This group typically only purchase proven products at good price points. They will wait until the price comes down or they accede to peer pressure.

Laggards: This group will purchase only if they must because they don't believe the product will solve their problem at any price. They are essentially non-customers. This group is only approached after mass adoption is achieved and the product needs a new market.

In his research, Moore noted that once a product has gone through all the innovators and the first paying customers, the early adopters, it reaches what he called "the chasm," a period when product sales abruptly halt. The challenge then is to get across the chasm of no sales to reach the mainstream customers on the other side and achieve mass adoption by this broader market. For disruptive technologies to successfully cross the chasm, Moore asserted that entrepreneurs must identify multiple tiny niche market applications for the technology so that a critical mass of demand can be created that will spark a flashpoint or tornado that propels the total market to immediately adopt the technology as the standard. This is no easy task because success will be a function of perceived benefit to the customers, price, distribution intensity, switching costs, the customer learning curve, and the ability to effectively demonstrate the product value before purchase. Customer Discovery Processes are typically used to gain the necessary key insights into customer needs and reveal new applications.

11.3 Introduction to the Business Model Canvas

The Lean Startup Method has become the most common approach used by startups in Silicon Valley principally due to the efforts of venture capitalist and Stanford adjunct professor Steve Blank. He grounded the methodology in a framework known as the Business Model Canvas (BMC), first developed by Alex Osterwalder and Yves Pigneur for their book, *Business Model Generation* (2010). The BMC consists of a table of nine building blocks, each representing a concept such as "value proposition" or "customer segments." Figure 11.2 is a depiction of a sample canvas. Note that the boxes can be modified to meet the specific needs of the entrepreneur. For example, "key resources" might replace "key metrics" in a resource-heavy endeavor. The hypotheses the entrepreneur develops around each of the boxes become the basis for prototyping an MVP, which is quickly tested through interaction with customers. Then the prototype is modified until the right combination of product features and customer benefits is achieved. The primary value of the BMC lies in its ability to rapidly get the entrepreneur to an end state. Unlike existing companies that execute on a carefully devised business plan and business model, entrepreneurs generally start from a nearly blank slate to seek a repeatable and scalable business model (Blank, 2013). The BMC provides an easy framework to achieve that.

Because of their common language and logical methodology, the Lean Method, Customer Discovery, and the BMC have succeeded in reducing some of the risks for entrepreneurs and the venture capitalists who fund them. At the same time, they have also received some well-deserved criticism. For example, one criticism is that Lean theory was born out of the Total Quality Movement in manufacturing and operations, so it naturally lends itself more to incremental

Problem	Solution	Unique value proposition (UVP)	Unfair advantage	Customer segments
Top 3 problems you're addressing. Job to be done	Top 3 features and associated benefits that demonstrate the UVP	How are you uniquely different from everyone else?	What cannot be copied or bought?	First customer and secondary markets
	Key Metrics Key activities to measure.		**Distribution Channels & Partners** Path to the customer	
Cost structure Customer acquisition Distribution People		**Revenue streams** Lifetime value Gross margin Subscription		

product innovation or continuous improvement of existing products and processes rather than disruptive technologies (Womack et al., 1990). Another criticism attacks the Customer Discovery technique of getting "out of the building" and talking with customers to acquire iterative feedback on the product as it's being developed. This approach works well, again, with incremental innovations that are easily seen and understood, but it does not generally lead to disruptive innovation or new-to-the-world technologies and business models. As discussed previously, the reason is that customers don't always know what they want until they see it. They often don't realize that a new technology product or solution has value or is even possible. Therefore, as Felin et al conclude, it's important to have a compelling theory of value that is testable before engaging with customers (Felin et al., 2020).

11.4 Framing, Reframing, and Defining a Problem

Problem framing and reframing are concepts within the broader domain of design thinking. Design thinking strategies seek to achieve deep understanding of a problem and the customer who has it, thereby enabling a more effective and relevant solution (Beckman and Barry, 2015). Design thinking is very compatible with Lean Theory and Customer Discovery. The critical questions in design thinking are *what is* (what do we know?), *what if* (what's possible?) *What wows?* What works? The way the problem is framed determines the range of possible solutions. The frame/reframe technique for problem-solving has been a critical skill for science and technology entrepreneurs to acquire to counterbalance their extensive problem-solving engineering education and training that frequently leads them to leap too quickly to solutions, sometimes before deeply understanding the nuances of the problem. At its worst, the result can be solving the wrong problem. In a time of significant change with entire industries facing disruption, framing a problem in new ways can make all the difference in possible outcomes. For example, the lighting industry's replacement business is facing significant disruption by LED technology. To correctly frame the problem, it is important to first understand what the dominant logic in the industry is. Dominant logic is simply the rigidities or blinders in industry thinking that can prevent a company from looking at a problem in a new light (Bettis and Prahalad, 1995). The positive outcome of divergent framing activities is a set of unique stories that are then used to guide decision-making, resulting in innovative solutions that were not obvious from the original framing of the problem.

Liedtka and Ogilvie (2011) addressed the paradox that those engaged in design thinking must first put aside their existing frames and lenses to be able to observe a problem with fresh eyes so the problem can be reframed or given a new perspective. The basis for this observation technique is the same as that for Customer Discovery—ethnography, observing customers in their everyday environment, which requires inductive reasoning. For example, medical device companies often embed researchers in a hospital setting to observe how hospital personnel go about their work. The researchers look for points in a process where an individual may not have a tool or solution for something they need to accomplish, so they create a workaround to solve the immediate problem. The researchers' goal, however, is to identify and understand the problem as completely as possible. Based on the observation, the researcher hypothesizes what the problem is and then tests that hypothesis by engaging the individual being observed in conversation to gain more empathy (a Customer Discovery technique). The researcher will then proceed to reframe the problem based on those observations, yielding a different set of potential solutions.

Tversky and Kahneman (1986) argue that variations in the framing of options will yield systematically different preferences. An initial problem frame "How can our bank reduce customer churn?" will produce a different set of solution options from the alternate frame "How do our customers experience banking, and why are they leaving us?" The first question views customer churn as a mechanical problem so it will lead to solutions to retain customers. The second question requires deep customer empathy to answer because it addresses the customer experience with the bank, which may involve feelings and emotions. In the next section, we discuss how to develop that empathy.

11.5 Using Customer Discovery Methods to Develop Customer Empathy

Customer empathy is at the heart of the Lean Startup Method. Empathy is a deep understanding of customer needs that comes from entrepreneurs embedding themselves into the world of customers they want to serve. Empathy seeks to answer the questions *what is true?* and *what if?* Several abilities are associated with and necessary for empathy to occur. They include *integrative thinking,* or the ability to see all the possible contradictory options to solving a problem; *optimism,* the ability to assume that there is always a superior option to the one currently being considered; *experimentation,* the willingness to iterate perhaps hundreds of times to uncover the best solution; and *collaboration,* the ability to work with others who have skills the entrepreneur does not possess or who can view a problem from an entirely different perspective.

Ethnography is an important way to explore the social culture of groups of customers to gain empathy (Hammersley, 1990). A simple five-step approach to ethnographic research includes the following steps:

1 The researcher studies customers in their normal environment to spot problems.
2 The researcher then explains what was observed.
3 The researcher develops a hypothesis or theory from what was observed in 2.
4 The researcher tests the hypothesis with additional customers in the field.
5 The researcher draws conclusions based on a preponderance of the evidence gathered.

During observation, entrepreneurs must realize that it's common to view things through the lens of their own experience and to assume things to be true without evidence—in other words, to see things that aren't there. These biases must be avoided. Without building real customer empathy, it is likely the entrepreneur will solve the wrong problem. For example, one company experiencing declining product sales quickly framed its problem as "How can we sell more virtual reality (VR) devices?" This question contains some hidden assumptions that can be revealed by asking "why" questions to expose the real problem.

- How can we sell more VR devices?
  - *Why* do we want to sell more VR devices?
- Because VR sales are down.
  - *Why* are VR sales down?
- Because we have too much competition.
  - *Why* do we have too much competition?
- Because we're not introducing anything new and innovative.
  - *Why* aren't we introducing anything new and innovative?
- *Because we're behind in product development.*

By asking these "why" questions, the company discovered that the real problem is related to product development, not sales. With this new information in hand, the company can reframe the problem as "How can we improve the product development process so we can get new products to customers more quickly?" The results achieved with this exercise are a function of how the problem is framed in the first place. Deeply understanding customer needs will increase the likelihood of framing the problem correctly. In this case, this company will spend its time and money finding ways to accelerate the product development process to meet customer needs rather than finding more ways to sell products.

Given that new product definition accounts for as much as 80% of the final product cost, it is critical to terminate unfeasible projects early (Allen, 2020). Framing and reframing the problem correctly takes more time on the front end, but it facilitates early failures that are less costly and it increases the probability of a successful solution based on deeply understanding the customer.

To effectively and advantageously employ the Lean Startup methodology, it's important to first spend sufficient time in the ideation phase to determine how novel the idea is. The more novel the idea, the less the Customer Discovery phase will be directed solely by customers. Feedback and new product iteration will be slower and more costly. In addition, depending on the technology, achieving mass adoption to an industry standard may be a paramount goal.

In conclusion, most technology startups would benefit from at least some of the techniques found in the Lean Startup Methodology and the Customer Discovery Process. Those technologies that are the result of continuous innovation would benefit immensely from employing the full methodology to ensure that the customer's problem is solved in a way that completely meets their needs.

References

Allen, K. (2020). *Launching New Ventures*. Boston, MA: Cengage, 227.

Beckman, S., and Barry, M. (Winter 2015). Framing and re-framing: Core skills for a problem-filled world. *Rotman Management Magazine*, 67–71.

Benner, M. J., and Zenger, T. (March 7, 2016). The lemons problem in markets for strategy. *Strategy Science*, 1(2), 71–128.

Bettis, Richard A., and Prahalad, C. (January 1995). The dominant logic: Retrospective and Extension. *Strategic Management Journal*, 16(1): 5–14.

Blank, S. (May 2013). Why the lean startup changes everything. *Harvard Business Review*. https://hbr.org/2013/05/why-the-lean-start-up-changes-everything

Blank, S. and Dorf, B. (2012). *The Startup Owner's Manual: The Step-by-Step Guide for Building a Great Company.* Palo Alto, CA: K&S Ranch.

Felin, T. Gambardella, A., Stern, S., and Zenger, T. (August 2020). Lean startup and the business model: Experimentation revisited. *Long Range Planning*, 53(4). https://doi.org/10.1016/j.lrp.2019.06.002. ISSN 0024-6301

Hammersley, M. (1990). *Reading Ethnographic Research: A Critical Guide*. London: Longman.

Koen, P., Ajamian, G., Burkart, R., Clamen, A., Davidson, J., D'Amore, R., Elkins, C., Herald, K., Incorvia, M., Johnson, A., and Karol, R. (2001). Providing clarity and a common language to the "fuzzy front end." *Research Technology Management*, 44(2), 46–55.

Khurana, A., and Rosenthal, S. R. (1997). Integrating the fuzzy front end of new product development. *Sloan Management Review*, 38(2), 103–120.

Leatherbee, M., and Katila, R. (2020). The lean startup method: Early-stage teams and hypothesis-based probing of business ideas. *Strategic Entrepreneurship Journal*, 14(4), 570–593.

Liedtka, J., and Ogilvie, T. (2011). *Designing for Growth: A Design Thinking Tool Kit for Managers*. New York: Columbia Business School Publishing.

Moore, G. (1999). *Crossing the Chasm: Marketing and Selling High-Tech Products to Mainstream Customers*. New York: Harper Business.

Osterwalder, A., and Pigneur, Y. (2010). *Business Model Generation: A Handbook for Visionaries, Game Changers, and Challengers*. Hoboken, NJ: John Wiley and Sons.

Ries, E. (2011). *The Lean Startup: How Today's Entrepreneurs Use Continuous Innovation to Create Radically Successful Businesses*. New York: Crown Business, 93.

Tversky, A., and Kahneman, D. (1986). Rational choice and the framing of decisions. *The Journal of Business*, 59(4): S251–S278.

Womack, J. P., Jones, D. T., & Roos, D. (1990). *The Machine That Changed the World*. New York: Simon and Schuster.

12 Pricing, Promotion, and Place

Martin Klarmann, Andreas Kleinn, and Orestis Terzidis

12.1 Introduction

Marketing, defined comprehensively as "the whole business seen from (...) the customer's point of view" (Drucker, 1954, p. 39), is vital to the survival and success of most startups. For instance, Homburg et al. (2014) find that startups are more likely to get funded if their chief marketing officer has substantial marketing experience.

Therefore, this chapter seeks to guide on crucial marketing issues startups face. It focuses on three essential elements of what is traditionally referred to as the "Marketing Mix": price, communication (traditionally "promotion"), and sales (traditionally "place"). Notably, the marketing mix comprises a fourth element, "product". Product decisions are covered in other chapters and will not be discussed here.

This chapter assumes that a startup already has a validated product (or service) idea (Chapter 6) and a clear understanding of its value proposition (Chapter 5). Moreover, it has developed testable hypotheses about its business model (Chapter 8) and the customer target group (Chapter 10). Hence, this chapter mostly considers tactical and operational marketing issues; it is less devoted to strategic aspects. It focuses on marketing toward customers and not potential employees or investors. More specifically, while this chapter generally adopts a broad perspective on marketing for startups covering activities that focus on consumers ("business-to-consumers" or B2C) and businesses as customers ("business-to-business" or B2B), its focus lies on B2B startups. (It is mostly because the prevalence of B2B startups is much larger.)

12.2 Common Marketing Challenges of Startups

Startups famously suffer from a liability of newness and a liability of smallness (Freeman et al., 1983). "Liability of newness" (Stinchcombe, 2013) refers to the idea that younger firms face higher risks concerning the organization's survival than older firms. Independent of age, smaller firms are also more likely to fail – especially in some industries (Freeman et al., 1983) – the liability of smallness.

Given these liabilities, startups face several specific marketing challenges:

- *Lack of financial resources*
- *Lack of experience*
- *Lack of awareness*
- *Lack of legitimacy and reputation*
- *Lack of references*
- *Lack of (customer) data*

DOI: 10.4324/9781003341284-16

These specific conditions imply a vital marketing principle for startups: Startup marketing can only be approached in a way that sophisticates "learning by doing" through inexpensive marketing experimentation. Therefore, the following section will describe key principles of experimental marketing. The rest of the chapter then looks in three dedicated subchapters at specific challenges for startup regarding price, promotion (communication), and place (sales) decisions.

12.3 Experimental Marketing

As described above, startups face many challenges when marketing their product. In addition to gathering other primary data from the market (see Chapter 10 on market and competitor analysis), they need to adopt a mindset of "learning by doing" through inexpensive market experimentation. Moreover, they must do so quickly so as to not waste the limited resources and time they have to find customers for their idea.

Especially for founders from the natural and technical sciences, the lack of established best practices is sometimes difficult to accept. Given the highly developed state of their disciplines, they expect that there are scientifically accepted principles of marketing (and management) that they simply need to adhere to. However, importantly, there is no universal best practice regarding any aspect of marketing. Instead, context matters – a lot.

To complicate matters further, rookie marketers often succumb to what can be described as an aspect of the "naturalistic fallacy". They mistakenly assume that *the way the world is represents the way the world should be*. In this vein, as marketers without data and experience, startup founders often simply imitate the marketing activities of established firms – based on the mistaken assumption that these firms would only be doing these things if they worked. However, even established firms err a lot when it comes to marketing. The famous dictum (often ascribed to Ford) also holds for them: "50% of my marketing budget is wasted, but I don't know which half".

In other words, every startup needs to determine how to get the marketing right for its product and customers. Furthermore, a systematic approach to marketing experimentation is the most effective way to learn. In particular, the advent of A.I. in combination with data acquisition through the Internet has made experiments even more effective (Chintalapati & Pandey, 2022).

In the startup world, the principles from "lean startup" as described in Chapter 11 are widely accepted: build – measure – learn. We suggest a similar attitude for startup marketing experiments, as sketched in Figure 12.1. With this mindset, marketing decisions and market research are deeply entwined. In a way, any marketing plan (or communication approach or brand strategy) is a hypothesis that needs to be tested empirically.

Hypothesis development. Ideally, the starting point for any experiment is some hypothesis about the customers, product, or effectiveness of specific marketing activities. Without hypotheses that guide data collection and analysis, the experiment will be arbitrary. For instance, one could test a name for the startup by comparing the customer reactions to different options.

1 *Creating experimental stimuli.* The active intervention of the marketeer in the world characterizes an experiment. Technically, this is referred to as "experimental manipulation". For instance, if you want to test different company names, you could design ads that are similar in text and only differ in the mentioned company name.
2 *Creating experimental groups.* In any experiment, different groups are exposed to the different marketing options you are testing. This is called a between-subjects design. (Alternatively, you could use a within-subjects design, where all options are tested with the same group at different points in time, but that tends to complicate the analysis). Hence, you must define a mechanism for how experiment participants (e.g., potential customers) are assigned

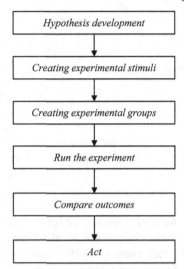

Hypothesis development

Creating experimental stimuli

Creating experimental groups

Run the experiment

Compare outcomes

Act

Figure 12.1 Experimental marketing.

to these groups. Ideally, potential customers are assigned randomly to each group, making all groups structurally equivalent. All observed differences are due to the differences in the marketing stimuli they experience. For instance, you could randomly use different company names in ads you show customers when they search for products in the respective category.

3   *Run the experiment.* The experiments should occur "in the field" with real potential customers. Only if this is not feasible (e.g., because your product only addresses a small number of B2B customers) could you run the experiment in a more artificial environment, such as click worker platforms (e.g., *Amazon Mechanical Turk*). An important question is related to the required sample size. The proper size depends on the true size of the effects you are studying (e.g., (Lakens, 2022)), but as a rule of thumb, you should have at least 30 data points in each group (otherwise, even simple statistical laws may not apply). Beware of arbitrarily stopping the experiments (e.g., check the data daily and stop the experiment when the evidence is consistent with your hypothesis) (Berman & Van den Bulte, 2022). Be aware that the experiments are there to overcome biases and prejudices.

4   *Compare outcomes.* Now analyze the data by comparing the different groups. Several statistical techniques can help to analyze the data (e.g., Schwarz et al., 2020). Often, simply by impartially looking at the results, you can get a good impression of what is happening. How evident are the group differences on a bar chart? If the group differences are not evident in any visual inspection of the data, they are likely negligible.

5   *Act.* All too often, evidence-based decision-making fails, because results are not used in decision-making. To make experimental marketing successful, you must ensure that results of your experiments are communicated well – together with actionable implications. Especially if your budget is limited, you should prioritize the best marketing option from the experiment until it is clear that the effectiveness of this option wears off and performance effects become markedly smaller.

There are dozens of possible marketing instruments that you can test in marketing experiments. Examples include (but are not limited to) advertising messages, product and firm names, advertising channels, sales channels, key product features, and homepages (especially the landing page).

Further Reads:

Bland and Osterwalder (2019) – Testing Business Ideas

What if experiments are not possible? For instance, with a highly customizable product, you may be unable to test prices using an experiment. Qualitative interviews with market experts are often a feasible alternative in these cases. In particular, experts can conduct thought experiments on the performance outcomes of different marketing options in these interviews. For instance, they could seek to judge the effect of different prices on sales.

12.4 Pricing

It is a challenge for startups to find a price due to their liabilities described above. Pricing affects the venture's profitability in several dimensions. Most significantly, the unit price minus the variable costs equals the contribution margin, which is the amount available to pay fixed costs and earn a profit. Pricing is a function of a startup's goals: To increase market share (lower price), maximize profit (raise prices or increase sales or lower overhead; or control demand), as it influences not only revenues but also the number of buyers, which can shape future demand and the diffusion process.

Pricing has several important characteristics that render it the marketing instrument that is possibly the most powerful (a similar list can be found, for instance, in Simon and Fassnacht (2018)). These characteristics also make pricing possible the most accessible marketing tool for startups.

1 The effect on customer behavior is strong.
2 The effect on customer behavior is fast.
3 The implementation costs of price changes are low.
4 Price reductions are difficult to reverse.

Among the many aspects of pricing, this chapter focuses on three. We believe these are particularly relevant for startups:

- Setting prices for new products
- Basic price differentiation
- Price discounts for early customers

12.5 Setting Prices

Identifying a sound and sustainable price for a startup's offering is a key challenge in the company's early days. In this section, we will present a few basic techniques that can be helpful here. Notably, the techniques available will result in a range of possible prices. They typically do not produce a single "correct" price.

Figure 12.2 illustrates that there is a theoretical lower bound and a theoretical upper bound for the price ranges. The cost structure of the startup determines the theoretical lower price bound. This reflects the simple idea that no product should have a price lower than the costs incurred in producing it. In the short term, this can be the product's variable costs, which will still mean selling at a loss. In the long run, the price must cover variable and fixed costs. It is a must-do exercise for startups to understand this "minimum price to stay in business".

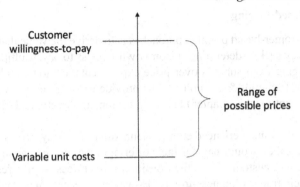

Figure 12.2 Possible price range.

The theoretical upper price bound is often referred to as "customer willingness-to-pay", the maximum amount of money customers are willing to spend for the startup's offering. Especially in B2B markets, customer willingness to pay should be relatively close to the "value-in-use" of the offering, which is the monetary value the customer will get from using the purchased product or service.

The price range between the lower and upper bounds is typically too broad to serve as a helpful guide when setting the price. There are many forces (e.g., strategic consideration, competition, investor requirements) that create a possible price range that is more concise. Nevertheless, the logic behind deriving the upper and the lower bounds also translates into two of the most popular price-setting mechanisms: cost-plus pricing and customer-based pricing.

Further Reads:

Simon and Fassnacht (2018) – Price Management, Strategy, Analysis, Decision, Implementation

12.6 Cost-Plus Pricing

The logic of cost-plus pricing is simple. Prices are calculated as a markup on costs. In some companies, it is applied as a simple heuristic such as "price=costs*1.5". Typically, average production costs are used, including at least those fixed costs that can be distributed relatively quickly across individual products. The advantages are clear. It is relatively simple to use, and customers consider it fair (Ebinger, 2023). However, it comes at a risk, especially regarding innovative products. Specifically, founders sometimes forget that the number of products sold also affects costs. You benefit from economies of scale and learning effects if you run a large operation. Hence, you already have to know about the demand to come up with a cost-based price. This can easily become a self-fulfilling prophecy. If you are pessimistic about demand, you will assume high costs, which implies a high price, leading to low demand.

These considerations highlight how important it is for entrepreneurs to understand the cost structure of their business. For instance, many software, machine learning, and A.I. startups face a cost structure dominated by fixed costs. The development of the software or the A.I. model is very resource-consuming. However, it can be easily rolled out to many customers once it is finalized. In fact, for software products, variable costs are close to 0. For these businesses, cost-based pricing will invariably lead to very low prices that may not reflect the value their offerings deliver.

12.7 Customer-Based Pricing

The key goal of customer-based pricing approaches is to derive the value that an offering brings to the customer. They seek to determine customer willingness to pay. Multiple approaches have been proposed ranging from surveys over price experiments, conjoint analysis, auctions, and value-based pricing (Schmidt & Bijmolt (2020) provide an overview). Two methods seem to be particularly relevant for this chapter (1) asking customers directly and (2) determining their value-in-use.

From our experience, inexperienced entrepreneurs often shy away from asking potential customers directly what they would pay for their offering. One fear is that such a survey would lose its validity because customers – in their desire for low prices – could respond strategically by understating their true willingness-to-pay. However, a recent meta-analysis suggests that these fears are mostly unwarranted (Schmidt & Bijmolt, 2020). Instead, the same meta-analysis provides evidence that another type of bias is present in a lot of these studies: hypothetical bias. The fictional setting of a price survey makes it easier to spend money than in a real-life purchase situation. As a result, there is an upward bias and not a downward bias when asking customers what they would be willing to pay.

The "Price Sensitivity Meter" is possibly the most employed of these price survey methods (Westendorp, 1976). Instead of asking customers one question of the type "How much would you pay for this product?", it consists of four questions. After presenting a short description of the offering, respondents are asked:

- At what price would you consider the product to be so expensive that you would not consider buying it? (Too expensive)
- At what price would you consider the product to be priced so low that you would feel the quality couldn't be very good? (Too cheap)
- At what price would you consider the product starting to get expensive, so that it is not out of the question, but you would have to give some thought to buying it? (Expensive/Pricey)
- At what price would you consider the product to be a bargain – a great buy for the money? (Cheap/A Bargain)

Plotting the cumulated frequencies of the answers, the optimal price range lies between the intersection of "pricey" and "too cheap" as the lower bound and "a bargain" and "too expensive" as the upper bound. The optimal price point is the intersection of "too cheap" and "too expensive". "Optimal" here means an equal tradeoff in willingness to pay within the acceptable price spectrum. The indifferent price point is the intersection of "a bargain" and "pricey" (Figure 12.3).

A second important approach to customer-based pricing is value-in-use pricing (for a detailed description, see for instance, Klarmann et al., 2011. The key idea behind this approach is to quantify the ultimate monetary benefits the customer will have if they adopt the startup's product. For instance, consider a firm that uses A.I. to automate creative processes. Let's say it saves customer firms €1000 freelancer costs per month. Then, the customer should not be willing to pay more than €1000 per month for the AI. €1000/month is called the value-in-use. Importantly, in many cases, identifying this value-in-use is far from being as straightforward as in this example. It will require the supplier firm to obtain a detailed understanding of customer cost structures (e.g., Wouters & Kirchberger, 2015). In particular, it entails understanding the customer's total costs of ownership for the product, which comprises the purchase prices, labor costs, and other costs related to the use of the product. Moreover, it also requires developing an

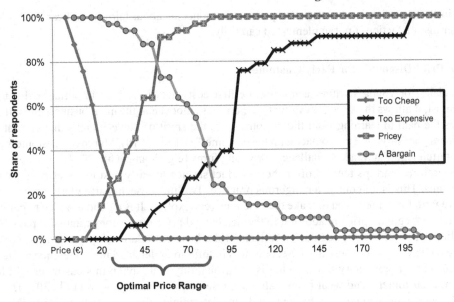

Figure 12.3 Van Westendorp method (Fertig, 2015).

in-depth understanding of the customers' current way of satisfying the need that the startup's offering satisfies.

Obtaining this information creates a lot of valuable insights for the supplier firm and enables customer learning at a very high level. At the same time, it also requires many resources, both from customers and suppliers. Moreover, it requires that the sales approach is also designed around the idea of selling value instead of selling a product or service. Therefore, it is not surprising that focusing on monetary customer value in sales-related conversations is not universally successful. It works best in periods of growth with a focus on acquiring new customers and if there is steady communication with customer finance departments (Klarmann & Wouters, 2023). Moreover, the value-in-use approach requires that prices can be customized to specific customers. If prices cannot be differentiated (e.g., if there are retail prices or prices are openly communicated), then the value-in-use approach is not easily applicable.

12.8 Basic Price Differentiation

Startups may use *price differentiation* as a pricing strategy to maximize their profits by charging different prices for the same product or service to different customers or groups of customers. This practice is based on the premise that customers may have different perceptions of value for a product or service and therefore different willingnesses to pay for a product or service. By charging a higher price to customers with a higher willingness to pay, startups can capture more value from these customers. Flatten et al. (2015) found that startups should focus on their price differentiation capability to improve performance.

Price differentiation can take different types, such as first-degree price differentiation, where the seller charges each customer the maximum price they are willing to pay. In second-degree price differentiation, the seller offers different pricing options based on the quantity purchased, and in third-degree differentiation, the seller charges different prices to customer segments based on their demographic characteristics or other observable traits. While price differentiation can increase profits for startups, it may also raise concerns about fairness and can lead to customer dissatisfaction if not implemented carefully.

12.9 Price Discounts for Early Customers

Especially for young startups, acquiring the first customers is of high importance. First and foremost, it allows the startup to validate the business model and the main business idea. It also paves the path to learning from the customer – in the spirit of Steve Blank's dictum that "no business plan survives first contact with the customer" (Blank, 2010). Moreover, customers give the startup legitimacy, a key challenge for young firms (e.g., Wang et al., 2014).

Therefore, startups tend to offer their product/service to early customers at considerable discounts. This is, of course, a dangerous practice. Two things seem particularly important in this regard. First, they need to make the discount very explicit. It is a good practice to communicate the "regular" price in addition to the discounted price the customer actually pays. This facilitates a return to the regular price later in the business relationship (or at least it gives some leeway for price increases). Second, it is helpful to understand the "reference value" of the customer in monetary terms. What is the probability that having this customer will help win new customers, and what is the value of these new accounts (Kumar et al., 2013)? Such a reference value can be an important guide for determining the magnitude of a possible discount. Only if customers really help the firm to get more business, they should get a discount.

12.10 Marketing Communication

Marketing communication of startups is one of the success factors and is vital to linking them with their target group. Its main objective is to effectively communicate the value proposition to potential customers, to create interest, and to pave the way to a possible transaction. For startups, it also means systematically addressing and minimizing the risks or concerns of potential customers, who may be worried about an unknown venture and its yet-to-be-proven products. Therefore, effective marketing communication is essential to build the necessary reputation and trust (Gruber, 2005). To meet these objectives, a startup marketer must provide the target group with the necessary information through appropriate channels.

Startups face specific challenges in marketing communication. Typically, they offer a new and unknown value proposition, which has immediate implications for planning marketing communication. It is often necessary to make assumptions about the target group and its preferences, and these assumptions must be tested quickly and cost-efficiently. Startup marketers often use very specific and sometimes unconventional approaches to engage with customers, gain insights, and promote the product.

From the customer's perspective, acquiring and applying new products or technologies carry various risks. Many buyers will think twice before they invest time, effort, or money in a product that is not proven. The "liability of newness" implications for marketing means that startups must explain their value proposition and focus on building credibility with their target audience (Gruber, 2004).

12.11 Target Market

Efficient marketing aims to reach as many potential customers as possible with limited resources. This implies tailored messaging and branding based on sound assumptions about the target group to minimize scattering losses. The assumptions are related to the needs and preferences for the product and the purchasing process.

In B2B, the product's end-user often differs from the buying decision-maker or the product lifecycle support team. If, for example, you sell on-premises software to a company, there will be the end-user (e.g., the accountants), the purchase decision-maker (e.g., the chief financial officer), and the IT department that will maintain, backup, and upgrade the system. A startup should be able to convince the relevant "buying center" members to purchase your product.

An example of precisely targeted marketing communication is Stripe, a payment processing platform, which effectively combined various marketing communication tools. They communicated a clear value proposition (simplifying online payments worldwide for businesses) and specifically targeted developers, who are often tasked with integrating payment options into online applications, shops, or websites. Stripe gained the trust of its audience by providing high-quality content (e.g., on its channels and blogs or Twitter) and engaging with the developer community through forums, open-source projects, and events (hackathons). Strategic partnerships with other players in the technology industry extended their reach and allowed them to gain credibility.

Frameworks That Help Entrepreneurs Understand Their Target Group

Jobs-To-Be-Done, Design Thinking, Customer Journey, Persona, etc.

12.12 Marketing Messages

As mentioned above, successful marketing communication will create a clear understanding of the value proposition, while communicating aspects that minimize the perceived risk. A clear structure, simplicity, and coherence of the messages are essential to minimize the customer's cognitive effort since the startup may only get a short opportunity to capture the customers' attention. The famous *elevator pitch* might have its name given the short time spent in an elevator to ensure the recipient (e.g., investor) fully gets what the startup offers.

Marketing communication is driven by desired outcomes and objectives and is tailored to the situation and specific needs. Among other things, marketing messages can be designed to attract attention, communicate the offer, differentiate the product from the competition, and initiate action in potential customers. Marketing messages can include the unique selling proposition, present benefits and features of the product, contain elements that create recognition, and prompt the audience to take a specific action. Depending on the nature of the product, prices can also be communicated, although it sometimes might not be practical in a B2B context. In addition, trust-creating elements such as track record, references, and awards can be mentioned, documenting the startup's performance and making it easier for decision-makers at the client's end to commit to the startup.

Startups should find ways to create visual recognizability, e.g., by integrating visual identity elements which may include brand, slogans, logos, imagery, and design. Building a brand as an anchor in the customer's mind that differentiates a company's offering from that of competitors is a long-term process and should be approached with the proper level and commitment of resources. After all, while it is difficult to change already established elements with recognizable features later, they do not create value in themselves and may be an inefficient use of a startup's limited initial resources.

Further Reads:

Simon Sinek (2009) – Start with Why

12.13 Communication Channels

Considering the target group, the content, and the industry, a marketer chooses the proper communication channels to reach the target customer and engage with it. Apart from unilateral channels where companies cast their messages to an audience, social media platforms with multilateral communication can be used by startups to leverage network effects (e.g., word-of-mouth and user-generated content [UGC]) and create visibility.

The word-of-mouth approach to entrepreneurial marketing communication is interesting for startups because it is more cost-efficient and aims at target groups that are often not easily accessible through traditional channels (Hills et al., 2010). Guerrilla, buzz, and viral marketing are unique forms of word-of-mouth marketing worth exploring (Morris et al., 2002).

Airbnb is an example of UGC. They encouraged hosts and guests to share their experiences and photos on the platform, creating a vast library of authentic content that showcases the available accommodations. This content helps build trust and credibility among potential users who can see real-life experiences shared by others, making it a powerful marketing tool.

In B2C and B2B, a wide range of digital and non-digital communication channels are available – including mailing lists, social media, video platforms, and the corporate website with search engine optimization (SEO) and search engine advertisement, as well as more traditional channels such as print, broadcasting media, business networks, and presence at trade fairs.

The Persona and customer journey methods help map, identify, and test hypotheses about the most effective marketing communication channels to reach their target audience. Selecting a suitable combination of channels and an appropriate advertising message should be subject to a constant feedback cycle and hypothesis testing. Matching metrics provide information about which message has performed well with which customer on which channel.

12.14 Place

"Place" is probably the most old-fashioned term to describe a marketing mix element. It is concerned with the design and organization of the ways (or "channels") through which the offering of a firm reaches the customer. When the marketing mix was developed in the retail sector, this was very much about finding suitable locations for stores, which justifies the term "Place". In today's time, where startups are born as global companies that can sell to nearly anyone on the planet almost instantly, the term has become almost misleading.

Therefore, while not starting with a "P", "Sales" is probably the best term to refer to this element of the marketing mix. That said, many startups also shy away from creating a sales position, preferring to name the associated activities with terms such as "Business Development", "Customer Success Management", or "Growth Hacking". This chapter looks at three sales decisions that we consider particularly relevant for startups.

- Sales channel design
- Sales funnel setup
- Sales analytics

12.15 Sales Channel Design

Sales channel design is about strategically developing the paths through which customers can procure a startup's offering. In established companies, this is often about identifying retailers or distributors that sell the product for the company. In the digital age, a "direct sales" approach is usually the best choice, where customers procure the product directly from the manufacturer (or service provider). Tesla is a recent example that illustrates this transformation. While most established car manufacturers use a complicated system of distributions, country organizations, and retailers to sell their cars to consumers, at Tesla, you order these cars directly from Tesla through a website.

Therefore, for startups, sales channel design is primarily about designing the customer acquisition process. Here, startups have a wide range of options at their disposal. Some of them are illustrated in Table 12.1. A nice overview can also be found in Weinberg and Mares (2015).

A key distinction that can be made is the distinction between inbound and outbound sales strategies. Inbound selling, a term popularized by a startup (HubSpot.com), refers to activities where the startup is mainly improving ways to be found by potential customers. As described in Table 12.1, this can be content marketing, where the firm provides potential customers with helpful material or optimizes Google's search results for certain search terms. Outbound selling is the more traditional idea of identifying potential customers and then approaching them proactively. While both approaches can be helpful, it is often thought (but difficult to establish empirically) that inbound strategies are becoming important as purchasers rely more on digital information sources (Lüders et al., 2023). Former HubSpot chief sales officer Marc Roberge has written a very insightful book on these issues and HubSpot's startup approach to sales (Roberge, 2015).

Table 12.1 Selection of different customer acquisition channels

Approach	Customer acquisition channel	Description
Inbound marketing	Content marketing	The startup produces content (e.g., blog entries, videos) that provides potential with important information in the general field where the startups is active.
	Freemium products	The startup provides its product in a basic version for free so that customers can try it out without risk. If customers are interested in more functionality, they have to become paying customers.
	SEO	Based on known functionalities of established search engines (particularly Google), the startup seeks to design its webpage so that is ranked prominently by search engines, ensuring it is easily found.
Outbound marketing	Search engine advertising	The startup bids on specific search terms at popular search engines (especially Google) so that its ads are shown when these terms are entered by potential customers.
	Display advertising	The startup invests in display advertising so that small banners with a well-designed communication message appear on certain websites that fit the startup's product or service.
	Social media advertising	The startup invests in social media advertising so that advertising messages appear in social media feeds (e.g., LinkedIn, Instagram) of users that meet certain targeting characteristics that the startup defined.
	Influencer marketing	The startup identifies and contracts influential personalities with many followers on suitable social media platforms or streaming platforms to promote their product or service during their appearances.

Further Reads:

Weinberg and Mares (2015) – Traction

Which customer acquisition channel a startup should use depends strongly on the product and/or service the startup is offering. Only experimentation can help a startup identify which customer acquisition channel is most effective. Once the most effective channel has been identified, it makes sense to focus most activities on this channel before starting to experiment again. An illustration of such experimental sales approaches can be found in the book "Traction" by DuckDuckgo founder Gabriel Weinberg (Weinberg & Mares, 2015).

12.16 Sales Funnel Setup

From a startup's perspective, the sales process itself can be viewed as a funnel. This is visualized in Figure 12.4. The logic of the sales funnel is that startups will end up with contacts that could become customers. These contacts are called "Leads". In the next step, the startup needs to validate whether these leads are suitable customers. This step is called lead qualification. For instance, some leads might simply lack the budget for the startup's product, or the contact of the startup has no decision-making power in the potential customer firm. If the lead satisfies a set of pre-defined criteria (typically verified in a phone call or video conference), the lead becomes a prospect. A generic but often-used set of criteria is called BANT (Budget, Authority, Need, and Timing).

The next step in the sales process is generating pitching opportunities among the prospects. Ideally, the startup gets the chance to present themselves and their product/service to the customer firm. If the customers are persuaded by the pitch presentation, they will ask for a formal offer. Often, a negotiation stage ensues, where the terms and conditions of the collaboration are agreed upon. Finally, if a negotiated contract is on the table, it is important to get the customer to sign it: the closing stage of the sales funnel.

Further Reads

Roberge (2015) – The sales acceleration formula: using data, technology, and inbound selling to from $0 to $100 million.

Notably, the sales funnel visualized in Figure 12.4 is a prototypical example. A startup will need to adapt it to the specific customer journey in their industry. For instance, if a large part of the customer acquisition process is semi-automated (e.g., through registration on a website), it will undoubtedly look different. However, it is helpful to define the stages of the acquisition process equally carefully.

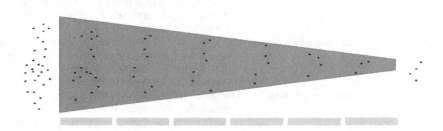

Figure 12.4 Sales funnel.

Only a well-defined sales funnel will allow a startup to use sales analytics in a way that uncovers problems in the acquisition process.

12.17 Sales Analytics

In line with the famous dictum often ascribed to Peter Drucker, namely that "what gets measured gets managed" and the importance of sales to any firm that starts up, it is essential to track some performance indicators concerning sales. A startup needs to carefully select a few of these metrics and observe them continuously.

Sales metrics can be divided into different categories. A first category of metrics refers to the sales funnel described in the previous section. First, it is helpful to monitor regularly (for example, weekly) the number of leads, prospects, pitches, etc., in the sales funnel. Second, conversion rates for the different stages should be monitored. For instance, if the conversion rate from presentations to offers is low (or goes down), this could point to problems with a startup's pitch presentation.

A second category of metrics refers to the customer relationship. Tracking customer satisfaction is important because it correlates with firm performance (e.g., Otto et al., 2020). Likewise, customer lifetime values (e.g., Fader et al., 2005), and customer engagement (e.g., (Venkatesan et al., 2017), are essential metrics to observe.

12.18 Conclusion

Startups operate in a difficult situation concerning marketing. They have to identify and balance different marketing measures such as price, communication, and sales. These actions are not only complex undertakings but also highly interdependent. They must be carried out with limited resources, knowledge, and other liabilities. A well thought through implementation of a comprehensive marketing strategy helps keeping track of the measures and their results. Such a strategy is necessarily based on a number of assumptions that need to be constantly re-evaluated. It is therefore valuable to set up low-cost marketing experiments and find ways of testing these assumptions and hypotheses. In this way, the various marketing activities can be developed with ever greater precision and effectiveness.

References

Albers, S., Mantrala, M. K., & Sridhar, S. (2010). Personal selling elasticities: A meta-analysis. *Journal of Marketing Research, 47*(5), 840–853. https://doi.org/10.1509/jmkr.47.5.840

Berman, R., & Van den Bulte, C. (2022). False discovery in A/B testing. *Management Science, 68*(9), 6762–6782. https://doi.org/10.1287/mnsc.2021.4207

Bijmolt, T. H. A., Heerde, H. J. Van, & Pieters, R. G. M. (2005). New empirical generalizations on the determinants of price elasticity. *Journal of Marketing Research, 42*(2), 141–156. https://doi.org/10.1509/jmkr.42.2.141.62296

Bland, D. J., & Osterwalder, A. (2019). *Testing business ideas: A field guide for rapid experimentation.* John Wiley & Sons. ISBN 978–1119551447

Blank, S. (2010). *No Business Plan Survives First Contact With A Customer - The 5.2 billion dollar mistake.*

Chintalapati, S., & Pandey, S. K. (2022). Artificial intelligence in marketing: A systematic literature review. *International Journal of Market Research, 64*(1), 38–68. https://doi.org/10.1177/14707853211018428

Deephouse, D. L., & Carter, S. M. (2005). An examination of differences between organizational legitimacy and organizational reputation. *Journal of Management Studies, 42*(2). https://doi.org/10.1111/j.1467-6486.2005.00499.x

Drucker, P. (1954). *Management:* Revised edition. Harper & Brothers Publishers.

Ebinger, D. (2023). *Value selling from the customer's perspective.* Karlsruher Institut für Technologie (KIT).

Fader, P. S., Hardie, B. G. S., & Lee, K. L. (2005). RFM and CLV: Using iso-value curves for customer base analysis. *Journal of Marketing Research, 42*(4). https://doi.org/10.1509/jmkr.2005.42.4.415

Fertig, D. (2015). *Bachelorthesis: Entwicklung und Evaluation eines Vertriebskonzeptes für mesana.* Karlsruher Institut für Technologie, Institut für Technik der Informationsverarbeitung (ITIV).

Flatten, T. C., Engelen, A., Möller, T., & Brettel, M. (2015). How entrepreneurial firms profit from pricing capabilities: An examination of technology–based ventures. *Entrepreneurship Theory and Practice, 39*(5), 1111–1136. https://doi.org/10.1111/etap.12098

Fleischmann, S. (2016). Evidenzbasiertes markenmanagement. *Evidenzbasiertes Markenmanagement.* Springer Gabler Wiesbaden. https://doi.org/10.1007/978-3-658-11998-0

Freeman, J., Carroll, G. R., & Hannan, M. T. (1983). The liability of newness: Age dependence in organizational death rates. *American Sociological Review, 48*(5), 692–710. https://doi.org/10.2307/2094928

Gruber, M. (2004). Marketing in new ventures: Theory and empirical evidence. *Schmalenbach Business Review, 56*(2), 164–199. https://doi.org/10.1007/bf03396691

Gruber, M. (2005). Process matters – Empirical evidence on the value of marketing planning in VC-backed startups. *Academy of Management 2005 Annual Meeting: A New Vision of Management in the 21st Century, AOM 2005,* Honolulu, Hawaii. https://doi.org/10.5465/ambpp.2005.18778659

Hills, G. E., Hultman, C. M., Kraus, S., & Schulte, R. (2010). History, theory and evidence of entrepreneurial marketing - An overview. *International Journal of Entrepreneurship and Innovation Management, 11*(1), 3–18. https://doi.org/10.1504/IJEIM.2010.029765

Homburg, C., Hahn, A., Bornemann, T., & Sandner, P. (2014). The role of chief marketing officers for venture capital funding: Endowing new ventures with marketing legitimacy. *Journal of Marketing Research, 51*(5), 625–644. https://doi.org/10.1509/jmr.11.0350

Kahneman, D., & Tversky, A. (1979). Prospect theory: An analysis of decision under risk. *Econometrica, 47*(2), 263. doi:10.2307/1914185. ISSN 0012-9682.

Klarmann, M., Miller, K., & Hofstetter, R. (2011). Methoden der Preisfindung auf B2B-Märkten. *Preismanagement auf Business-to-Business-Märkten,* 153–180. Hardcover ISBN 978-3-8349-1559-7

Klarmann, M., & Wouters, M. (2023). Benefits, discounts, features, and value as communication foci in selling: Exploring concepts, drivers, and outcomes. *Journal of Personal Selling and Sales Management, 43*(1), 46–64. https://doi.org/10.1080/08853134.2022.2082451

Kumar, V., Petersen, J. A., & Leone, R. P. (2013). Defining, measuring, and managing business reference value. *Journal of Marketing, 77*(1), 68–86. https://doi.org/10.1509/jm.11.0424

Lakens, D. (2022). Sample size justification. *Collabra: Psychology, 8*(1), 33267. https://doi.org/10.1525/collabra.33267

Lüders, M., Klarmann, M., Wouters, M., & Gerlach, A. (2023). How online information search behavior and the role of tacit knowledge differ across clusters of purchase situations. *Journal of Purchasing and Supply Management, 29*(4), Article 100862. https://doi.org/10.1016/j.pursup.2023.100862

Morris, M. H., Schindehutte, M., & LaForge, R. W. (2002). Entrepreneurial marketing: A construct for integrating emerging entrepreneurship and marketing perspectives. *Journal of Marketing Theory and Practice, 10*(4), 1–19. https://doi.org/10.1080/10696679.2002.11501922

Otto, A. S., Szymanski, D. M., & Varadarajan, R. (2020). Customer satisfaction and firm performance: Insights from over a quarter century of empirical research. *Journal of the Academy of Marketing Science, 48*(3), 543–564. https://doi.org/10.1007/s11747-019-00657-7

Pauwels, K., & D'Aveni, R. (2016). The formation, evolution and replacement of price–quality relationships. *Journal of the Academy of Marketing Science, 44*(1), 46–65. https://doi.org/10.1007/s11747-014-0408-3

Roberge, M. (2015). *The sales acceleration formula: Using data, technology, and inbound selling to go from $0 to $100.* John Wiley & Sons, Inc.

Schmidt, J., & Bijmolt, T. H. A. (2020). Accurately measuring willingness to pay for consumer goods: a meta-analysis of the hypothetical bias. *Journal of the Academy of Marketing Science, 48*(3). https://doi.org/10.1007/s11747-019-00666-6

Schwarz, J. S., Chapman, C., & Feit, E. M. D. (2020). Python for marketing research and analytics. In *Python for Marketing Research and Analytics*. Springer Cham. https://doi.org/10.1007/978-3-030-49720-0

Sethuraman, R., Tellis, G. J., & Briesch, R. A. (2011). How well does advertising work? Generalizations from meta-analysis of brand advertising elasticities. *Journal of Marketing Research*, *48*(3), 457–471. https://doi.org/10.1509/jmkr.48.3.457

Simon, H., & Fassnacht, M. (2018). Price management: Strategy, analysis, decision, implementation. In *Price Management: Strategy, Analysis, Decision, Implementation*. Springer Cham. https://doi.org/10.1007/978-3-319-99456-7

Sinek, S. (2009). *Start with why: How great leaders inspire everyone to take action*. Penguin. The golden circle. https://Tinyurl. Com/Golden-Circle-Sinek.

Stinchcombe, A. L. (2013). Social structure and organizations1. In James March (ed.) *Handbook of Organizations:* (Vol. 20, pp. 142–193). Routledge. https://doi.org/10.4324/9780203629130

Venkatesan, R., Petersen, J. A., & Guissoni, L. (2017). Measuring and managing customer engagement value through the customer journey. In Palmatier, R., Kumar, V., Harmeling, C. (eds) *Customer Engagement Marketing* (pp. 53–74). Palgrave Macmillan. https://doi.org/10.1007/978-3-319-61985-9_3

Wang, T., Song, M., & Zhao, Y. L. (2014). Legitimacy and the value of early customers. *Journal of Product Innovation Management*, *31*(5), 1057–1075. https://doi.org/10.1111/jpim.12144

Weinberg, G., & Mares, J. (2015). Traction how any startup can achieve explosive customer growth. In *News.Ge*. Pages: 250. Penguin. ISBN: 0698411870, 9780698411876

Westendorp, van P. (1976). NSS-Price Sensitivity Meter (PSM) - A new approach to study consumer perception of price. *Proceeding of the Esomar Congress*, Venice.

Wouters, M., & Kirchberger, M. A. (2015). Customer value propositions as interorganizational management accounting to support customer collaboration. *Industrial Marketing Management*, *46*, 54–67. https://doi.org/10.1016/j.indmarman.2015.01.005

Part V

Funding a Venture

13 Framing the Funding Challenge

Orestis Terzidis and J. Mark Munoz

13.1 Introduction

For technology ventures, financing is one of the significant determinants of success or failure (Bellavitis et al., 2017). Capital is needed to create new products while simultaneously searching for promising customer segments and building up the organization.

It requires time, a performing team, adequate development environments, and access to various networks to make progress. Consulting and engineering projects may generate revenues even at the early stages. They may make sense to create knowledge and networks, but they may also defocus the team from building up the core assets for a scalable business model. Very often, the situation of a technology venture is one where funding the venture from its own revenues is not an option, and it must attract external funding to achieve its goals.

The amount of capital required is related to the financing purpose, and this changes during the company's development. At an early stage, investments serve other objectives than at a later stage. For example, at an early venture stage, capital may have to be deployed to aggressively pursue business development and marketing goals as the business is being built. Different sources of financing serve diverse needs across different phases. In such cases, engagement with investors needs to be aligned with characteristics and preferences relating to risk, investment volume, and industry knowledge and networks.

Investors consider a variety of criteria when they decide to fund a venture. Two prominent perspectives are risk and return. At an early stage, there are significant risks. These risks relate to, for instance, the team, the market, the product, the competition, the supply chain, the partners, access to follow-up investments, and the general 'infancy risk' of the young venture (Kakati, 2003). Only investors willing to take elevated risks will provide capital in the first stages. As the project reaches certain milestones (e.g., a patent granted, a product released, a pilot customer acquired), the perceived risk is reduced. In such a case, the venture becomes more attractive to a wider base of investors.

13.2 Key Concepts

The financial objective of an investor is to generate an adequate return on the invested capital. At the same time, the investor tries to minimize the risk associated with the investment. The potential loss multiplied by the likelihood of this loss is a common way to operationalize risk. Risk in finance ranges from returns turning out lower than expected to losing the entire investment made.

DOI: 10.4324/9781003341284-18

13.2.1 Asset Classes

Investors distinguish between different asset classes with varying risk and return profiles. Typical examples are securities, stocks, bonds, and real estate. From the investor's point of view, new technology ventures are a specific high-risk asset class, as the probability of realizing a loss is relatively high. Factors like team performance, product development, or market conditions may cause a technology venture to fail. In addition, the failure rates also depend on the country, the industry, the macroeconomic environment, and other parameters. Overall, the failure rate is relatively high (see e.g., Ejermo & Xiao, 2014; Hor et al., 2021).

13.2.2 Risk and Return

Finance theory postulates that there is a positive correlation between risk and return. Higher return promises must compensate for higher risks, and thus venture capital investors will have high return expectations.

13.2.3 Debt and Equity

There are two distinct practices for funding a company: debt or equity. In the case of debt, the creditor expects repayment and interest. In the case of equity, the investors become co-owners (shareholders) of the venture, and there is no repayment expectation. Equity investors typically expect to increase the company's value and eventually sell part or all of their shares later with a significant gain.

Both types of capital providers – creditors and equity investors – use different ways to safeguard against the risk associated with their investment (Winton & Yerramilli, 2008).

13.2.4 Creditor Risk Management

Creditors increase the interest rate according to the increase in risk. The creditor's risk depends on the loan amount, the repayment period, and the overall creditworthiness of the debtor. For the payback period, there are three debt categories: short-term (typically up to 12 months), intermediate-term (up to ten years), and long-term (beyond ten years).

Especially for mid-term and long-term loans, creditors typically ask for securities. If the debtor cannot repay the debt and pay the interest, the creditor will dispose of the securities to satisfy his claims. Securities may be assets of the debtor (collateral, e.g., a building or a patent) or guarantees from another source that promised to resume the debt in case of a debt default of the original debtor (e.g., the security of a state bank or a private person). In financing early-stage technology ventures, mid-term and long-term debt financing is rarely used as the companies cannot provide sufficient securities (Han et al., 2009).

13.2.5 Equity Investor Risk Management

In case of failure, an equity investor is fully liable and may lose all the invested capital. Therefore, venture capitalists typically invest in many ventures simultaneously to diversify risk. Even if some companies fail and others hardly gain value, the portfolio will create profits if a few ventures are highly successful. Therefore, venture capitalists look for companies with high growth potential and accept the risks that come with young technology ventures.

As equity investors become owners, they also have control and governance rights. They can reduce information asymmetry and influence important decisions, in particular about the management team. In addition, equity investors seek to implement certain contractual rights that safeguard their investments.

Equity financing is highly relevant in the early stages of a company. In general, debt financing becomes more relevant at later stages when certain risks have been reduced, revenues create the necessary cash flow to pay back debt, and the focus on financial figures reduces information asymmetry (Hogan et al., 2017; Drover et al., 2014).

13.2.6 *Mezzanine Financing*

In French and Italian, the word 'mezzanine' literally means 'middle'; in architecture, the 'mezzanine' is an intermediate floor. Mezzanine financing is an intermediate form between equity investments and debt. It is a particular form of a loan with repayment and interest. However, in the case of mezzanine capital, the creditor accepts a much higher risk, in the extreme case, full liability. To compensate for the higher risk, the mezzanine lender often participates in the company's increase in value. A prominent example is a convertible loan. The lender can convert the loan into equity at certain conditions (e.g., with the next investment round).

In practice, a wide variety of mezzanine financing can be found. 'Silent partnership' is an important example. The lender is 'silent' and has no governance rights but otherwise functions like an equity investor. There are also agreements where the mezzanine lender participates in profits or revenues. Depending on their form and structure, mezzanine financing instruments are classified as either equity or debt for accounting purposes.

13.2.7 *Crowdfunding*

Crowdfunding enables entrepreneurs to collect money from a large number of people via online platforms. There are three structural elements: the ventures (or projects), the general public (the 'crowd'), and the crowdfunding platform. With crowdfunding, entrepreneurs have access to interested individuals in addition to business angels, venture capital funds, and banks (Lambert and Schwienbacher, 2010; Mollick, 2014). Crowdfunding can also be a way of cultivating a community around an offering, and venture or project owners can gain helpful market insights and access new customers through this online community.

Hundreds of platforms have emerged over the past years with different approaches. They include peer-to-peer lending, equity crowdfunding, rewards-based crowdfunding, donation-based crowdfunding, profit-sharing or revenue-sharing, debt-securities, and hybrid models.

13.3 The Financing Cycle and Stages of Technology Ventures

Entrepreneurship research suggests that technology ventures in their development go through different stages (Levie & Lichtenstein, 2010, p. 329). Often, these stages are related to the development of a product, the initial commercialization, a growth phase, and the establishment of a stable business (Kazanjian, 1988; Kazanjian&Drazin, 1990; Fernando, 2021). However, it is important to realize that there is no evidence for any deterministic sequence of development with a fixed pattern of stages. Each venture follows its own logic of growth (Levie & Lichtenstein, 2010).

The financing cycle is directly related to the development of the venture. The first phase is the 'pre-seed' phase. The first money typically comes from the entrepreneurs and their close ties ('3f' = friends, family, and 'fools'). In some countries, government programs provide pre-seed funding (e.g., BMWK, 2022). For technology ventures, it could also be some form of support from a university or research center. Typically, in this phase, the team creates a prototype, secures access to intellectual property (IP), approaches potential customers, and builds up a 'community of inquiry' (Shepard et al., 2021).

Once the team attains its first results, it approaches external financiers, often business angels, for a 'seed' investment. Business Angels are wealthy and well-connected individuals who provide funding to reach results (milestones) that prepare the venture for the subsequent financing round. Depending on the nature of the business, the milestones may be quite different. For a digital business model, it could be the first revenue to show market traction. For deep tech ventures, it could also be the next development step toward a marketable product or filing a patent.

Seed funding is the first equity funding stage. Often, business angel investments are 'boosted' with additional capital from institutional investors, including government-backed programs or banks.

If the team successfully reaches the goals of the seed stage, they enter the next financing round, often called 'series A'. Again, investment readiness for this round depends on the details of the business. For digital ventures, it typically implies proof of market traction. For other ventures, for instance in healthcare, the path to creating revenues is much longer, so the milestone may be tied to IP or some initial step in an official product approval procedure.

A venture capitalist typically provides the capital for series A financing. The investment is a significant amount of money triggering growth. The company hires employees and finds its way to efficient and scalable operations. Additional capital injections in further investment rounds (Series B, C, etc.) accelerate and amplify this process. Investors will ask for a monitoring system and potentially appoint experienced executives to manage the venture.

For many entrepreneurs, obtaining Venture Capital (VC) funding is a significant achievement and creates legitimacy for the new organization (Stuart, Hoang, and Hybels 1999). Investors are also an essential source of advice and contacts (Bellavitis, Filatotchev, and Kamuriwo 2014; Cumming, Fleming, and Suchard 2005; Sapienza, Manigart, and Vermeir 1996). VC funding and connections often fuel strong growth both domestically and internationally. A typical common goal of entrepreneurs and investors is to reach an exit, either in the form of an initial public offering or a sale of the company to a corporation. Many highly successful companies followed a similar funding cycle (e.g., Berger and Udell 1998), but ultimately, every venture writes its own story (Levie & Lichtenstein, 2010). Table 13.1 summarizes the development stages of a technology venture.

Table 13.1 Financing phases, typical activities, and typical funding sources

Phase	Typical activities	Funding source
Pre-seed	Lab prototype Secure access to IP Write a business plan Build a community of inquiry	3f Government programs University support
Seed	Register company Reach milestones (like a product prototype, first sales, or patent filing)	Business angels Government programs
Startup	Reach further milestones (sales targets, improve product economics, hire people, secure IP, secure suppliers)	Venture capitalists (Series A)
Growth	Secure profitability and scale business	Venture capitalists (Series B,C...)

13.4 Risks in Early-stage Technology Ventures

Early-stage ventures typically lack a track record, mature products, established customer rela-tionships, a well-coordinated organization, and an experienced management team. Turnovers, profits, and cash flow are uncertain (Kaserer et al., 2007; Damodaran, 2009). Six significant categories of risk need to be considered: team, market, technology, product, operations, and funding.

13.4.1 Team Risk

Team risk is associated with the team's competence, commitment, and cooperation.

In an early stage, the founders and the initial team are decisive for the success or failure of a venture. Entrepreneurship literature suggests that founders are heterogeneous in experi-ences and competencies, entrepreneurial imaginativeness, motivation and identity, affective responses, and enduring characteristics (Shepard et al., 2021).

In addition, team cooperation is vital, and miscommunication, divergent goals, and team conflict can be a significant risk for the young venture. For investors, the sense of confidence in the team is typically the most critical investment criterion (Wessendorf et al., 2019).

13.4.2 Market Risk

The venture's value proposition may not create an adequate willingness to pay in a sufficiently large market or may not reach the customer.

This risk has several facets. First, it has to do with whether the venture reaches a 'problem-solution fit' and whether the value proposition addresses a relevant need of the target customer (Blank & Dorf, 2020). Second, it has to do with whether customers show a willingness to pay for the value proposition. Only if the acceptable price of a product is high enough to create good profitability will the venture be able to capture value. Third, has to do with potential alternatives for the customer and hence market competition. The term 'product-market fit' (Blank & Dorf, 2020) indicates the degree to which a product satisfies strong market demand. Fourth, the customer segment must be big enough to generate suffi-cient revenues sustainably. Finally, a viable channel must reach the customer with affordable cost and time.

13.4.3 Technology Risk

The technology which is the basis of the value proposition may not reach an appropriate level of readiness for commercial use or may not be available for the venture.

Public organizations like space agencies use the 'Technology readiness levels (TRLs)' as a method for estimating the maturity of new technologies (Héder, 2017). The TRL depends on the technical concepts, the requirements, and demonstrated technology capabilities. TRLs are based on a scale from one to nine, with nine being the most mature technology.

In early-stage technology ventures, the technology to be exploited is typically in some early stage of development. It is crucial to assess prototypes and their performance and aspects like the technology's robustness, scalability, and safety and security.

New technology often is protected by IP rights. For a university spin-off, a critical patent may be the property of the university. The new venture must assure access to the IP, e.g., by licensing or acquisition.

13.4.4 Product Risk

Product risk is the risk of not being able to produce and deliver the product on quality, time, and budget.

Any development process has risks. It may turn out that the development process takes more resources or time than originally planned. The specification of the product may be overambitious, and there may be conflicting requirements. The technical architecture of the product may lead to limitations, and the availability of components may change over time.

13.4.5 Operational Risk

Operational risk is related to (cost-) efficient internal procedures, people, and systems for value creation and delivery.

Delivering the product or service to the customer requires a functioning organization. An efficient setup is necessary for a coordinated division of labor and an orchestrated flow of information and material. Even if the technology is mature and the venture has developed a good product with customers that are willing to pay, there are risks associated with setting up efficient and scalable operations.

Managing the costs associated with value creation is vital. Even if the development of a product or service is successful, there may be higher costs for manufacturing (for a physical product), human resources (for a conventional service), or computer resources (for digital services) than expected. Prototypes are expensive to produce and necessitate a high intentionality of finding value proposition at costs clearly below the market price.

13.4.6 Funding Risks

The venture may require more capital than planned to fund the product development, marketing activities, operations, and company building.

Running out of cash is a significant threat for the new venture. Investors will ask whether their investment will be sufficient to reach the next milestone. Such a milestone may be reaching break-even (creating enough revenues to have positive cash flow). In many cases, it means having enough capital to achieve the next step (e.g., acquire a pilot customer or file a patent) and raise more money in a follow-up investment round. This risk concerns the quality of financial planning and whether the time, scope, and budget for the next step are realistic and coherent.

All risk categories mentioned are interrelated and need to be strategically planned for. For instance, an incomplete understanding of customer needs may lead to an over-serving product with a very high cost. An immature technology may delay product development and leave the young venture without a marketable product. Divergent opinions about product or market strategy may lead to a thinly spread resources or an incoherent organizational setup. Lack of funding may compromise product quality, impede essential marketing and business development efforts, delay production, and lead to overall stakeholder dissatisfaction among others.

One of the most important tasks of an enterprise is to find adequate financial resources that match the venture goals and objectives. These financial resources need to be available at the precise time that it is needed. The type of funding option and provider determines its future course. Oftentimes, venture funding is one of the early obstacles ventures need to overcome. Taking on a holistic perspective of the funding options available and carefully weighing upon the challenges and opportunities they bring is essential to finding success.

References

Achleitner, A.-K. (2001) Start-up-Unternehmen: Bewertung mit der Venture-Capital-Methode. *Betriebsberater*, 56(18), pp. 927–934.

Achleitner, A.-K., and Nathusius, E. (2004) *Venture Valuation - Bewertung von Wachstumsunternehmen*. 1st edn. Stuttgart: Schäffer-Poeschel.

Bellavitis, C., Filatotchev, I., Kamuriwo, D. S., and Vanacker, T. (2017) Entrepreneurial finance: new frontiers of research and practice. *Venture Capital*, 19(1–2), pp. 1–16.

Blank, S., and Dorf, B. (2020) *The startup owner's manual. The step-by-step guide for building a great company*. Hoboken: Wiley (ProQuest Ebook Central).

BMWK (2022) The EXIST Business Start-up Grant. German Federal Ministry of Economic Affairs and Climate Action. Available online at https://www.exist.de/EXIST/Navigation/EN/Start-upFunding/EXIST-Business-Start-up-Grant/exist-business-start-up-grant.html, checked on 17 June 2022.

Brush, C. G., Manolova, T. S., and Edelman, L. F. (2008) Properties of emerging organizations: An empirical test. *Journal of Business Venturing*, 23(5), pp. 547–566.

Byers, T. H., Dorf, R. C., and Nelson, A. J. (2019) *Technology Ventures. From Idea to Enterprise*. Fifth edition, international student edition. New York: McGraw-Hill Education.

Chemmanur, T. J., and Fulghieri, P. (2014) Entrepreneurial finance and innovation: An introduction and agenda for future research. In *The Review of Financial Studies*, 27(1), pp. 1–19.

Damodaran, A. (2012) *Investment Valuation*. 3rd ed. Wiley Finance Series. Hoboken: John Wiley & Sons.

Damodaran, A. (2005) *Marketability and Value: Measuring the Illiquidity Discount, SSRN*. Hoboken: John Wiley & Sons. doi: 10.2139/ssrn.841484.

Drover, W., Wood, M. S., and Payne, G. T. (2014) The effects of perceived control on venture capitalist investment decisions: A configurational perspective. *Entrepreneurship Theory and Practice*, 38(4), pp. 833–861.

Eilenberger, G., Haghani, S. (2008) *Unternehmensfinanzierung zwischen Strategie und Rendite*. Berlin, Heidelberg: Springer (Academic network).

Ejermo, O., and Xiao, J. (2014) Entrepreneurship and survival over the business cycle: How do new technology-based firms differ? *Small Business Economics*, 43(2), pp. 411–426.

Feld, B., and Mendelson, J. (2011) *Venture Deals: Be Smarter Than Your Lawyer and Venture Capitalist*. Hoboken, New Jersey: John Wiley & Sons.

Fernando, J. (2021) Development Stage. Investopedia. Available online at https://www.investopedia.com/terms/d/developmentstage.asp, updated on 14 November 2021, checked on 15 June 2022.

Freear, J., Sohl, J. E., and Wetzel, W. E. (1995) Who bankrolls software entrepreneurs. *Frontiers of Entrepreneurship Research*, 16(4), pp. 85–94.

Han, L., Fraser, S., and Storey, D. J. (2009) The role of collateral in entrepreneurial finance. *Journal of Business Finance & Accounting*, 36(3-4), pp. 424–455.

Héder, M. (2017) From NASA to EU: The evolution of the TRL scale in Public Sector Innovation. *The Innovation Journal*, 22(2), pp. 1–23.

HighTech Startbahn (2017) *Activating Venture Capital for European Innovation*. 3rd Edition, pp. 2–7.

Hogan, T., Hutson, E., and Drnevich, P. (2017) Drivers of external equity funding in small high-tech ventures. *Journal of Small Business Management*, 55(2), pp. 236–253. doi: 10.1111/jsbm.12270.

Hor, S. C. T., Artemis C., Rui T. O., and Per D (2021) From the theories of financial resource acquisition to a theory for acquiring financial resources-how should digital ventures raise equity capital beyond seed funding. *Journal of Business Venturing Insights* 16, p. e00278.

Kakati, M. (2003) Success criteria in high-tech new ventures. *Technovation*, 23(5), pp. 447–457. doi: 10.1016/S0166-4972(02)00014-7.

Kaserer, C., Alfred, M., and Stefan, O. (2007) *Private Equity in Deutschland. Rahmenbedingungen, ökonomische Bedeutung und Handlungsempfehlungen. Abdruck des Forschungsgutachtens fe 3/06 'Erwerb und Übernahme durch Finanzinvestoren (insbesondere Private-Equity-Gesellschaften)' für das Bundesministeriu*. Norderstedt: Books on Demand GmbH.

Kazanjian, R. K. (1988) Relation of dominant problems to stages of growth in technology-based new ventures. *Academy of Management Journal*, 31(2), pp. 257–279.

Katz, J., and Gartner, W. B. (1988) Properties of emerging organizations. *Academy of Management Review,* 13(3), pp. 429–441.

Kazanjian, R. K., and Drazin, R. (1990) A stage-contingent model of design and growth for technology based new ventures. *Journal of Business Venturing,* 5(3), pp. 137–150.

Kotha, R. and George, G. (2012) Friends, family, or fools: Entrepreneur experience and its implications for equity distribution and resource mobilization. *Journal of Business Venturing,* 27(5), pp. 525–543.

Levie, J., and Lichtenstein, B. B. (2010) A terminal assessment of stages theory. Introducing a dynamic states approach to entrepreneurship. *Entrepreneurship Theory and Practice,* 34(2), pp. 317–350.

Mason, C. M. (1996) Informal venture capital: Is policy running ahead of knowledge. *International Journal of Entrepreneurial Behaviour & Research,* 2(1), pp. 4–14.

Mollick, E. (2014) The dynamics of crowdfunding: An exploratory study. *Journal of Business Venturing,* 29(1), pp. 1–16. doi: 10.1016/j.jbusvent.2013.06.005.

Van Osnabrugge, M., and Robinson, R. J. (2000) *Angel Investing: Matching Start-up Funds with Start-up Companies - The Guide for Entrepreneurs, Individual Investors, and Venture Capitalists.* San Francisco: Jossey-Bass.

Rudolf, M., and Witt, P. (2002) *Bewertung von Wachstumsunternehmen. Traditionelle und innovative Methoden im Vergleich.* 1st edn. Wiesbaden: Betriebswirtschaftl. Verlag Dr. Th. Gabler GmbH.

Shepherd, D. A., Souitaris, V., and Gruber, M. (2021) Creating new ventures: A review and research agenda. *Journal of Management,* 47(1), pp. 11–42.

Sohl, J. E. (1999) The early-stage equity market in the USA. *Venture Capital,* 1(2), pp. 1–20.

Wessendorf, C. P., Kegelmann, J., and Terzidis, O. (2019) Determinants of early-stage technology venture valuation by business angels and venture capitalists. *International Journal of Entrepreneurial Venturing,* 11(5), pp. 489–520. doi: 10.1504/IJEV.2019.102259.

Wilmerding, A. (2003) *Deal Terms: The Finer Points of Venture Capital Deal Structures, Valuations, Term Sheets, Stock Options and Getting Deals Done.* John Wiley & Sons.

Winborg, J., and Landstrom, H. (1997) Financial bootstrapping in small businesses: A resource-based view of small business finance. In *Babson College-Kauffman Foundation Research Conference.* Babson Park.

Winton, A., and Yerramilli, V. (2008) Entrepreneurial finance: Banks versus venture capital. *Journal of Financial Economics,* 88(1), pp. 51–79.

14 Funding Process for Technology Ventures

Christoph P. Wessendorf

14.1 Introduction

Technology ventures are a major source of change that affects our daily lives, businesses, and society as a whole. They create new industries and force old ones to adapt to the new conditions by being able to respond quickly to changes in the market or the environment (Egeln, 2000). This change, on the other hand, doesn't just happen with a strong entrepreneurial team and new technology; it also requires enough funds to create an innovative business. Ventures that are based on technology, in particular, need a lot of capital to fund research and development and a great interdisciplinary team (Pary & Witmeur, 2018). They encounter huge uncertainties regarding customer demand and product-market-fit (Lynn & Heintz, 1992). It can be hard to get these needed funds, especially in the early stages of a company's life-cycle (Kaserer et al., 2007). Yet, most ventures securing a seed-financing are not able to raise more capital after the initial funding, even if they've made progress on building a business model and can show they have the potential to grow and generate revenue.

In order to prepare, set up, and run the funding process, the technology entrepreneur who wants to raise funds needs to answer three important questions: Why am I raising capital, when do I need to start the funding process and how can I run the process in a tight and targeted manner. With the answers to these questions, three strong design principles drive the funding process: strategic clarity (why to raise funds), investor readiness (when to start the funding process), and an understanding of main activities within the fundraising process (how to run a tight process) (Hor et al., 2021).

Clarify your values, mindset, expectations, and goals to figure out **why you're trying to raise capital**. This will increase the chances of a successful fundraising campaign (Hor et al., 2021).

Thus, "before rushing into preparing pitch materials, meeting investors, and hammering out funding terms, it is critical to get your mindset, expectations, math, and strategy right" (Cremades, 2016). Most of the time, entrepreneurs won't get past the first meeting, even if their business is ready for investors, if they can't explain why they want to fund raise and what their business goals, next steps, expectations, and exit plan are. So, figuring out why you want to raise funds is a very important first step that will make it more likely that the fundraising goes well. In addition, entrepreneurs should very early on reflect on the ideal source of funding, which is highly specific to each venture's development phase and business model. While debt financing might not be an option for all ventures, it certainly is for some of them. The same holds true for retained earnings or subsidies. As venture capital is certainly one funding source that can provide a significant amount of capital already in the early stage, financing by venture capital and private equity investors deserves particular attention.

DOI: 10.4324/9781003341284-19

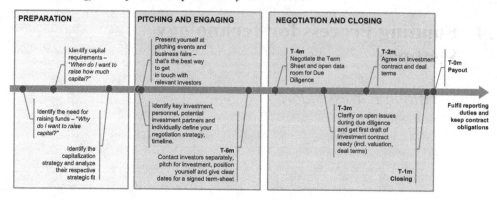

Figure 14.1 Phases of the funding process highlighting main activities. Illustration by the author.

Assess your business's scalability, sustainability, and structure to determine **when you're ready to raise capital**. Investor readiness increases your chances of successfully raising financing (Hor et al., 2021). The reflection on the "why" will also need to cover the financing strategy, i.e., the preferences for a specific type of funding.

A key part of being ready for investment, according to C. Mason & Kwok (2010), is defined as "the investability of the businesses that do seek external finance." More importantly, the high rejection rates of business angels and venture capitalists were mostly blamed on the businesses not being financially sound or not being able to meet the investors' needs (C. M. Mason & Harrison, 2003; Riding, 1993; Stedler & Peters, 2003). Douglas and Shepherd (2002) break down investor readiness into three parts: technology readiness, market readiness, and management readiness. This is called "investability." So, for a new business to be investable, it needs to have a product (technology) that can grow to serve a large market (user base) and a team (management) that is ready and able to carry out the business plan. More importantly, the target investor must see all three elements at the same time.

All of the above suggestions are aimed at making sure that the business is ready for investment or that investors can invest in it. A technology entrepreneur should also keep a close eye on the outside world to figure out when the best time is to start a fundraising campaign.

To run **an effective funding process**, you need to organize your network, prove your credibility, and involve your funding sources. Knowing how to run a process well will make it more likely that your fundraising campaign will be successful (Hor et al., 2021).

These three design principles will have an effect on the three main stages of the funding process (Hor et al., 2021). Strategic clarity and investor readiness are of particular importance when preparing for fundraising, thus in the Preparation-phase. As preparation marks the first phase of the process, a clear strategy and optimal timing will also be decisive for all later phases of the process. Still, these later phases, which are Pitching, Engaging, Negotiating, and Closing, need to take into account one more thing to be successful: How well and efficiently the entrepreneur runs the process (Figure 14.1).

Even though it's not a part of the funding process itself, the time after closing should be on the mind of the entrepreneur when they are raising funds. After acquiring enough funds to continue developing the business, the technology entrepreneur needs to keep the promises made to investors. In the investment contract, he agreed to reach certain milestones and invest the capital he raised. He also has to send reports and meet other contract requirements. Beyond that, he needs to be aware that the terms that were negotiated and agreed upon will affect future funding rounds.

14.2 Preparation

14.2.1 Identifying the Need for Raising Funds

As a first step in fundraising, the entrepreneur should reflect on mindset, values, and expectations. This clarity drives the process. By answering "why do I want to raise capital," the entrepreneur not only sets the main objective, such as "raising capital to go to market due to first positive client feedback," but also creates the context to answer questions about capital requirements, timing of the fundraising process, sources of capital to be chosen, and value add provided to the fund provider (Hor et al., 2021).

14.2.2 Identifying Capital Requirements

Identifying capital needs depends on the firm's financial state and fundraising time. Due to its lack of track record and uncertainty about its future development, early stage ventures may benefit from triangulating various methodologies to determine their capital needs (Kaserer et al., 2007).

First, an entrepreneur could think about the strategic initiatives (i.e., value steps) he wants to implement to get his endeavor to the next level, such as "implementing a marketing strategy for Germany" or "to expand the current business globally" (Feld & Mendelson, 2011). He must estimate investments and running costs for each initiative. The needed capital equals the total value of defined initiatives' investment and operating costs (preferably until break-even).

Second, an entrepreneur should anticipate and plan his firm with a cash flow statement. If he needs external investment, the company's free cash flow pre-investment will be negative. Negative free cash flows equal the necessary capital.

An entrepreneur may also consider how much capital he is willing to raise given his grasp of pre-money firm valuation, i.e., every Euro raised x will diminish his own equity in the company as investors receive *x/post-money valuation.*

14.2.3 Identifying the Capitalization Strategy

The technology entrepreneur must consider debt, equity, and a mix of both when capitalizing his firm (Eilenberger & Haghani, 2008). These types of finance can, for example, come from business angels or venture capital funds (VC funds), who invest in high-growth enterprises.

The entrepreneur may choose venture capital financing. The investment size, the venture's significant risk, and the lack of collateral and credit history may justify this. Further, according to the trade-off theory of capital structure (de Rassenfosse & Fischer, 2016), debt providers are generally not pursuing lending to pre-profitability ventures, as lenders are only sharing losses but not participating in gains, as equity holders regularly do. As this is a prevalent scenario for technology entrepreneurs, this chapter will focus on venture finance (which includes funding from venture capital investors as well as, in a later stage of development, private equity investors). Yet, it needs to be pointed out that the source of funding is strongly dependent on the venture's development phase and business model.

Next, the entrepreneur must decide if venture capital is right for his business and growth objectives. There are various pros (such as access to a strong network of entrepreneurs and fund partners as well as management support and coaching) and disadvantages (such as a defined and often complex investment procedure) to consider.

Once the entrepreneur is clear on his need for venture capital, he should analyze the anticipated step in company development to determine if it constitutes a "value step," or a step that dramatically changes the firm's characteristics and value. This is a crucial characteristic for venture capital investments, as investors want to improve portfolio firm value.

14.2.4 Providing Value to the Fund Provider

The entrepreneur should consider how his venture benefits investors. An investor wants (risk-adjusted) return first. Investing possibilities are plenty.

Thus, the entrepreneur should consider other factors that may appeal to investors. This can be determined by analyzing the investor's investing strategy, purpose, and investment focus (including company development stages, the business models, or the geographical areas the fund focuses on). In this scenario, he should explore a strategic fit (e.g., a corporate investor looking for complementary technology or product) or a technology fit (e.g., a venture capital investor that only invests in software ventures will in general not be interested in a hardware firm). The investment horizon of the fund must match the entrepreneur's proposal. A venture capital fund that must pay its investors in two years (the end of the fund) will not invest in a firm with a 5–7-year exit plan. The entrepreneur should understand potential investors' motivations before contacting them and seeking funding.

This may limit the number of equity sources for a particular business, but it ensures a strategic fit, common understanding, and shared goals once a VC invests.

14.3 Pitching and Engaging

14.3.1 Establish Contact and Apply

Once an entrepreneur is clear on the *why* and *when* and decided on the venture's funding strategy and capital requirements, he will need to get in contact with relevant business angels and venture capitalists. As the variety of investors is large, it should be well-planned and given ample time (Feld & Mendelson, 2011).

In a first step, the entrepreneur will establish a long-list of potential investors by researching their investment focus (e.g., area, industry, development stage, investment sum) and investment approach. This must match the capitalization strategy and capital needs. He'll expand this list by networking. The identified investors can be reached by phone, LinkedIn, or a fund's dedicated email address. Further, the entrepreneur should participate in pitch events and business plan competitions to meet possible investors.

14.3.2 Presenting Your Venture

The entrepreneur must showcase his idea and vision to potential investors to gauge their interest and suitability for the fundraising process. The enterprise is pitched or a pitch deck is sent. A pitch deck is a short presentation that introduces potential investors to a venture's backdrop, value proposition, business strategy, and finances. This is usually a Power Point presentation with no more than 15 slides.

Investors often pre-screen pitch decks. Because the risk is higher than usual, investment decisions must be based on a thorough understanding of the companies and their markets. First, a company's incoming documents are checked for errors or misunderstandings. They must meet minimum formal requirements (i.e., investment focus), economic potential, or attractiveness. This initial screening phase rejects most company proposals and enterprises. Only those who pass this level are invited for a personal presentation, phone conversation, or more thorough investigation.

These pitch sessions can indicate an investor's interest and fit. Some investors refuse to invest. For others, the entrepreneur may decide the (personal) fit isn't perfect. Other investors may be interested in the business but cannot comply with the investment process, e.g., they may not be willing to invest in the next six months but are open to investing afterward. The entrepreneur can then shortlist possible investors after analyzing the individual sessions.

Online resources describe the "ideal pitch deck" for certain areas or sectors. Entrepreneurs should research these based on their venture or ask the investor what information they want from the pitch.

14.4 Negotiation and Closing

14.4.1 Negotiate the Term-sheet to Set Out Key Investment Conditions

Fundraising involves intense contract negotiations. The entrepreneur should consult a lawyer to thoroughly understand the terms' impact on the deal and the venture.

The process involves two steps. First, the term-sheet. A signed term-sheet specifies investment requirements. Here, the parties agree on the investment's basic criteria, such as a value interval, contractual rights, or investment amount. A venture capitalist only cares about economics and control when negotiating an investment. Economics refers to an investor's return in a liquidity event (e.g., an Initial Public Offering (IPO)) and the conditions that affect it. Control refers to methods that allow an investor to exercise control over a corporation or veto-specific actions (Feld & Mendelson, 2011).

Even though the term-sheet is not legally enforceable, it is done to obtain a common understanding of the deal's scale and structure and to avoid knock-out criteria in subsequent discussions. Once all parties agree on basic conditions, which can take weeks, a lawyer incorporates them into an investment contract in a second step. Here, a term-sheet of 15–20 pages might turn into a 60+ page contract with all relevant information.

14.4.2 Performing the Due Diligence

Once all parties are sure the endeavor is worthwhile, due diligence begins. The venture team receives a list of corporate details the investor wants to know. This may include the financial track record of sales and profits, debt liabilities, the existing customer base, a competitor analysis, marketing strategy and material, explanations on the company's operations (cost controlling, inventory control, decision processes, etc.), information on the present owner structure, documents confirming that legal obligations are being followed, or even information on the private income situation of the founders and guarantors (Feld & Mendelson, 2011; van Osnabrugge & Robinson, 2000). In essence, the venture capitalist wants to know everything that influences the risk he is incurring by investing in order to carefully appraise it. He can also seek legal or expert advice. In this phase, it is vital for the founders that they do not hold back or conceal relevant information which means that they should freely and honestly discuss the company's strengths, flaws, and situation from the initial contact with the investor on.

14.4.3 Negotiating the Investment Contract

The investment contract is next. The signed investment contract officially closes the deal by including all terms negotiated between the investor and the venture. Its objective is to protect both parties from investment risks. It also outlines the investment amount and firm valuation, which is tricky for a technology venture, in particular in the early stage (Wessendorf, 2021). Complex contracts require legal assistance. Several terms that entrepreneur should focus on during negotiations may have major financial ramifications on a subsequent exit or the entrepreneur's share in the venture (Feld & Mendelson, 2011). These provisions balance the entrepreneur's incentives, manage decision-making, and protect the investor's financial downside (van Osnabrugge & Robinson, 2000). This chapter explains simply the most crucial deal terms founders should know to negotiate.

14.4.3.1 Liquidation Preferences

Liquidation of the corporation offers the biggest risk to all parties. Because debt providers' claims are generally prioritized in a liquidation, the equity owner must obtain certain financial rights for himself. A typical agreement guarantees the venture capitalist at least his initial investment or his proportional part of liquidation proceeds (Feld & Mendelson, 2011). But liquidation preferences can also take on several other forms.

14.4.3.2 Vesting

The venture's management team is crucial to its success. Founder exit is another risk for the business. Vesting clauses stipulate that founders' shares aren't entirely theirs until a particular time or after reaching specific milestones (Feld & Mendelson, 2011). In case of an early exit, a founder would forfeit his portion of the company's value, giving him a significant incentive to stay and work for the venture's success.

14.4.3.3 Anti-Dilution and Pre-Emptive Rights

If the company doesn't grow as expected, a future financing round may have to be valued lower. Down-rounds weaken existing investors' shares and threaten their rewards. The investment contract usually guarantees early investors the same price as future investors to avoid penalizing them for taking early risks. Anti-dilution terms maintain the initial investor's ownership percentage steady without paying more than later investors. Pre-emptive rights are the right to buy new shares at a certain price (Feld & Mendelson, 2011).

There are several well-written books which particularly focus on the legal aspects of fundraising and give a good overview of deal terms and the contractual process (e.g., Feld & Mendelson, 2011; Wilmerding, 2003). These books are a good source of knowledge for the entrepreneur in order to develop a basic understanding of the negotiation dynamics and underlying rationale.

14.5 Implications of Fundraising Post-closing

14.5.1 Fulfill Reporting Duties and Keep Contract Obligations

After a venture capitalist or business angel invests, the entrepreneur will have extra tasks that affect the venture's operations.

First, investors will want regular updates on the venture's performance and growth (van Osnabrugge & Robinson, 2000). Such reports might be quantitative (e.g., sales pipeline, profit and loss statement, cash flow statement), qualitative (e.g., marketing and sales activity, development progress), or a blend of both.

Second, decisions that affect the firm's progress will be made formally (van Osnabrugge & Robinson, 2000). This decision-making will engage new shareholders (i.e., investors) at a shareholder meeting or quiet procedure. Investors will exercise voting rights (e.g., pro-rata in accordance with their stake in the company).

Firms receiving equity must often generate extensive financial statements, especially if the investor is an institutional VC fund. In this instance, financial statements must meet certain criteria for proper investor control (Feld & Mendelson, 2011). In addition, the investor might require an auditor to review the books and examine the financial statements for its proper reflection of the firm's financials.

14.5.2 Further Funding Rounds and Implications on Operations after Closing

In most circumstances, the first fundraising round isn't enough to maintain successful technology ventures' growth. The venture must continue to prioritize a value-focused strategy. This means it focuses on value-driving aspects of its existence, such as attractive financial Key Performance Indicators (KPIs) like equity ratio and profitability, high growth outlooks in sales and profits, and increasing cash reserves, as well as an outstanding team, increasing market shares and customer base, secured intellectual property. It entails keeping up with financing and maintaining contacts. Positive news about the business makes it desirable and may shorten investment cycles. Keep company presentations and materials updated to present the company in its best light at all times.

Founders must also remember that further financing will likely mean selling more of the venture's shares, reducing their own interests and influence. A high number of shareholders can also complicate operational capacities and slow down crucial decision processes, reducing flexibility and increasing effort in corporate development. Early stage ventures should consider these factors while negotiating their first investment to strengthen their clout in further talks.

References

Cremades, A. (2016). *The Art of Startup Fundraising: Pitching Investors, Negotiating the Deal, and Everything Else Entrepreneurs Need to Know*. John Wiley & Sons.

de Rassenfosse, G., & Fischer, T. (2016). Venture debt financing: Determinants of the lending decision. *Strategic Entrepreneurship Journal, 10*(3), 235–256.

Douglas, E. J., & Shepherd, D. (2002). Exploring investor readiness: Assessments by entrepreneurs and investors in Australia. *Venture Capital: An International Journal of Entrepreneurial Finance, 4*(3), 219–236.

Egeln, J. (2000). Die volkswirtschaftliche Bedeutung junger Unternehmen. In G. Buttler, H. Herrmann, W. Scheffler, & K.- I. Voigt (Eds.), *Existenzgründung* (pp. 3–32). Physica.

Eilenberger, G., & Haghani, S. (2008). *Unternehmensfinanzierung zwischen Strategie und Rendite*. Springer.

Feld, B., & Mendelson, J. (2011). *Venture Deals: Be Smarter Than Your Lawyer and Venture Capitalist*. John Wiley & Sons.

Hor, S. C., Timothy, Chang, A., Torres De Oliveira, R., & Davidsson, P. (2021). From the theories of financial resource acquisition to a theory for acquiring financial resources—how should digital ventures raise equity capital beyond seed funding. *Journal of Business Venturing Insights, 16*, Article e00278. https://doi.org/10.1016/j.jbvi.2021.e00278

Kaserer, C., Achleitner, A.-K., von Einem, C., & Schiereck, D. (2007). *Private Equity in Deutschland. Rahmenbedingungen, ökonomische Bedeutung und Handlungsempfehlungen. Abdruck des Forschungsgutachtens fe 3/06 "Erwerb und Übernahme durch Finanzinvestoren (insbesondere Private-Equity-Gesellschaften)". für das Bundesministerium der Finanzen*. Books on Demand GmbH.

Lynn, F., & Heintz, S. (1992). Where does your new technology fit into the marketplace? *Journal of Product Innovation Management, 9*(1), 19–25.

Mason, C., & Kwok, J. (2010). Investment readiness programmes and access to finance: A critical review of design issues. *Local Economy, 25*(4), 269–292.

Mason, C. M., & Harrison, R. T. (2003). "Auditioning for money": What do technology investors look for at the initial screening stage? *The Journal of Private Equity, 6*(2), 29–42.

Pary, N., & Witmeur, O. (2018). New Technology-Based Firms and Grants: Too Much of a Good Thing? In *Technology Entrepreneurship* (pp. 177–200). Springer International Publishing.

Riding, A. (1993). *Informal Investors in Canada: The Identification of Salient Characteristics.* Industry, Science and Technology Canada.

Stedler, H., & Peters, H. H. (2003). Business angels in Germany: An empirical study. *Venture Capital: An International Journal of Entrepreneurial Finance, 5*(3), 269–276.

van Osnabrugge, M., & Robinson, R. J. (2000). *Angel Investing: Matching Start-up Funds with Start-up Companies - The Guide for Entrepreneurs, Individual Investors, and Venture Capitalists.* Jossey-Bass.

Wessendorf, C. P. (2021). *Indicating Value in Early-Stage Technology Venture Valuation.* Springer Fachmedien.

Wilmerding, A. (2003). *Deal Terms: The Finer Points of Venture Capital Deal Structures, Valuations, Term Sheets, Stock Options and Getting Deals Done.* Aspatore Books.

15 Understanding How Capital Providers Think

Yu Wei Ye

To raise money successfully, entrepreneurs must know the capital providers' motivation and objectives. They also need to understand the investment criteria and process of capital providers. In Chapter 14, we discussed what technology ventures should expect and prepare and how they start the funding process. This chapter will discuss what factors are essential to capital providers, how they make their decisions, and why it's crucial to enhance two-way understanding and communication between capital providers and entrepreneurs in technology ventures.

15.1 Introduction

Starting a technology venture is incredibly hard. Prior research shows that new ventures face more significant problems than other firms, such as lacking resources and capabilities for building competitive advantage and performance (Yeoh and Roth, 1999). High-tech startups are especially vulnerable and easy to fail, with less than half lasting five years (O'Shea and Stevens, 1998).

Among all the significant factors that affect the survival and success of entrepreneurial ventures, financing is one of the most critical issues (Hogan et al., 2017). However, while people hear too many stories that capital providers act as white knights saving entrepreneurs, realities usually differ from these myths.

There are many reasons for capital providers' hesitation when providing money. Besides the high failure rate of technology ventures, capital providers also have difficulty exiting their investments. Most high-tech startups initially do not generate profits to pay dividends (Lazonick, 2009). While venture capitalists can reply with an exit in the form of either an initial public offering (IPO) or acquisition (Cumming and Johan, 2008), there are high barriers to doing so (Cefis et al., 2022). Therefore, capital providers must screen for entrepreneurial ventures to enhance the value of investment activities. In other words, capital providers need to be able to find the one or two haystack needles that have the potential to generate the greatest rewards (Gutmann, 2019).

Thus, funding-seeking entrepreneurs must understand capital providers' criteria (Hall and Hofer, 1993) and the motivations behind their behavior. Some essential questions that may help strengthen understanding include: What is vital to the capital provider? What are their decision-making models, and what is the 'logic' that applies?

15.2 The Difference between Funding Sources

Despite the difficulty in raising money, different sources of funding exist. Each funding source has its criteria for choosing the target. Technology ventures need to consider their development stages, the type of funding available at that stage, and what they'd like to trade off for funding.

DOI: 10.4324/9781003341284-20

There probably are significant variations in the ways that various investor types make decisions (Lerner et al., 2007). Subsidy or grants from the government or organizations may choose the company that has the potential to create jobs in a new sector (Czarnitzki and Lopes-Bento, 2013). An early-stage angel investor may seek an exciting, unique opportunity (Wiltbank et al., 2009). Debt provided by banks and specialized finance companies usually needs collateral (Gan, 2007). Retained earnings constitute a substantial funding source (Thirumalaisamy, 2013) and convey information about companies' growth prospects (Gilchrist and Himmelberg, 1995). In recent years, there have been some new types of funding sources. Equity crowdfunding platforms have played a central role in investment. However, their behavior is still somewhat regarded as a black box (Löher, 2017). Venture debt lending, a financial tool at the intersection of venture capital (VC) and traditional debt, is also used by tech ventures (De Rassenfosse and Fischer, 2016).

High-tech ventures are fond of external equity financing (Hogan et al., 2017), which may be partly due to the reason that, compared to lenders who share in losses but do not benefit if the firm performs well, equity holders have the chance to share gains if the firm is successful (De Rassenfosse and Fischer, 2016). Empirical evidence from market-based economies such as the United States (Coleman and Robb, 2012) and the United Kingdom (Moore, 1993) confirm the preference for external equity for high-tech startup ventures.

For ventures in the startup stage, VC is the primary source of financing and leverage (Cumming et al., 2023). This funding source can fill the void between sources of funds needed for innovation and traditional, lower cost, and available sources of capital (Zider, 1998). While the ventures enter a more stable stage, they may attract more external funding from private equity (PE) (PE) (Cumming et al., 2023). VC usually invests in the relatively early stage of the technology venture, while PE invests in the relatively late stages. Therefore, VC and PE may have different requirements for entrepreneurs. However, the difference between VC and PE seems to diminish since investors may show similar interest in investment targets.

Understanding how the VC/PE industry works is crucial for entrepreneurs. For example, VC/PEs may be concerned more with the return for their limited partners (Manigart and Wright, 2013), while entrepreneurs may focus more on technology and products (Clarysse et al., 2011). The introduction of funding may lead to restructuring the corporate governance structure, limiting future free financing. Entrepreneurs may be forced to give up equity if expected performance is not achieved. This conflict can make collaboration between entrepreneurs and capital providers challenging.

15.3 The Expectations from Capital Providers and Entrepreneurs

From a venture capitalist's perspective, it is essential to acquire an attractive return for VC participants (Barry, 1994). Thus, sufficient upside potential from the invested ventures is needed to generate high returns.

The ideal venture should be in an attractive industry with an attractive market, product, and business model. The ideal entrepreneurs are supposed to have some characteristics in common (e.g., Brandt and Stefansson, 2018; Braun, 2020; Cope et al., 2004): They have a good reputation; they can tell a convincing story; they show approved competence and skill; they build and maintain a diverse team with open ideas; they have a clear goal but still maintain flexibility; most of all, they know the trade-off of funding and have realistic expectations about process and outcome.

From an entrepreneur's perspective, they may be frustrated by suffering an unfair deal process and equity position (Zider, 1998). Sometimes, VCs/PEs may remove entrepreneurs or impose the threat of these things over their heads to strong-arm the entrepreneurs into certain decisions (Wasserman, 2008).

However, this perception by entrepreneurs may be only partially objective since not all entrepreneurs understand that VCs/PEs are in a position of power mainly because they are usually the only source of capital and can influence the network (Zider, 1998). Due to this dominant position, they prioritize picking up qualified ventures with potential success and excellent managers who can deal with uncertainty (Loch et al., 2008).

Another reason for potential conflict between the capital providers and entrepreneurs is the structure of funding. Most VC/PEs have limited years of partnerships (Bhattacharya and Ince, 2012), with several more years' extension at the discretion of the fund's board of advisors or the general partners (Sahlman, 1990). In this case, entrepreneurs may be forced to make hasty decisions because VCs/PEs have liquidity pressure and want to get their money out before the end of the investment period.

Although the capital providers and the ventures are indeed a kind of alliance (Chang, 2004), the goals of both parties don't always align (Higashide and Birley, 2002). Many perspectives, including resource-based, capabilities, institutional, and network theories, may offer insights to further the understanding of the behavior of VC firms (Wright et al., 2005). Entrepreneurs should fully understand their ventures' advantages and disadvantages and find suitable capital providers with record deals with similar ventures. It's critical to increase the matching degree to ensure the success of the financing.

15.4 How Capital Providers Pick Up Their Favorite Targets

Capital providers build up their seeking criteria for investment targets through continuous practice. However, the criteria and the process vary regarding investors' differences (Block et al., 2019).

15.4.1 Does the Business Plan Matter?

The business plan is the most crucial document for venture capitalists to assess the investment opportunity (Kirsch et al., 2009). It also serves as a means of communication. Apart from opportunity, particular claims about intellectual property, market size, and other strategic elements, business planning documents also include non-opportunity-specific information regarding organizational and human capital (Kirsch et al., 2009).

However, the prior findings suggest the time venture capitalists spend on the business plan may not be as high as imagined. For example, a study by Hall and Hofer (1993) found that venture capitalists spent an average of fewer than six minutes on the stage of initial screening and less than 21 minutes on the stage of proposal assessment. In the initial stage, they verify if the ventures align with the VC's requirements and the industry's long-term growth and profitability. In the second stage, they look at the source of the business proposals.

15.4.2 Does the Network Matter?

Studies indicate that a significant portion of venture capitalists' deal flow originates from their networks (Gompers et al., 2020). The best deals often come from a network including trusted investors, entrepreneurs, and professors, especially in the technology industry. Expert assistance is quite helpful in producing quantity and then sifting for quality (Gompers et al., 2020). Those that have already been reviewed by persons known and trusted are easier to receive a high level of interest (Hall and Hofer, 1993).

Since VCs rely on their networks to source opportunities, it is nearly impossible for entrepreneurs to break into the VC firm's doors without any connections (Gompers et al., 2020). Entrepreneurs should identify people in the VC network and integrate into the right social and professional networks, otherwise obtaining funding may be difficult.

15.4.3 Does the Capital Provider Type Matter?

Prior studies (Knockaert et al., 2010) show three VC investor clusters that accordingly concentrate on technology, finance, and human capital. Knockaert and his peers (2010) found that: In the first group, the vital factors include the degree of protection that the technology can receive and the investment manager's relationship with the entrepreneur; the second group pays more attention to the potential return in the business plan; in the third group, the critical factors in the selection process are human factors, such as the leadership capacities of the entrepreneur and the quality (e.g., complementarity and experience) of the team. Other factors, such as the market's size and geographic scope (global or regional), and the judgment of the technology (general-purpose technology or not), seem to have less impact on the VC's decision (Knockaert et al., 2010).

Venture capitalists can also be categorized by the funding sources: private, public, and co-investment (Pierrakis and Saridakis, 2019). The amount of public money varies according to government intervention (Pierrakis and Saridakis, 2019), while private money has followed a strongly cyclical pattern (Jeng and Wells, 2000). For example, recent research shows that early-stage VC activity decreased by 38% in the first two months following the COVID-19 pandemic, despite late-stage VC activity not changing significantly (Howell et al., 2020).

15.5 Why Do Some Seemingly Promising Firms Fail to Secure Funding?

Even if the ventures and entrepreneurs meet all the criteria of VCs, there is no guarantee that a seemingly promising venture will have the chance to get external funding. A survey found that for each eventually closed deal a VC firm considers, on average, 101 opportunities (Gompers et al., 2020).

15.5.1 Heterogeneity at the Firm's Level

There is increasing recognition that new high-tech ventures may be heterogeneous regarding their starting resources and business models (Mustar et al., 2006). Some are subject to long development times; some may require much greater capital and resource investment than other ventures.

There are also persistent differences in levels and rates of development between different sectors of the economy (Harris, 1985). For example, some firms from the manufacturing, agriculture, and energy/utilities sectors may have limited opportunities to get funding since their sales cycles, market potential, and growth trajectories are incompatible with VC's targets (Sarycheva and Muro, 2021).

However, even those attractive-looking technology companies may not be able to secure such funding if they don't exhibit the rapid growth path venture capitalists seek (Sarycheva and Muro, 2021).

15.5.2 Preferences of Valuation Model

The valuation reflects enterprise quality and entrepreneurs' cost of financial capital (Hsu, 2007). VCs rely on methods used to value investments and the information used to arrive at valuations

(Wright et al., 2004). However, there are no uniform valuation models. Potential financial and strategic rewards are highly uncertain, and VCs also lack appropriate measurements to select and evaluate their target companies accurately (Yang et al., 2009).

In practice, venture capitalists rely on prior experience of success and failure to develop their criteria and routines (Yang et al., 2009); thus, they have their preference in selecting the valuation model, which leads to different results. Notably, valuing new firms is notoriously challenging, and every approach carries some degree of uncertainty (Yang et al., 2009).

15.5.3 Timing for Funding and Exiting

The prior study also shows that 'timing' for searching for funding is critical as VC's aggregate deal volume and size often decline substantially in recessions (Howell et al., 2020). The sensitivity of early-stage VC investment to market conditions, evident in recessions spanning four decades from 1976 to 2017, prompts inquiries on the pro-cyclical nature of VC (Howell et al., 2020).

The most recent example is the considerable volatility that the VC industry experienced in the past several years. From 2018 to 2020, the total value of venture funding in tech declined by 13%, but almost doubled in Q1 2021 from the same period in 2020, over twice the growth rate of other sectors (Schallehn and Johnson, 2021). However, with the layoffs spread across the tech industry in 2022, tech-startup investors expect a big 'reset' that may create two years of both pain and opportunity (PitchBook, 2022).

The timing of the exit is also important. Only the successful exit can be seen as a realized return. IPOs become the widely accepted way of exit due to their openness (Draho, 2004), but it is also the way most affected by the economic environment and industry cycles (Angelini and Foglia, 2018). Thus, it is necessary to look systematically at the determinants and the drivers behind the kind of ebbs and flows we have seen in the cycles (Gompers and Lerner, 2004).

15.6 Bridging between Capital Providers and Entrepreneurs

Khanin and Turel (2015) propose that venture capitalists and entrepreneurs may experience two types of conflict: One is driven by perceived inequities in economic and social exchange, and another is about the allocation of control rights and relationship issues by the perceived inequities in power relations. In addition, Collewaert and Fassin's (2013) research shows that perceived unethical behavior among partners triggers conflicts through increased fault attribution or blaming, increasing the likelihood of a negative partnership outcome such as failure or another form of involuntary exit.

A mutual understanding is necessary to solve the issues mentioned above. Huang and Knight (2017) developed a theoretical model based on the exchange theory (e.g., Blau, 1964; Cropanzano and Mitchell, 2005). This model highlights the multifaceted relationships that entrepreneurs and investors share (both affective and instrumental dimensions), and the bidirectional exchanges of social and financial resources used to build these relationships over time.

It's in each party's interest to realize that reciprocal exchange benefits relationship development. Indeed, the goal of a VC firm has never been just to focus on the financial aspects but also on how they integrate into their portfolio and leverage their experience and knowledge to support the founding management team.

Another realistic approach is introducing prospect theory (e.g., Kahneman and Tversky, 2013) into decision-making and relationship maintenance. By converting the simple profit and loss value into a comprehensive prospect value, VC institutions, and entrepreneurial enterprises can construct a multi-objective optimization model (Gunantara, 2018) to maximize the comprehensive prospect value, achieving stronger long-term results cooperation.

15.7 Summary

An objective and comprehensive understanding of the relationships between entrepreneurs and capital providers is essential to avoid unnecessary communication costs and unrealistic expectations. For entrepreneurs who want external funding to develop their ventures, it would be of great value if they do a background check to know more about the capital providers' attributes and working styles. They benefit from the weighing between financing and strategic fit, with prioritization of critical success factors. Meanwhile, as the global macro environment changes, the financing environment of the capital market will also change accordingly. Therefore, it is necessary to keep track of the dynamics at any time. Those who understand and satisfy all the necessary financing criteria can come to the table with a strong negotiating position.

References

Angelini, E., & Foglia, M. (2018). The relationship between IPO and macroeconomics factors: An empirical analysis from UK market. *Annals of Economics and Finance*, *19*(1), 319–336.

Barry, C. B. (1994). New directions in research on venture capital finance. *Financial Management*, *23*(3), 3–15.

Bhattacharya, D., & Ince, O. (2012). Last Exit Before Toll: Venture Capital Funds and Liquidity Pressure. Available at https://ssrn.com/abstract=2024277.

Blau, P. (1964). *Exchange and power in social life*. New York: Wiley.

Block, J., Fisch, C., Vismara, S., & Andres, R. (2019). Private equity investment criteria: An experimental conjoint analysis of venture capital, business angels, and family offices. *Journal of Corporate Finance*, *58*, 329–352.

Brandt, M., & Stefansson, S. (2018). *The personality venture capitalists look for in an entrepreneur: An artificial intelligence approach to personality analysis*. M.Sc. thesis, KTH Royal Institute of Technology, Stockholm, Sweden.

Braun, A. (October 7, 2020). VCs Consider This Trait Most Important When Choosing Entrepreneurs to Invest In. Retrieved from https://www.entrepreneur.com/leadership/vcs-consider-this-trait-most-important-when-choosing/356109.

Cefis, E., Bettinelli, C., Coad, A., & Marsili, O. (2022). Understanding firm exit: A systematic literature review. *Small Business Economics*, *59*(2), 423–446.

Chang, S. J. (2004). Venture capital financing, strategic alliances, and the initial public offerings of Internet startups. *Journal of Business Venturing*, *19*(5), 721–741.

Clarysse, B., Wright, M., & Van de Velde, E. (2011). Entrepreneurial origin, technological knowledge, and the growth of spin-off companies. *Journal of Management Studies*, *48*(6), 1420–1442.

Coleman, S., & Robb, A. (2012). Capital structure theory and new technology firms: Is there a match? *Management Research Review*, *35*(2), 106–120.

Collewaert, V., & Fassin, Y. (2013). Conflicts between entrepreneurs and investors: The impact of perceived unethical behavior. *Small Business Economics*, *40*(3), 635–649.

Cope, J., Cave, F., & Eccles, S. (2004). Attitudes of venture capital investors towards entrepreneurs with previous business failure. *Venture Capital*, *6*(2–3), 147–172.

Cropanzano, R., & Mitchell, M. S. (2005). Social exchange theory: An interdisciplinary review. *Journal of management*, *31*(6), 874–900.

Cumming, D., & Johan, S. (2008). Information asymmetries, agency costs and venture capital exit outcomes. *Venture capital*, *10*(3), 197–231.

Cumming, D., Kumar, S., Lim, W. M., & Pandey, N. (2023). Mapping the venture capital and private equity research: A bibliometric review and future research agenda. *Small Business Economics*, *61*(1), 173–221.

Czarnitzki, D., & Lopes-Bento, C. (2013). Value for money? New microeconometric evidence on public R&D grants in Flanders. *Research Policy*, *42*(1), 76–89.

De Rassenfosse, G., & Fischer, T. (2016). Venture debt financing: Determinants of the lending decision. *Strategic Entrepreneurship Journal*, *10*(3), 235–256.

Draho, J. (2004). *The IPO decision: Why and how companies go public*. Edward Elgar Publishing.

Gan, J. (2007). Collateral, debt capacity, and corporate investment: Evidence from a natural experiment. *Journal of Financial Economics*, *85*(3), 709–734.

Gilchrist, S., & Himmelberg, C. P. (1995). Evidence on the role of cash flow for investment. *Journal of Monetary Economics*, *36*(3), 541–572.

Gompers, P. A., & Lerner, J. (2004). *The venture capital cycle*. MIT Press.

Gompers, P. A., Gornall, W., Kaplan, S. N., & Strebulaev, I. A. (2020). How do venture capitalists make decisions?. *Journal of Financial Economics*, *135*(1), 169–190.

Gunantara, N. (2018). A review of multi-objective optimization: Methods and its applications. *Cogent Engineering*, *5*(1), 1502242.

Gutmann, T. (2019). Harmonizing corporate venturing modes: An integrative review and research agenda. *Management Review Quarterly*, *69*(2), 121–157.

Hall, J., & Hofer, C. W. (1993). Venture capitalists' decision criteria in new venture evaluation. *Journal of Business Venturing*, *8*(1), 25–42.

Harris, D. J. (1985). The theory of economic growth: From steady states to uneven development. In *Issues in contemporary macroeconomics and distribution* (pp. 378–394). Palgrave Macmillan.

Higashide, H., & Birley, S. (2002). The consequences of conflict between the venture capitalist and the entrepreneurial team in the United Kingdom from the perspective of the venture capitalist. *Journal of Business Venturing*, *17*(1), 59–81.

Hogan, T., Hutson, E., & Drnevich, P. (2017). Drivers of external equity funding in small high-tech ventures. *Journal of Small Business Management*, *55*(2), 236–253.

Howell, S. T., Lerner, J., Nanda, R., & Townsend, R. R. (2020). *Financial distancing: How venture capital follows the economy down and curtails innovation*. National Bureau of Economic Research.

Hsu, D. H. (2007). Experienced entrepreneurial founders, organizational capital, and venture capital funding. *Research Policy*, *36*(5), 722–741.

Huang, L., & Knight, A. P. (2017). Resources and relationships in entrepreneurship: An exchange theory of the development and effects of the entrepreneur-investor relationship. *Academy of Management Review*, *42*(1), 80–102.

Jeng, L. A., & Wells, P. C. (2000). The determinants of venture capital funding: Evidence across countries. *Journal of Corporate Finance*, *6*(3), 241–289.

Kahneman, D., & Tversky, A. (2013). Prospect theory: An analysis of decision under risk. In MacLean, L.C. and Ziemba, W.T. (Eds) *Handbook of the fundamentals of financial decision making: Part I* (pp. 99–127). World Scientific Publishing, Hackensack.

Khanin, D., & Turel, O. (2015). Conflicts and regrets in the venture capitalist–entrepreneur relationship. *Journal of Small Business Management*, *53*(4), 949–969.

Kirsch, D., Goldfarb, B., & Gera, A. (2009). Form or substance: The role of business plans in venture capital decision making. *Strategic Management Journal*, *30*(5), 487–515.

Knockaert, M., Clarysse, B., & Wright, M. (2010). The extent and nature of heterogeneity of venture capital selection behaviour in new technology-based firms. *R&d Management*, *40*(4), 357–371.

Lazonick, W. (2009). The new economy business model and the crisis of US capitalism. *Capitalism and Society*, *4*(2), 1–70.

Lerner, J., Schoar, A., & Wongsunwai, W. (2007). Smart institutions, foolish choices: The limited partner performance puzzle. *The Journal of Finance*, *62*(2), 731–764.

Loch, C. H., Solt, M. E., & Bailey, E. M. (2008). Diagnosing unforeseeable uncertainty in a new venture. *Journal of Product Innovation Management*, *25*(1), 28–46.

Löher, J. (2017). The interaction of equity crowdfunding platforms and ventures: An analysis of the prese-lection process. *Venture Capital, 19*(1–2), 51–74.

Manigart, S., & Wright, M. (2013). Reassessing the relationships between private equity investors and their portfolio companies. *Small Business Economics, 40*(3), 479–492.

Moore, B. (1993). *Financial constraints to the growth and development of small high-technology firms.* Department of Applied Economics, Small Business Research Centre, University of Cambridge.

Mustar, P., Renault, M., Colombo, M. G., Piva, E., Fontes, M., Lockett, A., ... & Moray, N. (2006). Con-ceptualising the heterogeneity of research-based spin-offs: A multi-dimensional taxonomy. *Research Policy, 35*(2), 289–308.

O'Shea, M., & Stevens, C. (1998). Governments as venture capitalists. Organisation for Economic Coop-eration and Development. *The OECD Observer,* (213), 26–30.

Pierrakis, Y., & Saridakis, G. (2019). The role of venture capitalists in the regional innovation ecosystem: a comparison of networking patterns between private and publicly backed venture capital funds. *The Journal of Technology Transfer, 44*(3), 850–873.

PitchBook. (2022, July 13). PitchBook – NVCA Venture Monitor (Q2, 2022). Retrieved from https://pitchbook.com/news/reports/q2-2022-pitchbook-nvca-venture-monitor.

Sahlman, W. A. (1990). The structure and governance of venture-capital organizations. *Journal of Finan-cial Economics, 27,* 473–521.

Sarycheva, A., & Muro, M. (September 29, 2021). Beyond VC: Financing technology entrepreneur-ship in the rest of America. Retrieved from https://www.brookings.edu/blog/the-avenue/2021/09/29/beyond-vc-financing-technology-entrepreneurship-in-the-rest-of-america/.

Schallehn, M., & Johnson, C. (September 20, 2021). Why Venture Capitalists Are Doubling Down on Tech-nology. Retrieved from https://www.bain.com/insights/why-venture-capitalists-are-doubling-down-on-technology-tech-report-2021/.

Thirumalaisamy, R. (2013). Firm growth and retained earnings behavior–A Study on Indian firms. *Euro-pean Journal of Business and Management, 5*(27), 40–57.

Wasserman, N. (February, 2008). The Founder's Dilemma. Retrieved from https://hbr.org/2008/02/the-founders-dilemma.

Wiltbank, R., Read, S., Dew, N., & Sarasvathy, S. D. (2009). Prediction and control under uncertainty: Outcomes in angel investing. *Journal of Business Venturing, 24*(2), 116–133.

Wright, M., Pruthi, S., & Lockett, A. (2005). International venture capital research: From cross-country comparisons to crossing borders. *International Journal of Management Reviews, 7*(3), 135–165.

Wright, M., Lockett, A., Pruthi, S., Manigart, S., Sapienza, H., Desbrieres, P., & Hommel, U. (2004). Venture capital investors, capital markets, valuation and information: US, Europe and Asia. *Journal of International Entrepreneurship, 2*(4), 305–326.

Yang, Y., Narayanan, V. K., & Zahra, S. (2009). Developing the selection and valuation capabilities through learning: The case of corporate venture capital. *Journal of Business Venturing, 24*(3), 261–273.

Yeoh, P. L., & Roth, K. (1999). An empirical analysis of sustained advantage in the US pharmaceutical industry: Impact of firm resources and capabilities. *Strategic Management Journal, 20*(7), 637–653.

Zider, B. (1998). How venture capital works. *Harvard Business Review, 76*(6), 131–139.

Part VI
Team and Organization

16 Team Building – It Is All about People, the Mission, and Values

Margaret A. Goralski and Krystyna Górniak-Kocikowska

16.1 Introduction

In 1954, when James Killian, the then tenth President of Massachusetts Institute of Technology, who was also a scientist himself with a deep interest in science and technology, was asked by the President of the United States to commence a study "of the country's technological capabilities to meet some of its current problems," he created the Technological Capabilities Panel (TCP) by gathering 42 of the nation's brightest scientists (Dean 2017, 48). Killian hand selected each member of the panel for their scientific and/or technological expertise, their clearance level, and the degree of secrecy involved in the many projects that they would undertake. One of the men chosen was Edwin "Din" Land, founder of Polaroid. Land decided to have just five men to serve on his panel utilizing one of his favorite management theories – "that any committee should fit within a taxi" (Dean 2017, 49). Killian reported directly to the Central Intelligence Agency (CIA).

On future CIA projects, each team of people worked on a portion of a project in a discreet location unknown to others on the project. They may have known their end goal, but very few knew the entire mission. The workforce depended on workers coming together because they believed in the strength of the organization for which they worked and believed that they were members of a unique team of men personally chosen to complete a critical mission. Management of the team was extremely complex and directed overall by a very few men (Dean 2017). The second CIA science and technology program team, code-named Oxcart, was even smaller than the one formulated by Killian. Kelly Johnson and Ben Rich decided to remove the door that separated two of the teams. It worked so well that they removed all the doors so that solving a problem became as easy as yelling across the room (Dean 2017, 61).

When Tony Hsieh, co-founder of an internet advertising network, LinkExchange, was asked during an interview at Stanford University why he sold the company to Microsoft in 1998 for $265 million, his response was that in honesty he had run out of friends. The organization had been built by adding friends along the way as their area of expertise was needed and then during expansion as people were required. Hsieh went on to found and become CEO of Zappos, an online shoe and clothing company. In 2009, Zappos was bought by Amazon for $1.2 billion dollars. Hsieh stayed on as CEO until 2020 when he retired at the age of 46. He did not build this organization on friendships. He used innovation and acquired knowledge from his past experiences as a leader to build a strong and robust organization.

Today, when we speak about formation of workforce ecosystems, we refer to ecosystems that combine teams of internal employees, external contractors, service providers, gig workers, and even software bots (Altman et al. 2021); individuals and groups of people are again being chosen to work on specific projects based on their particular area of expertise. As noted in the

DOI: 10.4324/9781003341284-22

above reference to teams that were created by TCP, the CIA, and Hsieh, workforce ecosystems or teams constructed of people with unique talents were developed prior to the Covid pandemic and will be continued long after the pandemic subsides. Yet, Covid has in some ways expanded the possibilities due to leaders being forced to make critical decisions swiftly to keep business and the economy thriving at a time of deep disruption.

16.2 Workforce Ecosystems

Some of the same characteristics of team formation that were put in place by Killian, Johnson, Rich, Hsieh, and others prevail today in the formulation of unique ecosystems of workers who implement a specific plan regardless of their geographic location on the planet and whether they are internal or external contractors. As the workforce increasingly becomes dependent on external workers, new management practices, systems, and processes need to be designed to incorporate these employees into what until now had been dominated by internal employees. There is a tension to reconcile the two realities of internal and external factions working together on the same project.

Altman, Schwartz, Kiron, Jones, and Kearns-Manolatos (2021) explored how various organizations viewed augmenting internal employees with external workers to fill gaps and add value back to the organization. WPP, a British multinational company, visualizes its workforce as concentric rings and doesn't limit itself to the innermost rings of internal employees; Workday, an American enterprise software company, uses a continuum analogy to include contingent workers and freelancers; and the U.S. National Aeronautics and Space Administration (NASA) includes gig workers who may work at NASA for a season while also working at other jobs at the same time as they are part of the NASA team. The terminology may be different, the workforce may not be called a workforce ecosystem, but more and more organizations are including external workers into the overall make-up of teams to add value and specific areas of expertise.

In addition to Amazon's one million employees worldwide, there are two million independent owners who offer merchandize through the Amazon marketplace. While remaining independent, these owners complement Amazon's business while adding value to the Amazon marketplace (Altman et al. 2021). There are both complementarities and interdependencies that exist in these new workforce ecosystems. Additionally, Amazon has approximately 200,000 robots physically working alongside humans in its warehouses (Altman et al. 2021). NASA has virtual bots that are employees within its Information Technology system. The bots are given unique IDs and issued virtual employee badges (Altman et al. 2021, 9). Technology can also become a worker by completing tasks that had previously been performed by humans. There is a lively discussion taking place in artificial intelligence circles around the status of virtual (robotic) employees getting paid for their work, etc., as well as other ethical issues related to this new phenomenon.

An angel investor and member of the board at Launchpad Venture Group uses yet another word, patchwork, when talking about startup ventures with limited resources utilizing a variety of talent to get the job done.

> You end up thinking about … the various ways you can use talent: part-timers, temps, the platforms, the agencies, the remote developers, advisers, … lawyers, … bankers…. Every hire that a startup makes is a financial bet. Having a bigger patchwork allows you flexibility.
>
> (Altman, et al. 2021, 4)

and makes the venture's risk smaller.

These ecosystems usually include people of diverse talents, background, experience, and perspectives to maximize the possibilities being explored. This diversity leads to innovative solutions. However, diverse teams do not always work together harmoniously. There are challenges that come with diverse ecosystems of workers. Nonetheless, evidence proves that diversity improves performance (Satell and Windschit 2021). Leaders need to build teams that are diverse and yet unified enough to work efficiently together to get results.

A workforce ecosystem is not necessarily the creation of a completely new structure. It is a new approach that regards the organization and relationships between structures already engaged in fulfilling the company's goals, especially in interactions between internal and external workforces, humans and artificial intelligence. In that sense, a workforce ecosystem can be the mental plane on which the structural configuration of a company is strategized, irrespective of whether the company is a startup or a well-established one. It seems, however, that startups can benefit greatly from following the workforce ecosystem model. It could make it easier for them to deal more efficiently with the variety of hurdles they will encounter while establishing themselves. Following are more detailed remarks regarding some of the most vital aspects of a workforce ecosystem, such as leadership, mission, values, and culture.

16.3 Leadership, Mission, Values

James Killian, Kelly Johnson, Ben Rich, and the scientists and engineers that worked together with them believed strongly in what they were doing. These leaders, among others, like John Parangosky, national reconnaissance pioneer, were men who were called together into a joint effort to form a TCP, design the U-2, and/or design and deploy a photo reconnaissance satellite. They did it because they believed in the mission of the people and organizations that they worked for – the U.S. President, the Navy, the CIA. Parangosky showed a unique ability to assemble and manage a team that included government workers and private contractors. Killian wrote that

> the United States was capable of almost any engineering accomplishment that it considered necessary to national survival. It possessed in its manpower and industrial base the power to achieve almost any single goal it set, provided only that it was willing to concentrate its energies and resources on that goal.
>
> (Dean 2017, 48)

Tony Hsieh believed that organizations were more likely to innovate and thrive when they unleashed the potential of individuals and the power of self-organizing teams. He believed that an organizational model must distribute its decision-making authority to self-organizing circles made up of employees who act as "human sensors" to allow the organization to be more adaptable, innovative, and resilient. Hsieh strongly believed that employees must find the intersection of what they are good at, what they are passionate about, and what adds value to the organization (Hsieh 2017).

Hsieh considered three dimensions to be foundational: culture and values, purpose, and market-based dynamics. Self-organization is about having an entrepreneurial mind-set. One study found that successful female entrepreneurs had three unique characteristics: tolerance of ambiguity, intellectual curiosity, and emotional intelligence (Orr and Lewis n.d.). All these are important characteristics for self-organization. Hsieh quoted Charles Darwin, "It's not the fastest or strongest or most intelligent of species that survives. It's the one most adaptable to change" (Hsieh 2017).

Altman ct al. state that entities within an ecosystem rely upon others to get work done and accomplish shared objectives. You can see by the above examples of the scientists and engineers that gathered to work under the men of the CIA and the self-organized employees of Zappos, that these are not new objectives. The success or failure to each of these goals is dependent on the ability of the people and recently even the bots to collaborate effectively. The interdependencies and self-organization of each part is fundamental to a workforce ecosystem. There are challenges in orchestrating a large, diverse workforce especially when they are housed in many geographic locations and answer to many different cultural norms and entities.

What holds these diverse workforces together is the common culture – the objective to be met or the goal to be accomplished. The team must have shared beliefs and a trust in the mission and the values of the organization to hold the project together. Altman et al. ask how an organization can maintain quality in a world in which an organization is just buying a slice of someone's time. The mission and the organizational values must be strong enough to make one responsible for delivering whatever expertise she or he has agreed to.

Leaders need to identify the shared values that are important and build change upon a common ground that exists within all workers on a project. Managers need to articulate their organizations mission and hire people who are inspired to dedicate their talents to that mission (Satell and Windschit 2021). Hsieh believed so strongly in the importance of mission and value that a person could be hired or fired based on whether they were living the organization's core values, independent of their job performance.

The environment of work is undergoing profound change. New technologies, especially artificial intelligence and automation, are overturning entire sectors of industry. There is a great paradigm shift that is taking place. Culture and values are how an organization honors its mission. Values are a critical element of strategic intent. Future success will depend on an organization's ability to articulate a higher purpose.

16.4 Culture

Peter Drucker, management consultant, educator, and author believed that culture was vital to the sustainability of an organization and its societal values. As organizations include external workers into their ecosystems, internal employees feel threatened or, in some cases, leave the organization to become "free agents" themselves. A prime example of this is nurses within a hospital system vs. traveling nurses who are paid more even though they may have the same or fewer qualifications and duties than internal nurses. This often causes a schism in the workforce and multiple layers of treatment by managers or supervisors.

Culture is shaped by the rules that reside in the mind of each employee. Each interprets a situation in their own way and decides how to react based on observations and situations. An organization's cultural strength is determined by the similarity of the rules in the minds of its employees. The culture is weak if the rules vary among individuals – each acting in his or her own self-interest and strong if there is a sense of commonality where the rules are interpreted similarly (Martin 2022).

When a new ecosystem is introduced into the organization, the culture must shift. How to smoothly incorporate new talent into an existing workforce becomes a challenge with internal employees resisting change and external employees being blindsided by a culture that has established rules that are yet unknown to them. Culture can be changed, but that would take time and effort. Change would be slow and incremental.

Roger Martin, strategy advisor, suggests small incremental cultural changes like sitting at a round table rather than a rectangular one during a brainstorming session. Alex "Sandy" Pentland (2012) and his team at the MIT Human Dynamics Laboratory identified group dynamics that characterized high performance teams – "energy, creativity, and shared communication" (Pentland 2012). The team found that the "best predictors of productivity were energy and engagement outside of formal meetings" (Pentland 2012) so even changing the coffee break of employees to a time when all could meet socially for conversation increased the performance of teams. Lack of these types of opportunities was one of the things that employees complained about most during the pandemic.

One way to change the culture of an organization is to have the ecosystem work together on a project as a coherent team in the same way as consultants on a project would bring together a team of people to reach a specific goal. Internal and external workers would move freely from one project to another with teams formulated based on accomplishing the best results. When the project is complete, the team would be dismantled, internal workers would move to a new project, and external workers would fill the gaps. Importance is placed on the project and its successful results not on whether the team members are internal or external. It is possible that internal workers may eventually become redundant and a new concept of the corporation, or a new business model where teams of freelancers, humans, or bots, or humans and bots, may be assembled for a project and then realigned creating a new configuration of the workplace ecosystem may be created.

Most organizations have faced profound and accelerating disruptions. Employees are being asked to work toward a common goal. Teams are being asked to dream big and define what is needed to make a transformation happen (Sancier-Sultan 2022). Many organizations have tried to replicate the ecosystem success of technological giants like Apple and Amazon, but some have struggled and failed. Ecosystems are complex. An organization needs to define an approach that captures maximum value for their organization. They can define their ecosystem strategy by assessing trends and characteristics in the market and their "fit" within a given ecosystem. An organization needs to assess its own value-creation agenda and decide if they want to create new products or services, grow their core business, build a new solution, or improve their efficiency (Dietz, Khan and Rab 2021, Sengupta et al. 2019). Once the internal strategy is defined, then organizational leaders can decide how to create and adapt an ecosystem that is specific to their needs.

16.5 Corporate Engagement with Entrepreneurial Innovation

Innovation and competitive pressure are driving organizations to tap into entrepreneurial ecosystems in their regions (Budden and Murray 2022). These ecosystems include corporations, entrepreneurs, governments, investors, and research institutions. It is important for organizations to become trusted partners with a commitment to building relations with entrepreneurial leaders within their own organization as well as with external players.

As discussed earlier in this chapter, many entrepreneurs begin their journey with friends and family and then expand by building an ecosystem of others – angel investors, venture capitalists, attorneys, accountants, bankers, etc. Some entrepreneurs also include governmental agencies in their ecosystem if there are set asides or opportunities for growth.

Budden and Murray (2022) require organizational leaders who want to engage with innovation ecosystems to ask themselves these questions: What they want to acquire from the ecosystem engagement, whom they want to engage with and who from their organization will engage, and how they are going to engage to ensure effective interactions.

While leaders are striving to understand what they want to acquire from the ecosystem engagement, there may be diverse answers dependent on what benefits they desire for the entire organization.

An organization may want to enhance its own internal innovation by expanding outward into startup activities that will benefit both the organization as well as startups in the region. Organizational leaders must ask themselves what they can bring to the table – such as funding or ideas on what customers need. Organizations can provide startups and entrepreneurs expertise to navigate governmental regulations or knowledge about supply chains, and how to scale up when the time comes (Budden and Murray 2022). They should be looking for the same ecosystem complementarities and interdependencies as discussed earlier in this chapter in order for the organization and entrepreneurial venture to succeed.

Startups explore new solutions to emerging problems, but not all startups are the same (Aulet and Murray 2013; Budden and Murray 2022). Some are innovation-driven enterprises (IDEs), and others are small business entrepreneurships or small and medium enterprises. IDEs would be those that most large organizations would partner with as they experiment, learn, gain information, and determine which paths to explore and which ones to abort. (See Budden and Murray for more specifics about various stages of startups.) Most regions in the United States already have communities that exist where entrepreneurs gather in shared spaces and ecosystem programs. An organization could form a larger array of relationships within these communities and then narrow the relationships down to those that offer the best solutions for each entity. This type of immersion also ensures that organization representatives and entrepreneurs have an opportunity to discuss the possibilities and decipher how to form an ecosystem of competitive advantage.

16.6 Conclusion

Within this chapter, we have discussed team building on various levels beginning with a very structured system of bringing men together to work harmoniously on specific governmental projects. Then, we turned the discussion to Tony Hsieh, a man with a brilliant mind who had definite researched ideas for successful team formulation, implementation, and evaluation.

As team building has emerged into design for creation of successful ecosystems, we have drawn some conclusions from previously successful team building into the new ideal of an engaging ecosystem that fills internal gaps in an organization and allows internal and external workers within an ecosystem to come together regardless of geographic location or culture. It is the mission and values of an organization that allow successful results to emerge in these ecosystems through project-focused strategies.

Some schisms exist when a new ecosystem is introduced into an organization. Diversity brings excellence but also rifts that must be addressed. The cultural rules under which an organization exists in the minds of its internal employees, must shift to embrace new incumbents whether human or robotic or the ecosystem will fail. There are strategies for change, but change is slow and incremental. Treating organizations as immutable would be a serious mistake.

As corporations understand that innovation is essential to their growth and sustainability, new ecosystems are occurring between organizations that can bring expertise, funding, and dependable industry data to entrepreneurs and entrepreneurial ventures that can experiment, learn, revise, and create feedback loops for new innovative solutions to problems existing or in the future. With the right preparation and by understanding what the organization wishes to achieve through these entrepreneurial ecosystems, partnerships can create successful new liaisons (Pentland 2012). Ultimately, team building and successful workforce ecosystems will depend on people, the mission, and values.

References

Altman, Elizabeth J., Jeff Schwartz, David Kiron, Robin Jones, and Diana Kearns-Manolatos. 2021. "Workforce Ecosystems - A New Strategic Approach to the Future of Work." *MIT Sloan Management Review and Deloitte.*

Aulet, Bill, and Fiona Murray. 2013. *A Tale of Two Entrepreneurs: Understanding Differences in the Types of Entrepreneurship in the Economy.* May. https://www.issuelab.org/resources/15236/15236.pdf.

Bettencourt, Luis M. A., Jose Lobo, Dirk Helbing, Christian Kuhnert, and Geoffrey B. West. 2007. "Growth, Innovation, Scaling, and the Pace of Life in Cities." *PNAS* 7301–7306.

Budden, Philip, and Fiona Murray. 2022. *Strategically Engaging with Innovation Ecosystems.* July 20. https://sloanreview.mit.edu/article/strategically-engaging-with-innovation-ecosystems/.

Dean, Josh. 2017. *The Taking of K-129.* New York: Random House LLC.

Dietz, Miklos, Hamza Khan, and Istvan Rab. 2021. *How Do Companies Create Value from Digital Ecosystems?* https://www.mckinsey.com/capabilities/mckinsey-digital/our-insights/how-do-companies-create-value-from-digital-ecosystems.

Hsieh, Tony, interview by Aaron De Smet, and Chris Gagnon. 2017. *Safe Enough to Try: An Interview with Zappos CEO Tony Hsieh* (October 19).

Martin, Roger L. 2022. *A New Way to Think – Your Guide to Superior Management Effectiveness.* Boston: Harvard Business Review Press.

Orr, Evelyn, and James Lewis. n.d. *Korn Ferry.* Accessed January 11, 2023. https://www.kornferry.com/institute/ceo-insights-can-organizations-gain-edge-tapping-female-entrepreneurial-talent.

Pentland, Alex. 2012. *The New Science of Building Great Teams.* April. https://www.mckinsey.com/industries/financial-services/our-insights/how-the-best-companies-create-value-from-their-ecosystems.

Sancier-Sultan, Sandra. 2022. *Turning a Transformation into a Reinvention.* December 14. https://www.mckinsey.com/~/media/mckinsey/email/rethink/2022/12/2022-12-14d.html.

Satell, Greg, and Cathy Windschit. 2021. *High-Performing Teams Start with a Culture of Shared Values.* May 11. https://hbr.org/2021/05/high-performing-teams-start-with-a-culture-of-shared-values.

Sengupta, Joydeep, HV Vinayak, Miklos Dietz, Violet Chung, Xiang Ji, Lingxiao Xiao, and Luke Li. 2019. *How the Best Companies Create Value from Their Ecosystems.* November. https://www.mckinsey.com/~/media/mckinsey/industries/financial%20services/our%20insights/how%20the%20best%20companies%20create%20value%20from%20their%20ecosystems/how-the-best-companies-create-value-from-their-ecosystems-final.pdf.

Wessendorf, Christoph Philipp, Jens Kegelmann, and Orestis Terzidis. 2019. "Determinants of Early-Stage Technology Venture Valuation by Business Angels and Venture Capitalists." *International Journal of Entrepreneurial Venturing* 11 (5): 489–520.

17 Entrepreneurial Leadership

Edward Agbai

17.1 Introduction

In today's digital world, what we know, or experience gathered in the past, could become unreliable if not improved upon or finding new ways to get things done. Collaborations and interface with others in the business environment to understand stakeholders' unique requirements and the inherent weaknesses and strengths in the system become the bedrock for understanding the unique entrepreneurial environment. Relying on the old ways without understanding the needs of stakeholders could end up re-enforcing stunted growth. In most cases, when the inventive and up to the minute ways take a foothold, it will take us by surprise, and in native African setting, the ancestors or the village people as blamed for failure of lack of preparedness.

Take instances between Tesla and GM motors of the USA, Volkswagen of Germany, or Toyota of Japan. Between Elon Musk and managers in these automobile companies, who can boast of experience in the auto industry? Our answer is as good as mine, but today, Elon Musk has changed the automobile industry's narrative and dynamics. The other automobile companies run from pillar to post as Tesla gives them a chase for their money. Five to ten years from now, if most traditional car companies do not try the evolutionary approach and build better cars, they will doubtlessly become bankrupt if it is not already happening. At the same time, tech companies (Tesla, Apple, Google) will take the revolutionary approach and take over the market.

The mid and later year of the third decade of the 21st century will see pressing needs for full integration into the digital ecosystem for vehicles, opening new revenue streams for the tech industry as the automaker overhauls its human-to-machine interface. The two years of the pandemic have witnessed leapfrogging of digital transformation while automakers face escalating challenges from Covid-19 setbacks and struggle to rebound. Young customers demand product innovation, more significant supply chain resilience, and a memorable customer experience.

Technology is increasingly defining the way businesses run and conduct activities today. In today's global workplace, micro and small-scale enterprises, the need for technology has never been greater than before. The long-term economic growth and prosperity of developing economies need the active participation of all, including entrepreneurs whose business performance needs to be examined. Entrepreneurs in the tech space are fast becoming an essential stakeholder as employers of labor and revenue-generating outfit that increases the country's Gross Domestic Product of their countries (Ratten, 2018; Vinsel & Russell, 2020). Entrepreneurs played significant roles in providing solutions for societies and businesses by exploiting entrepreneurial opportunities.

Over the years, startups have gained increasing attention globally because of their role in various economies (Global Entrepreneurship Monitor, 2012). In Africa, startups play vital roles in the economic development of their communities. However, cultural limitations have hindered

DOI: 10.4324/9781003341284-23

their progress in lower- and middle-income countries (Iganiga, 2010). Such limitations include the distribution of social wealth in education and health (Ibru, 2009). Nevertheless, startups contribute to their countries' rural and urban economic development through significant involvement in credit schemes and job creation through micro-enterprises (Hammawa & Hashim, 2016).

Entrepreneurship is felt generally as a developmental & progressive idea for the business world (Shane, 2003). Hence, entrepreneurial activities are essential for rural economic transformation and poverty alleviation mechanisms in developing economies to create diverse opportunities for entrepreneurs. Effective utilization of human resources for their benefit is one of the most critical challenges business organizations face in the contemporary and trendy industrialized world, where entrepreneurs are edged-on toward micro business growth and development in the rural economy (Histrich & Ramadani, 2017; Soloveva, 2022). Entrepreneurial activities do not negate any gender participation, nor is it only for men. Instead, somewhat economic hardship enables more women to look toward entrepreneurship activities to mitigate the economic hardship (Hammawa & Hashim, 2016; Ranhagen, 2021).

Tracking the values and practices that leadership brings to an institution could be challenging, a leader needs to be committed to the services he/she provides and must be able to communicate that value and its attendant vision to the followers and stakeholders alike. The technology industry is a growing industry, and the leadership provides direction and focus to team members and the organizations. The tech profession has diverse and varied domains and areas of specialties within its fold; these diverse bases of IT practitioners need strong leadership to drive change and embrace innovation.

Increasingly the technological sector is characterized by frequent technology turnovers to improve better user interface and reduce delivery time. These improvements address problems of internal controls arising from increased demands for transparency, accountability, and active stakeholders' engagement. The tech stakeholders have vested interests in the industry because improved performances lead to positive outcomes for the entire businesses. However, innovations are happening at a jet leading a dynamic mix. Closely related to innovations are increased demand for tech products and external factors like changing demography, government policies, and globalization.

Expectation management is at the fulcrum of the tech management, leaders need to be constantly reminded of the fundamental role tech play in the lives of people as data are generated daily in terabytes. The core responsibility of the leader is to make the objective of the growth and innovation clear to stakeholders (Agbai, 2018). Leadership is at the core of driving changes at all levels of the tech domains, and it is spread across the broad spectrum of management in the various tech organizations.

In this chapter, we will examine the various leadership principles in relation to the tech and entrepreneurship landscape. Leadership is crucial in shaping organizational culture within the context of developing processes and procedures and its implementation.

How do leaders harness the potential that exists within the tech space and use it to drive innovations? The leaders need to be abreast of the new changes and what they portend. The technology turnovers have not spared any industry from education, health, manufacturing among others. What leadership principles will be suitable for the technological and entrepreneurial space and how will the principles adapt to the changes. There are various principles that speak to how leaders accept changes and use the changes to better manage the team and followers.

17.2 The Concept of Leadership

Certain variables can contribute to the success of a business in any given industry, leadership, strategy, structures, systems, and human resources are among such variables. Leadership determines who should be involved in the day-to-day running of the business and strategy indicates what to do at every point. Structure provides outlines of how the business is organized to meet the demand of the industry and systems put in place what is required for operation and implementation of the strategy. The strongest of these variables is leadership as it takes leadership to develop and implement strategies, build structures and systems, and lead human resources toward the achievement of the desired goals.

The concept of leadership is linked to theories – the expectancy theory, the goal theory, and equity theory: expectancy theory for self-efficacy and engagement, while the goal theory for recognition, goal settings, and pride.

Effective leadership is about commitment to excellence and striving to continuously meet quality standards. It is the act of helping group members attain productivity, good quality, patients' satisfaction, and job satisfaction (Dubrin, 2013; Greenawald et al., 2022). Leaders get things done through other people and getting things done is important for business and economic growth (Kubica, 2014; Olson, 2022). The leaders need to develop some skills that will enable them to lead and develop teams as mentors. Leadership starts with self-awareness and answering some salient questions like (a) what I am good at? (b) what do I enjoy doing best? Answers to these questions provide a guide to the leader on why he/she is in leadership.

17.2.1 What Is Leadership?

The "So what?" Questions in entrepreneurial leadership – Leaders must study the trends and opportunities for improvement in contemporary tech changes, models, and practices. They need to create innovative ways of conducting business and responding to change in the advent of technology (Naimi-Sadigh et al. 2021; Pepper, 2010). For example, vital elements such as business processes, leadership, and culture have been valuable in addressing organizational change globally because of technological advances (Pepper, 2010). The "So what?" questions in the field of leadership pertain to what are the essential components of change that can influence whole systems approaches? (Naimi-Sadigh et al. 2021; Pepper, 2010), what novelties in change management are valuable to driving transformation in the tech industry? (Radwan, 2010), what are the competencies needed to explore, exploit, and transfer valuable knowledge within the team and beyond (Hajro & Pudelko, 2010; Zhao & Anand, 2013).

Leadership comes with responsibilities; the responsibilities are derived from existing standards set out in various codes of ethics related to the tech and entrepreneurial landscape. In Leadership, four words are the pillar to successful lead: honesty, trustworthiness, integrity, and respect. The credibility and reputation of the leader traverses all spectrum of the leadership attributes, the leader's credibility and reputation are assets that are valued and become evident in diverse situations that happen within the socio-cultural and economic spectrum of the business.

The ability to inspire confidence and support from team members is foundational in leadership to achieve set objectives. Hersey et al. (2008) defined leadership as the process of influencing the activities of team members at the individual or group level. This means that leadership in the tech and entrepreneurial landscape is important for the following reasons:

- Influencing the behavior of team members: A leader exhibits effective leadership skills to quickly build rapport, thus leading to the motivation of team members.
- Aligning priorities of the team with the organization's objectives: A leader can prioritize activities for the team geared toward achieving set objectives.
- Leadership skills are necessary to implement effective time management policies to improve the efficiency of team members and other stakeholders.

- Leadership skills allow the leader to plan for changes that may occur during the implementation processes and procedures.

The leadership behaviors, skills, and activities required vary from one business within the tech space to another. The demography within the organization, its complexities, the project under-taken, and the business location affects its degree of variety. The need to continually monitor emerging trends put leaders under considerable pressure. The pressures are from competitors and other external factors. This puts stress on daily leadership activities needed to balance resources and schedule with entrepreneurial success in mind.

The domains in the tech industry have special skills needed and this leads to specializations as analyst, scientists, and engineers. The practitioners depicted by the character Miebi or Tekena move on the corporate ladder as analysts, then team lead, then manager and director or CEO. It is expected that Miebi/Tekena moves from entry level to leadership, knowing a bit of everything within the tech industry. If the analyst turned leader decides to focus more on his/her area of specialty, then other areas of the business suffer. Watkins (2012) opined that newly minted and emerging leaders struggle within these two frames (analyst and leadership doing specialist roles and not generalist role). The immediate challenge for these leaders is a shift in mindset from leading his or herself to overseeing the full spectrum of business functions within the tech and entrepreneurial space. To control the structure, the new leader needs the input of team members on important decision-making processes. These team members provide unique and relevant knowledge to the decision-making processes.

Peter Northouse in his book Leadership: Theory and Practice (2013) viewed leadership as a phenomenon that resides in the context of interaction between the leader and the follower. He opined that leadership can be observed in the leader's behavior and can be learned, where leaders can take decisions that are suitable for the whole business and select talented team members to mentor. For new leaders, the scope and complexity of the task dramatically increases in ways that can leave them feeling overwhelmed and uncertain (Watkins, 2012). During such periods, they need to imbibe leadership principles that focus on acquiring new skills and conceptualized frameworks.

Imbibing the principles of leadership are germane concerns for stakeholders in the tech industry. The future belongs to those who can develop peak performance through skills optimization and accepting diversity and dynamic changes through innovations (Dunn et al. 2012; Yun et al. 2020). The future belongs to leaders who awaken the geniuses in the team and evoke the potential to succeed in a high turnover, volatile, uncertain, complex landscape and know how to keep these businesses from descending into chaos. To achieve seamless and effective migration, the new leader needs to do the following.

- Establish direction by creating a vision, clarifying the big picture, and setting strategies.
- Align people by communicating goals, seeking commitment from team members, and build-ing coalitions.
- Motivate and inspire other team members by empowering subordinates and satisfying the unmet needs of the workforce.

Furthermore, the transitory process allows the new leader to embrace migration mindset. The seven seismic shifts as espoused by Goman (2014) are stages of growth and process involved in the migration for new leaders. When seismic shifts occur as part of growth and transitory processes, the leader needs to be put in context the following:

- Build collaboration strategy around the human element (build the human capacity)
- Use collaboration as organizational change strategy (leverage on existing organizational structure)

- Make visioning a team sport (embrace team effort in goal setting)
- Utilize diversity in problem solving (team dynamics)
- Help people develop relationship (build lasting relationship); and
- Focus on building trust.

The principle of leadership is anchored on the right choice's leaders take and the leadership style adopted. The leaders need to;

- Choose the realistic goals that the business needs to pursue.
- Choose the modalities for team members to motivate to pursue goals.
- Choose activities needed to coordinate and achieve the goals.
- Outline modes of decision-making because leaders need to set clear targets for the team.

17.3　Knowledge Management Potential of Leaders

Knowledge management (KM) is the activity concerned with strategy and tactics to manage human-centered assets. KM is the practice of organizing, managing, and utilizing all the knowledge and information contained with the business to achieve the set goals (Egbedoyin & Agbai 2020). It is divided into two categories – explicit and tacit. Explicit knowledge is any knowledge that can be documented, achieved, or codified with the assistance of IT. Tacit knowledge is the knowledge that human beings possess.

A leader needs to be knowledgeable because knowledge is seen as a capital, like intellectual capital (IC) and asset such as land asset (Schyns et al., 2011). A knowledgeable leader needs to apply KM to manage business assets, like IC assets.

The IC asset model as espoused by North & Kumta (2014) is segregated into human, customer, process, and growth element that is housed in two distinct categories of human capital and organization/structural capital. It assumes that knowledge is scientific and needs a scientific approach to resolve issues related to it. The drawback of this model is that it does not factor in the political and social aspect of KM. It rather adopts a mechanistic approach meaning that the KM can be developed into an objective element rather than being a socio-political phenomenon. Leadership effectiveness largely depends upon context; change to the context affects the leadership outlook (Okafor, 2019).

The interpersonal skill mirrors how leaders engage in self-assessment before stepping out to start team building process and group formation. Leadership is about being human because you can only lead people. Interpersonal skills include good communication skills, conflict arising from personality clash, and its resolution mechanism, delegation of duties, critical decision skills, and managing teams. Interpersonal skill development is about self-awareness, discovering one's weaknesses and trying to work on areas that need improvement. Leading is beyond being smart; it involves relationship management skills with empathy, organizational awareness, ability to develop and influence team members. Additionally, leading is about developing others and encouraging teamwork. These skillsets are anchored on the leader's trust level and sense of character.

Trust – is a belief and faith that persons have in each other (Wong, 2013; Okafor, 2019), it can be related to the ability of team members to count on each other to perform and support the team goals of the team. When there is trust, there are shared values demonstrated in behaviors. In leadership, trust is important and mutual.

Investing time to build trust is the foundation for an endearing relationship between the leader and the team member, because a trustworthy leader builds a trustworthy team. When trust exists in a team, the leader does not have to be in every place. For the leader, implementing the virtues of trust is key (Green, 2012; Okafor & Fadul, 2019). When trust between leaders and team members is high, performance increases in a positive direction.

Character – Kubica and La-Forest (2014) opined that character is the sum of the characteristics possessed of a person. It is the total being and personality embedded in moral qualities, ethical standards, and principles. The character of a leader is how they treat the team members; the respect for their personality integrity speaks to their sense of character. Moving a little deeper to the realm of emotional and social intelligence, the degree to which the leader displays these traits is by understanding the feelings of personality with the team and showing empathy through the connection with their emotions. To realize the power of collective team effort, the leader needs to optimally maximize the abundance of talent at their disposal.

17.4 Implementing Tech Leadership Principles

Post pandemic, it is evident that the future of tech industry resides in the hands of leaders who understand the system to shape the envisaged future. The innovations are becoming more sophisticated and complex for non-tech savvy stakeholders. It behooves industry leadership to adapt with complexities. It portends adopting an adaptive leadership style that mutates among different leadership styles. Adopting system thinking in adaptive leadership requires principles to lead (Edo et al., 2020). Adopting the adaptive leadership style is critical for implementing complex systems to achieve sustainability in the tech landscape that proactively addresses future challenges. Five major leadership principles are discussed herein.

17.4.1 Clarity of Purpose

The globe is witnessing technological advancement in ways never seen before, a system with clear mandate of technology adoption is desirous in the tech landscape. Leaders are encouraged to provide a clear, compelling, and purposeful roadmap that reflects the tech industry core values. Tech leaders should empower team members to clarify the big picture of where the industry is heading to build team coalition.

17.4.2 Credibility of Leadership

The leaders should be willing to act with courage and take risk when the need arises. It speaks to their credibility when they champion and orchestrate change. Leaders are saddled with the responsibility to identify and nurture team members with the envisaged capacity and discipline needed to drive sustainable changes. The leaders should empower team members by sharing control of authority. Engaging every team member, providing direction, and communicating its purpose. Leading involves creating opportunities for trust building and relationships development. The credibility of the leaders is a strong ingredient that propels team members to interact openly and get the work done. Relationships foster increased collaboration, understanding, mutual accountability, and trust. Leaders that are self-aware can demonstrate empathy in dealing with unique challenges of team members. Empathy provides a foundation for integrity, trust, credibility, and quality relationships.

17.4.3 Integrity in the Tech Industry

High-performing leaders align the goals of the organization to their personal and team goal. Coherence in the system creates space and energy for creativity, innovation, and transformation. Team values are important in a frequent tech turnover environment. In such complex systems, the human resources, relationships, and structures flow in a complicated mix that is rarely predictable. Therefore, strong core values are essential for team adaptability and flexibility.

In frequent technology turnovers, challenge exists in demonstrating leadership that supports creative tension in the systems because tough decisions will be made to set clear direction and sense of purpose. When such engagement occurs without direction and sense of purpose, groups flounder because boundaries are unclear. What is more, when direction occurs without engagement, the result is a superficial consensus that saps energy which blocks creativity.

Embracing diversity is another area of industry integrity. If the tech industry is viewed as pyramids, stakeholder expectations must be at the top, stakeholders' interest and diversity must be accommodated transparently (Rintamäki, 2018; Sithira, 2016). Stakeholders should be educated, informed, and empowered in managing the expectation of new innovations (Rintamäki, 2018; Sithira, 2016).

17.4.4 Accountability for Performance

Accountability is the act of responsiveness and taking ownership of a role in an activity. It is the principle that all team members are willing to bear the consequences of their actions, be it good or bad. Accountability by leadership is difficult but when leadership becomes accountable to stakeholders and team, they improve performance within the organization. An accountable leader pays greater attention to details and expects the same from the team. At the industry level, leaders are accountable for system performance (Edo et al., 2020). The collective accountability of the team drives positive outcomes. Attention to details involves all aspects of the project lifecycle, from initiation to closeout phases.

Accountable leadership focuses on implementations and decision-making processes to figure out the leads and lags in the process. It allows for holistic participation of stakeholders and accommodates diverse ideas. People who feel engaged become willing to contribute to team's set goals, work harder, and are more productive. The silver lining in highly accountable and performance teams are the unalloyed corporation leaders get from the team when there is efficient systemic performance.

The twin factors of assessment and evaluation are tools leaders use to measure meaningful results. They focus on the achievable rather than results and measurement, with attention on the lessons and high points. Striking the balance between the need for meaningful measurement anchored on values, with the acknowledgment that measures must be appropriately developed, timed, and interpreted, is a challenging yet critical task for today's leaders in tech industry.

17.4.5 Implementing Decisions

One abiding principle of effective leadership is the ability to implement decisions. When decisions are reached at any level, it is the responsibility of the leader to implement them. Communication by the leader ensures that roles, duties, and responsibilities are clear and does not give room for conflict/disconnects/inconsistencies.

It is important to set deadlines and distribute the manpower resources evenly to solve team's problems and take corrective actions aimed at resolving team's difficult issues. The leader needs to build consensus on issues affecting the team, consult widely before making decisions to achieve greater participation of team members.

There are two guiding principles for implementing decisions to achieve sustainability. Good practices dictate that both principles are developed and practised for self-perpetuation and industry sustenance. Adherence to good practice requires self-awareness of the leader's mindset and readiness to change in the following areas:

1 **Identity.** Identify the team's strength and weaknesses, optimize the strength, and improve on the weaknesses. Focus on the big picture and align the team's goal to organizational goal. Provide a linkage and connection of the team to the organization's vision.
2 **Information.** Provide information openly and without ambiguities. See information sharing and open communication as a tool for relationship building. The essence of timely information sharing cannot be lost in the healthcare system as timely information saves lives. Providing accurate information should be a priority for the leader as the more open the flow of the information the easier it is to convert data into meaningful knowledge.

The newfangled tech leaders are confronted with emerging challenges related to the evolving technological advancement happening before us. These challenges entail:

• Setting and programming objective
• Motivating and aligning effort
• Co-ordinating and controlling activities
• Developing and assigning talent
• Accumulating and applying knowledge
• Amassing and allocating resources
• Building and nurturing relationships
• Balancing and meeting stakeholder demands

Leadership suitable for the tech industry needs to aggregate the six levels of intelligence as contained in global competency index that set the conceptual stage for developing leadership intelligence. These levels of intelligence include intellectual intelligence (IQ), emotional intelligence (EQ), cultural intelligence (CQ), meta-cognitive intelligence (MCQ), existential intelligence (XQ), and moral intelligence (MQ) (Dunn, et al., 2012; Yun et al. 2020). The leaders need to operate in this level of intelligence on a conceptual basis to increase their global acumen, leadership skill, and potential of contemporaneity (Dunn et al., 2012; Yun et al. 2020).

17.5 Adopting Futuristic Tech Changes

Emerging technologies are technologies that may or may not yet be in use but whose potential could be significant in replacing technologies used presently. Tech leaders would differentiate themselves by absorbing feedback, create team loyalty, and embrace new technology. Kotter (2007) opined that leadership that is forward looking and futuristic needs to adopt a change strategy as outlined below:

Establishing a sense of urgency – The technological advancement and innovation driving change need to be adopted. This creates a sense of urgency for the less developed economies in leveraging technology. To create this sense of urgency, the leadership should start sensitizing team members and the entire workforce on the need to develop a robust and improved procedure for technology adoption.

Forming a powerful guiding group – A high powered and efficient team with sufficient mandate would be set up to serve as the steering committee to articulate short- and medium-term action to achieve the desired and rapid changes desired.

Creating a vision – If the vision of the organization does not align with the present realities, the steering committee and the entire leadership structure would need to rethink the vision of the new strategy vis a vis the vision of the organization. Since business strategies are derived from the vision of the organization, the new articulate vision should capture the sustainable development goals 2030 objective and align with the protection of the environment for the benefit of the company and its stakeholders.

Communicating the vision – When the new vision is articulated, all should align with the change, driven by top management, a comprehensive communication management plan should be developed to inform member of staff of the new vision and market the vision for the changes and its impact on company profile to the entire workforce.

Empowering others to act on the vision – To drive the point for changes, the leadership needs to empower departmental and sectional leaders to develop their team goal and align such goals to the new vision. Continuous engagement with key stakeholders is necessary to creating the right synergy among various teams in the organization to guarantee sustainability.

Planning for and creating the short-term wins – To measure successes, the leader needs to create short-term goals, provide timelines for achieving these goals, and follow-through with the teams to achieve these goals (Okafor, 2019). The achievement of these short-term goals becomes the springboard for achieving greater goals.

Institutionalizing new approaches – This should be based on new visions, the alignment of the business strategy and wins in the short-term goals. Processes that produced these results are institutionalized to provide documented evidence for the new approach to serve as a beacon for future teams.

The introduction of new technologies will herald rapid changes to improve team performance. Schein (2002) identified three stages in the change process, which are unfreezing by creating motivation to change, changing by learning new concepts, and refreezing by internalizing these new concepts.

In learning to accommodate the new changes, there may be delays in the execution **of** various sub-projects because different people have different capacity to adopt to new teams, new technologies, and new regulations; this is the second stage of **learning new concepts**. With time, blending happens, lessons learned, and learning curves smoothed, the old and new fuses together as one unit. This is the **refreezing and** final stage of the change process.

To survive in this ever-changing technology environment, leaders must constantly differentiate themselves, absorb team feedback, develop services that create loyalty, and adopt new technologies. Leaders desirous of leading in the future need to adopt strategies that embrace emerging technologies and digital transformation using strategic management in furthering their team advantage and learning capabilities. These strategies thrive around the vision, plan, action, and strategy of strategic management. Steps that leaders could consider taking include.

- Identify the future customer and clientele base.
  - Assess current benchmark in relation to where you want to be. Map out major evolution and look out for opportunities.

Analyze and prioritize significant evolution in the medical and digital transformation space.

  - Assess assets, skillset, culture, and readiness by focusing on the intangible assets (Services).
    - Learn, measure, re-assess, scale, innovate. Align existing strategies to a desired road map to where you need to be as an organization.

- Design and develop for innovation, optimization, agility, and leveraging on economies of scale and institutional knowledge to connect technologies.
  - Get top management and leadership buy-in on processes and procedures. Move from the known to the unknown, simple to complex tasks.

17.6 Conclusion

For the tech leadership, global leadership theory will continue to be relevant in the immediate and distant future. For the idea of technology change and the implications for businesses as advances are made in technology (Aggarwal, 2010). The survival of the business and its ability to remain sustainable is anchored in part to its leadership and its commitment the entrepreneurship (Adekiya et al., 2016). The entrepreneur is encouraged to articulate a vision and ready to adapt to change occasioned by factors external to the business (Adekiya et al., 2016). Visionary leadership is at the heart of the need to craft reforms as a strategy for long-term sustainability of the firm (Lassalle & McElwee, 2016). The entrepreneur needs to drive the process and initiative through actions and plans that are geared toward a 56 culture that endears professionalism and competence (Adekiya et al., 2016; Lassalle & McElwee, 2016; Mohamad et al., 2015). The leaders of business startups should lead by example and command a high level of enthusiasm and zeal toward achieving set targets and growing the business.

References

Adekiya, A. A., & Ibrahim, F. (2016). Entrepreneurship intention among students. The antecedent role of culture and entrepreneurship training and development. 141 *International Journal of Management Education, 14,* 116–132. doi:10.1016/j.ijme.2016.03.001

Ademokun, F., & Ajayi, O. (2012). Entrepreneurship development, business ownership and women empowerment in Nigeria. *Journal of Business Diversity, 12*(1), 72–87.

Agbai, E. (2018). Pathway to Entrepreneurship Training Towards Addressing Youth Unemployment in Nigeria. *Walden University Dissertation-ProQuest.* https://scholarworks.waldenu.edu/dissertations/5153

Aggarwal, C. C., & Wang, H. (Eds.). (2010). *Managing and mining graph data* (Vol. 40). New York: Springer.

Dubrin, A. J. (2013). *Leadership: Research findings, practice, and skills,* 7th ed. Boston: Houghton Mifflin.

Dunn, T. E., Lafferty, C. L., and Alford, K. L. (2012). Global leadership: A new framework for a changing world. *S.A.M. Advanced Management Journal, 77*(2), 4–14 proquest.com/openview/106ff21fd474159d e721285fe57728f3/1?pq-origsite=gscholar&cbl=40946

Edo, O. C., Okafor, A., & Justice A. E. (2020). Corporate taxes and foreign direct investments: An impact analysis. *Public Policy and Administration Research, 10*(9) 51–62. doi:10.7176/PPAR/10-9-07

Egbedoyin, F. S., & Agbai . E.P. (2021). The role of leadership in tacit knowledge transfer in the Nigeria oil and gas industry. *African Journal of Engineering and Environmental Research, 2*(1), 90–109. https://ajoeer.org.ng/otn/ajoeer/qtr-1/2021/07.pdf

Goman, C. (2014). Collaborative leadership. *Leadership Excellence, 31*(4), 35.

Greenawald, M. H., Jeremiah, M., & Mertes, C. (2022). How to be employed "well": Optimizing your professional satisfaction. *Family Practice Management, 29*(5), 29–34.

Hammawa, Y. M., & Hashim, N. B. (2016). Women-micro entrepreneurs and sustainable economic development in Nigeria. *Journal of Business and Management, 18,* 27–36.

Hisrich, R. D., & Ramadani, V. (2017). Effective entrepreneurial management. *Effective Entrepreneurial Management.* Springer

IBRU, C. (2009). *Growing micro finance through new technologies.* Federal University of Nigeria, Owerri, Nigeria.

Iganiga, B. O. (2010). Evaluation of the Nigerian financial sector reforms using behavioral models. *Journal of Economics, 1*(2), 65–75.

Kotter, J. (2007). Leading change: Why transformation efforts fail. *Harvard Business Review, 85*(1), 96–103. https://hbr.org/2007/01/leading-change-why-transformation-efforts-fail

Kubica, T., & LaForest, S. (2014). Intrapersonal skills. *Leadership Excellence, 31*(4), 70. https://search.proquest.com.library.capella.edu/docview/1534108206?acccountid=27965

Lassalle, P., & McElwee, G. (2016). Polish entrepreneurs in Glasgow and entrepreneurial opportunity structure. *International Journal of Entrepreneurial Behavior and Research, 22,* 260–281. doi:10.1108/IJEBR-01-2016-0012

Mohamad, N., Lim, H., Yusof, N., & Soon, J. (2015). Estimating the effect of entrepreneur education on graduates' intention to be entrepreneurs. *Education and Training, 57,* 874–890. doi:10.1108/ET-03-2014-0030

Naimi-Sadigh, A., Asgari, T., & Rabiei, M. (2021). Digital transformation in the value chain disruption of banking services. *Journal of the Knowledge Economy, 13* (2), 1–31. https://doi.org/10.1007/s13132-021-00759-0

North, K., & Kumta G (2014). *Knowledge management: Value creation through organizational learning.* 2nd Edition. Springer Texts in Business and Economics.

Ogundele, G. F., Abdulazeez, R. O., & Bamidele, O. P. (2014). Effect of pure and mixed substrate on oyster mushroom (Pleurotus ostreatus) cultivation. *Journal of Experimental Biology and Agricultural Sciences, 2,* 2S.

Okafor, A. (2019). Refocusing on the success enabling factors in mergers and acquisitions. *European Scientific Journal 15(16) 172–190.* doi:10.19044/esj.2019.v15n16p17

Okafor, A., & Fadul J. (2019). Bank risks, regulatory interventions and deconstructing the focus on credit risk. *Research Journal of Finance and Accounting, 10*(8) 67–75. doi:10.7176/RJFA

Olson, M. (2022). *The rise and decline of nations: Economic growth, stagflation, and social rigidities.* Yale University Press, New Haven, Connecticut, USA.

Peter, G. N. (2013). *Leadership, theory and practice.* 6th Edition. Sage Publications Inc, Washington, DC, USA.

Ranhagen, U. (2021). *Transport hubs connect the city: A story from Gothenburg in Chapter 2 Space and Place.* Sciences Building, Upper Campus University of Cape Town, South Africa.

Ratten, V. (2018). *Sport entrepreneurship: Developing and sustaining an entrepreneurial sports culture.* Springer, **New York City**, USA. https://link.springer.com/book/10.1007/978-3-319-73010-3

Rintamäki, S. (2018). Stakeholder expectations of CSR–Case Olvi Group. https://urn.fi/URN:NBN:fi-fe201801262353

Schein, E. H. (2002). Models and tools for stability and change in human systems. *Reflections, 4*(2), 34–46. https://www.researchgate.net/profile/Edgar-Schein/publication/247713050_Models_and_Tools_for_Stability_and_Change_in_Human_Systems/links/53fe2adc0cf283c3583bce40/Models-and-Tools-for-Stability-and-Change-in-Human-Systems.pdf

Soloveva, A. (2022). *Illegal charters and aviation law.* Taylor & Francis, New York, USA.

Vinsel, L., & Russell, A. L. (2020). *The innovation delusion: How our obsession with the new has disrupted the work that matters most.* Currency, New York, USA

Watkins, M. D. (2012). How managers become leaders. *Harvard Business Review, 90*(6), 64–72.

Wong, Z. (2007) *Human factors in project management: Concepts, tools, and techniques for inspiring teamwork and motivation.* 1st Edition. San Francisco, CA: Josey-Bass.

Yun, J. J., Kim, D., & Yan, M. R. (2020). Open innovation engineering—Preliminary study on new entrance of technology to market. *Electronics, 9*(5), 791. https://doi.org/10.3390/electronics9050791

Zhao, Z. J., & Anand, J. (2013). Beyond boundary spanners: The 'collective bridge'as an efficient interunit structure for transferring collective knowledge. *Strategic Management Journal, 34*(13), 1513–1530. doi:10.1002/smj.2080

18 Building an Organization

Rafael Augusto Seixas Reis de Paula and
Roger (Rongxin) Chen

18.1 Introduction: Organizational Theory at a Glance

The organizational theory was born in the sixties and was initially used to explain the division and control of labor in established firms. Nevertheless, its application can help to understand young and growing startups. Lawrence and Lorsch (1967) laid one of the foundations of Organization Theory.

The initial research of Lawrence and Lorsch – in the sixties proposed that a firm is an open system in which the behaviors of the members are interrelated, interdependent with the formal organization, the tasks to be performed, the personalities of other individuals, and the unwritten rules on the proper conduct of the members. They explain that as a firm grows, it becomes more complex with different departments and divisions, and the functioning of these separate parts (e.g., research and development, commercial, and production) must be integrated to make the whole system viable. These parts – organizational functions – of the system must also be linked to realize the entire purpose of the firm.

Revisiting the classic works of Lawrence and Lorsch (1967), Galbraith, Downey, and Kates (2002), and Mintzberg et al. (1989), we can summarize that this theory attempts to explain how firms might organize groups, subgroups, and individuals, who interact with each other, most efficiently and effectively. In other words, how to organize human's tasks to accomplish the firm's goals.

There is no successful firm without an appropriate organization of human's tasks. From a practical view, we are interested in understanding how to organize a startup, mainly human tasks. The main point is that entrepreneurs, even the most efficient ones, might not do all the startup tasks. They will need support and know how to arrange and manage human tasks. In this sense, organizational theory can help us. Here, we focus on this theory and its practical implications for startups. We highlight conceptual lenses relating to better organization of startups, challenges, tips, and advice to implement these concepts.

Firms need to be organized, for example, to implement and support their product development processes, to improve their capabilities to explore and exploit market opportunities, and to serve customers. These tasks comprise the startup's daily activities. The literature considers that a startup navigates a non-straightforward route, which demands the capacity to deal with uncertainty and continuous shifting in the firms' strategies and business models (Amit & Zott, 2001; Alvarez & Barney, 2007; Gruber et al., 2008). Consequently, entrepreneurs must be able to deal with unpredictable changes (e.g., competition and customer needs).

In this way, considering the importance of organizational theory, how does a startup team need to be organized to conduct its business tasks?

There is not just one answer to this question. Literature and practical approaches have shown us that entrepreneurs must consider at least three conceptual lenses: (a) the startup team needs to

DOI: 10.4324/9781003341284-24

be able to engage in communities of developers, professionals, and users; (b) the startup team, instead of being guided by a detailed predefined work plan, is orientated by an experimentation perspective (step-by-step, based on continuous testing and learning), and (c) the startup team needs to be flexible, adjusting according to each startup project (e.g., different product development projects demand distinguished project teams). The details are discussed below.

18.2 Key Conceptual Lenses

The classical principle of organizational theory argues that each firm will define its specific organizational form according to its interests and objectives. If you are a startup leader, do not try to copy what another startup is doing. It is not a guarantee of success. As Donaldson (2006) remembers, there is no best way to organize. How to organize, for example, the human tasks to perform the product development processes or to boost the capabilities efforts depends upon the contingencies of the firm.

As the definition of Ries (2012), startups aim to create new products and services under extreme uncertainty. Startups operate in a turbulent context characterized, for instance, by innovative products or technologies not thoroughly managed (Tushman & Anderson, 1986), ambiguous or not well-structured markets (Santos & Eisenhardt, 2009), and unclear or previously unknown attributes (Hargadon & Douglas, 2001).

In this scenario, a relevant problem for entrepreneurs is defining the appropriate organizational form for their startups, considering their contingent aspects in a high-uncertainty context. Therefore, it is hard to determine how entrepreneurs might organize their startup teams, and it is impossible to define a perfect organizational form for startups. By the way, there is no perfection for any firm, especially startups.

However, how do we deal with this non-perfection? Are there any guides to follow? Scholars and practitioners acknowledge that one of the main advantages of startups, compared with established firms, is that startups are more agile, flattened, and fast. The literature has robust discussions (e.g., Benner & Tushman, 2015; Cooper, 2017) that can help us. The discussions initially focused on the established firms' efforts to develop highly innovative products. However, here, we can translate the main conceptual lenses to the startup's context. In this way, we present three of them and discuss their practical impacts.

18.2.1 Non-Boundary Performance

Based on the findings from Benner and Tushman (2015), innovative firms need to be able to engage communities of developers, professionals, and users. Although innovation projects in the past also considered the within-firm as the focus, alternative ecosystem perspectives push innovation increasingly outside of firms' boundaries. Adner (2017, p. 42) defines the ecosystem as "the alignment structure of the multilateral set of partners that need to interact for a focal value proposition to materialize."

In this way, we assume that a *non-boundary performance is the capacity of the startup to organize its teams to establish successful links with external partners to generate and capture value propositions.*

We can understand the innovation process and exploration efforts as a capacity of the startups to establish interfirm arrangements (e.g., as discussed by open innovation literature – see Chesbrough, 2017), going beyond the firms' boundaries. Innovation management is focused on opening up the innovation processes and combining internal and external technologies, knowledge, and resources to create business value. Startups can gain a lot by fostering external partnerships, as their resources and market reach are limited (Huizingh, 2011; Gassmann, Enkel & Chesbrough, 2010).

Chesbrough, Vanhaverbeke, and West (2014), Bianchi et al. (2015), Usman and Vanhaverbeke (2017), and many other scholars have tried to understand how startups successfully organize and manage external partnerships with large firms. According to them, adopting a non-boundary organization startup can, for example, amplify their opportunities to explore new markets and technologies, save on R&D costs, accelerate the market entrance, and capitalize on large firms' reputations.

18.2.2 Flexibility

Some scholars have indicated that if an innovative firm wants to develop a new product, the firm must follow a process, which has a linear bias in many situations. For Garud, Tuertscher, and Van de Ven (2013), more precisely, firms need to organize their resources and project team according to a "sequence of events that unfold as ideas emerge, are developed, and are implemented" (Garud, Tuertscher & Van de Ven, 2013, p. 774).

The established firms' literature on this topic – flexibility – can bring important insights for us. Gomes et al. (2020) and Cooper and Sommer (2016) highlight that a new product development process must be defined in a situation where each project is unique and has its routing. In other words, the activity process depends on the nature and characteristics of each project. In this way, the project team might skip or combine the stages and decision points to tailor the product development process to each project.

For Gomes et al. (2020), considering a new product development process, a firm might calibrate the process according to the different sources of uncertainty in a given project. Based on this principle, we acknowledge that flexibility can bring significant benefits to startup teams, such as being agile, reducing redundant activities and errors, and tailoring their tasks.

Considering Cooper's classic definition of flexibility (2017), for us, *flexibility is a startup's capacity to adjust its teams according to each project, strategy, or business model, responding to the firm's contingencies.*

Recently, the literature has tried to understand in more detail the startup context. Startups typically face many uncertainties, requiring entrepreneurs to pivot and adjust their directions and strategies. As a result, startups need to change their tasks and projects accordingly. Many times, these changes are unpredictable and force entrepreneurs to be flexible. Besides, startups must frequently customize their product development process to serve specific niche markets or satisfy unique customer needs. Serving these unique customers and market needs has important implications for how startups are organized. Furthermore, strategic flexibility is crucial for firms' survival. Firms depend on customers for the needed resources to survive and thrive. As a result, firms are forced to be flexible when the environment is dynamic and frequently changes (Gong et al., 2021). This is especially true for startups. Most startups are new to their markets. They are exploring to find new products or new business models. These exploration processes are uncertain and force startup teams to be flexible in their search and daily tasks (Shepherd & Gruber, 2021).

18.2.3 Experimentation Perspective

The organization of startup tasks faces many uncertainties. As a result, the organization of startups needs to follow experimentation, not predefined steps (e.g., traditional stage gate process), such as go-kill criteria. In a startup's daily life, developing a rigid plan with a long-range view is not viable. With the development of the Internet, Big Data, and Data Analytics, business experiments have become essential, especially for startups, to develop new products, search for customers, reduce costs, increase product quality, etc.

Startups' experimentation method typically is centered around the customer journey, that is, different areas where customers become aware of and use a firm's products. The experimentation method uses A/B testing data analytics and relies on firm's websites (including mobile apps), social media, etc. This method is necessary to test new products, raise customer awareness of products, develop new and retain existing customers, and increase customer usage or purchases of the products.

Many studies analyze how to design and set up business experiments. Anderson and Simester (2011) indicated that business experiments should follow the rules based on at least three elements: focusing on individuals, short-term results, and simplicity. Other scholars discuss how to conduct analytics experiments. For example, Kohavi and Thomke (2017) discussed how to set KPIs (key performance indicators or hypothesized results) of experimentation and select key areas to test in the experiments. Furthermore, Chen and Lee (2022) argue that business experiments are far beyond just tests; they require firms to build holistic activity systems that involve best practices before, during, and after conducting business experiments.

Business experiments have helped firms to identify opportunities and quickly grow from small startups to global giants. For example, it took Google and Amazon only five years to increase their revenues from 0 to $1 billion, Facebook six years, and Spotify eight years (Grothaus, 2019). All these firms heavily relied on business experiments when they were startups to search for opportunities, develop products, and grow their businesses. Similarly, Optimizely (2019) surveyed more than 800 managers and executives from the U.S., the UK, and Germany. The survey showed that firms doing more experiments enjoy higher revenue growth.

Based on Sommer, Loch, and Dong (2009), *the experimentation perspective is the capacity of a startup to employ its teams to conduct business' experiments, actively search for new opportunities, and adjust their plans, applying unique and original problem-solving as further information becomes available.*

18.3 Lessons to Implement the Key Conceptual Lenses: Challenges, Advice, and Tips

Considering the non-boundary performance, flexibility, and experimentation perspectives, we need to understand how entrepreneurs organize their startups to structure their product development process and develop their capabilities to explore markets. Therefore, we present these three concepts lenses based on our experience from twenty years of mentoring and supporting the creation and growth of more than four dozen entrepreneurs.

18.3.1 Non-Boundary Performance in Practice

If you are an entrepreneur, you are not isolated and cannot do everything necessary for your startup. The startup tasks, mainly exploring new knowledge, as noted, might encompass an ecosystem approach, following an open and collaborative approach. You may not do all the necessary activities and possess all resources and knowledge. You can cooperate, for example, with other startups, established firms, public or private scientific and technological institutions, government actors, accelerators, venture capitalists, and other actors of an ecosystem.

Imagine that you are exploring a new market and have identified a relevant business opportunity. However (as occurs in most cases), you only have limited resources (e.g., initial technologies or products and limited marketing capabilities). In many situations, you do not need to own all the required resources; you might co-develop the possible solutions with partners to explore the opportunities. A complementary alternative is to join a community or ecosystem (in the IT sector, this is a common practice, but nowadays, it is also applied to other sectors). Imagine, for example, that you are a biotech startup and have discovered a new route to develop a relevant drug. You may need additional knowledge, expertise, and business infrastructure to support you. An intelligent decision is to organize within a group of firms and select the best partners for you.

Although the non-boundary collaborative approach is an essential strategy for startups, entrepreneurs should be fully aware of and capable of dealing with challenges in collaboration. Such challenges are especially acute when entrepreneurs collaborate with established large firms; these firms have different organizational cultures, operational processes, and strategic priorities. For example, entrepreneurs may find that their collaborative established firms are very slow and rigid in decision-making and adjusting actions; this may force the entrepreneurs to slow down their speed of execution or causing the startups missing opportunities in changing business environments.

Entrepreneurs may also be overwhelmed by partner firms' complex organizational structures and setups. This can cause difficulties for the entrepreneurs to find the appropriate departments or decision-makers to help startups implement cooperation. Also, many large firms follow fixed annual budgeting and resource allocation practices. Suppose entrepreneurs approach large established firms for collaboration outside such resource allocation windows. In that case, it will be difficult for the entrepreneurs to find departments or units within large established firms to cooperate. Because of this, entrepreneurs need to identify strong supporters or sponsors in the collaborative partner firm to help startups navigate the complex organizational structure or resource allocation processes, and provide necessary introductions and support.

Besides, entrepreneurs may find challenges when their collaborative firms change their strategic directions or priorities during the cooperation, affecting, for example, the commitments, resources, and personal and other supports to the cooperation, causing difficulties for startups to pursue their strategic objectives from the cooperation. To mitigate such uncertainties, entrepreneurs need to identify their strategic intention and clarify the responsibilities of collaborative firms and terms of cooperation to minimize the losses caused by the changes.

In summary, while searching for market opportunities and developing new venture businesses, startups should do more with other firms. Startup teams need to take an open collaboration approach, proactively seeking and engaging with the ecosystem's actors, thus leveraging the essential resources and capabilities required for startups. At the same time, startups must also develop capabilities for managing collaboration challenges and uncertainties.

18.3.2 Flexibility in Practice

Many startups intend to decide what competencies to develop, which process to follow in their product development or project execution, and how to establish appropriate procedures to guide their tasks.

Considering the uncertainties that startups face in their projects or product development tasks, entrepreneurs might implement agile methodologies and tools (e.g., scrum, kanban, extreme programming, lean development). For example, at the beginning of a product development project, the entrepreneurs may know they need to develop a product with specific features or functions. After customers see the prototype or try the initial version of the product, the entrepreneurs may learn that customers have other needs or require other features. Under this circumstance, entrepreneurs must be flexible in adjusting their processes and team setups to work on product development.

Furthermore, many startup teams work on products or activities that are highly customized to specific niche markets or customer groups. Meeting such unique demands frequently requires startups to customize their projects and tasks, which demand specific processes and task arrangements, which further requires startups to adjust organization structure to match the particular contingencies of the projects.

For example, suppose you have an Edutech startup interested in offering two new solutions to educate children in different countries. Consider that one of your services is to provide an IT solution to teach for free a specific program language for poor children in a public school in a Latin American country. The second is the same IT solution, which is paid for and available for private schools in the same country. In both situations, you might apply lean software development methodologies. You will, for example, aim to eliminate waste, deliver, test, and learn fast. However, your project team will vary.

In the first example (program language for poor children), the project team might comprise representatives for some public funding. Your team might consider that some children will not have in their homes a basic infrastructure to use your solution (they could, for instance, demand an IT laboratory in public schools), and many other specificities. To go further in these two new service development projects, you must perform different tasks, business models, external patterns, users, etc. As a result, you will need to adjust the structure and the makeup of these two project teams to better satisfy the different demands of these two projects.

However, there is a limit on startup flexibility. As startups scale up their business, they must consider formalizing and relying on appropriate, effective information systems to improve operation consistency and efficiency. There are several reasons for this transition.

Internally, as startups grow their business, they serve more customers and their business volume increases. This leads to complexity in operations. Company activities tend to involve more people and departments, require more coordination and communication. This can lead to challenges such as increased costs, lower efficiency, and problems with production, customer service, and inventory management. On the external side, as startups grow, their customers change from early adopters to mainstream customers. Compared with early adopter customers, mainstream customers are more price-sensitive and demand higher quality and consistency in their products and services.

These internal and external challenges require growing startup companies to make great efforts to tackle the internal operation complexity and the external new customer demands. To mitigate these challenges, startup companies need to establish formal procedures and operating policies. The startup companies also need to adopt appropriate information systems to help its activities. Internally, these formal operation policies and information systems can help to control costs, standardize operations, and improve operation consistency and product/service quality. These efforts, especially the high-quality information systems can also help the startup companies manage information flow, and capture operational insights and improve organizational learning. Externally, standard operation and information systems also help startup companies better manage customer interactions and services. They can make the customer services and interactions more predictable, transparent, and follow standard procedures. All these benefits will further help startup companies to further grow their businesses. In sum, although flexibility is an important characteristic of startup companies, flexibility needs to be gradually balanced by formalization and good information systems as startups scale up their business.

18.3.3 Experimentation Perspective in Practice

Considering a startup context, entrepreneurs cannot plan all the startup tasks. They will face many difficulties if they intend to follow rigid plans and specific milestones (e.g., testing the prototypes and supporting the first customers). It is typically challenging for startups to follow traditional business plans strictly. Defining, for example, a detailed five-year plan for a new product development process is, in most times, difficult and unnecessary.

In the early phases of new startup activities, entrepreneurs can use experiments to understand customer insights, identify target customers, and develop new products. As entrepreneurs successfully find initial target customers and initial products that satisfy these early customers, they will enter a growth or scale-up phase. At this phase, experimentations will be expanded to other areas, such as recruiting new and retaining existing customers, improving customer experiences using the products, and increasing referrals.

To implement these business experiments, entrepreneurs need to learn and establish best practices before, during, and after the experiments. For example, before the experiments, entrepreneurs need to clarify the goals of the experiments and rely on deep customer behavior insights to guide experimental design. Once the experiments start, entrepreneurs need to set clear criteria and policies to guide the scale-up of successful experiments. For those that fail to show the expected results, set a precise time limit for continuing or terminating the experiments. In other words, entrepreneurs must decide how long they will continue experimentation that does not generate the expected results.

After the experiments, entrepreneurs also need to establish effective practices to assess experiment results and develop insights. Since different teams within a startup may do different experiments, it is important to coordinate the experimentation efforts of different teams. Entrepreneurs must set clear strategic priorities and develop effective mechanisms to synchronize different experimental efforts, thus creating synergy among various experimental efforts. To achieve this, entrepreneurs can establish cross-functional teams to coordinate such experimental efforts. In many firms, such teams are called growth teams, which lead and coordinate cross-functional growth experiments and efforts design.

18.4 Final Comments

In startup success cases, entrepreneurs do not assume all responsibilities *"from idea to the market."* Entrepreneurs have a difficult mission in organizing their internal teams. Fortunately, the literature has offered relevant insights for people interested in understanding startup organizations. Despite the high level of uncertainties that startups face, entrepreneurs might find conceptual and practical guidance in this chapter to support their initial paths.

In sum, when organizing startups, entrepreneurs need to consider: (a) a non-boundary approach (i.e., the startup team nor the entrepreneurs will be responsible for performing all tasks. It is more effective to be engaged, for example, in a co-developing network), (b) flexibility (i.e., each project demands a specific team), (c) adoption of an experimentation perspective (i.e., avoid detailed work plan for startup activities. Go step by step, testing, learning, and moving ahead).

References

Adner, R. (2017). Ecosystem as structure: An actionable construct for strategy. *Journal of Management*, 43(1), pp. 39–58.

Alvarez, S.A., and Barney, J.B. (2007). Discovery and creation: Alternative theories of entrepreneurial action. *Strategic Entrepreneurship Journal*, 1(1–2), pp. 11–26.

Amit, R., and Zott, C. (2001). Value creation in e-business. *Strategic Management Journal*, 22(6–7), pp. 493–520.

Anderson, E.T., and Simester, D. (2011). A step-by-step guide to smart business experiments. *Harvard Business Review*, 89(3), pp. 98–105.

Benner, M.J., and Tushman, M.L. (2015). Reflections on the 2013 decade award—Exploitation, exploration, and process management: The productivity dilemma revisited ten years later. *Academy of Management Review*, 40(4), pp. 497–514.

Bianchi, M., Croce, A., Dell'Era, C., Di Benedetto, C.A., and Frattini, F. (2015). Organizing for inbound open innovation: How external consultants and a dedicated R&D unit influence product innovation performance. *Journal of Product Innovation Management*, 33(4), pp. 492–510.

Chen, R., and Lee, J.Y. (2022). Business experiments as activity systems, far beyond tests. In *California Management Review (insight)*. Available online at https://cmr.berkeley.edu/2022/07/business-experiments-as-activity-systems-far-beyond-tests/, checked on 23 December 2022.

Chesbrough, H., Vanhaverbeke, W, and West, J. (2014). *New frontiers in open innovation*. Oxford: Oxford University Press.

Chesbrough, H. (2017). The future of open innovation: The future of open innovation is more extensive, more collaborative, and more engaged with a wider variety of participants. *Research-Technology Management*, 60(1), pp. 35–38.

Cooper, R.G., and Sommer, A.F. (2016). The agile–stage gate hybrid model: A promising new approach and a new research opportunity. *Journal of Product Innovation Management*, 33(5), pp. 513–526.

Cooper, R.G. (2017). Idea-to-launch gating systems: Better, faster, and more agile: leading firms are rethinking and reinventing their idea-to-launch gating systems, adding elements of agile to traditional stage-gate structures to add flexibility and speed while retaining structure. *Research-Technology Management*, 60(1), pp. 48–52.

Donaldson, L. (2006). The Contingency Theory of Organizational Design: Challenges and Opportunities. In: Burton, R.M., Håkonsson, D.D., Eriksen, B., Snow, C.C. (eds) *Organization Design. Information and Organization Design Series*, vol 6. Springer, Boston, MA.

Galbraith, J.R., Downey, D., and Kates, A. (2002). *Designing dynamic organizations: A hands-on guide for leaders at all levels*. New York, NY: Amacom Books.

Garud, R., Tuertscher, P., and Van de Ven, A. H. (2013). Perspectives on innovation processes. *Academy of Management Annals*, 7(1), pp. 775–819.

Gassmann, O., Enkel, E., and Chesbrough, H. (2010). The future of open innovation. *R&d Management*, 40(3), pp. 213–221.

Gomes, L.A.V., Seixas Reis de Paula, R.A., Figueiredo Facin, A.L., Chagas Brasil, V., and Sergio Salerno, M. (2020). Design principles of hybrid approaches in new product development: a systematic literature review. *R&d Management*, 52(1), pp. 79–92.

Gong, Y., Le, Y., Zhang, X., Chen, X., and Zeng, H. (2021). Organizational adaptability influenced by practice strategy, environmental dynamism, and absorptive capacity. In *Complexity*. Available online at https://downloads.hindawi.com/journals/complexity/2021/4241485.pdf, checked on 23 December 2022.

Grothaus, M., (2019). "It Took amazon 5 years to make its first $1 billion, and only 2 days to make its latest billion", *Fast Company*. Available online at https://www.fastcompany.com/90310332/it-took-amazon-5-years-to-make-its-first-1-billion-and-only-2-days-to-make-its-latest-billion, checked on 23 December 2022.

Gruber, M., MacMillan, I.C., and Thompson, J.D. (2008). Look before you leap: Market opportunity identification in emerging technology firms. *Management Science*, 54(9), pp. 1652–1665.

Hargadon, A.B., and Douglas, Y. (2001). When innovations meet institutions: Edison and the design of the electric light. *Administrative Science Quarterly*, 46(3), pp. 476–501.

Huizingh, E.K. (2011). Open innovation: State of the art and future perspectives. *Technovation*, 31(1), pp. 2–9.

Kohavi, R., and Thomke, S. (2017). The surprising power of online experiments. *Harvard Business Review*, 95(5), pp. 74–82.

Lawrence, Paul R., and Lorsch, Jay W. (1967). Differentiation and integration in complex organizations. *Administrative Science Quarterly*, 12(1), pp. 1–47.

Optimizely Survey (2019). Mastering the Digital Experience Economy, 2019. Available online at chrome-extension://efaidnbmnnnibpcajpcglclefindmkaj/https://www.optimizely.com/contentassets/8c077f40b8034671a1f03e480b427a8e/atl_ebook_digital_experience_economy.pdf

Ries, E. (2011). *The lean startup: How today's entrepreneurs use continuous innovation to create radically successful businesses*. Currency.

Santos, F.M., and Eisenhardt, K.M. (2009). Constructing markets and shaping boundaries: Entrepreneurial power in nascent fields. *Academy of Management Journal*, 52(4), pp. 643–671.

Shepherd, D., and Gruber, M. (2021). The lean startup framework: Closing the academic–practitioner divide. *Entrepreneurship Theory and Practice*, 45(5), pp. 967–998.

Sommer, S.C., Loch, C.H., and Dong, J. (2009). Managing complexity and unforeseeable uncertainty in startup companies: An empirical study. *Organization Science*, 20(1), pp. 118–133.

Tushman, M.L., and Anderson, P. (1986). Technological discontinuities and organizational environments. *Administrative Science Quarterly*, 31(3), pp. 439–465.

Usman, M., and Vanhaverbeke, W. (2017). How startups successfully organize and manage open innovation with large companies. *European Journal of Innovation Management*, 20(1), pp. 171–186.

Index

Note: **Bold** page numbers refer to tables and *italic* page numbers refer to figures.

A/B testing 77, 78, 178
academics 5, 69, 72, 82
accelerator programs 22
accountability 165; by leadership 170; for performance 170
Acquisition-Behavior-Conversion process 76
actualization view 9
adaptive leadership style 169
Adner, R. 176
adoption-diffusion curve *107*, 107–108
agile development 107
Ajzen, I. 68
Alexiou, C. 40–41
Alibaba 78
Allen, J. P. 76
Altman, E. J. 158, 160
Amazon 158, 161, 178
American Marketing Association 91
Anderson, E.T. 178
Anderson, J. 41
anti-dilution 144
Apple 100, 161
application: identification 48–51; selection 49–51
Armstrong, N. E. 4
Armuña, C. 25
artificial intelligence 3, 46, 158–160
asset classes 132
augmented reality 3, 46
automation 160
Avery, G. C. 70

B2B *see* business-to-business (B2B)
B2C *see* business-to-consumers (B2C)
Bacigalupo, M. 19
Bailetti, T. 74–75
BANT (Budget, Authority, Need, and Timing) 124
Benner, M.J. 176
Berne Convention 33, 34, 36
Bianchi, M. 177
big data 76, 178
Bird, B. 25, 27

Blank, S. 11, 120
blockchain 3, 46
BMC *see* business model canvas (BMC)
BML *see* build-measure-learn (BML)
bootstrapping 13
Brem, A. 52, 75
Briggs, R. O. 62
Budden, P. 161
build-measure-learn (BML) 76, 105
business: experiments 178; infrastructure 179; opportunity 178–179; plan 12, **12**; processes 166; relationship 120; strategies 171–172; value 63, 176–177; *see also* business model
business model 10–11, *53*, 113, 177; canvas as design tool 75–76; characteristics of 74–75; definition of 53, 74–76; description of 74; design process 78, **79**; development 4; experimentation 76–78; innovation 74, 76–78; research, theoretical foundation of 74; sections 76
business model canvas (BMC) 11, 38, 74–76, 108–109
Business Model Generation (Osterwalder and Pigneur) 108
business-to-business (B2B) 92, 96, 113, 115, 121, 122
business-to-consumers (B2C) 122

Camuffo, A. 77, 78, 82
capitalization strategy 141–142
capital providers 132, 147, 149, 151–152; business plan matter 149; description of 147; difference between funding sources 147–148; and entrepreneurs 148–149; expectations from 148–149; network matter 149–150; type matter 150
capital requirements 141–142
Cardinal, L. B. 85
Catalani, M. S. 81–82
causation 84; *vs.* effectuation 82–83, *83*; entrepreneur 84; hybrid approach combining 86, *86*; logic 83, 84

Cavallo, A. 52
Central Intelligence Agency (CIA) 157–160
change process 172
character 47, 167, 169
Chen, R. 178
Chesbrough, H. 53, 177
China: patent law 35; strategic approach 35
Clerico, G. F. 81–82
codes of ethics 166
coherence 121, 169–170
collaboration/collaborative 8, 13, 23, 27, 41, 55, 63, 110, 124, 167–169; firms 179; strategy 167
Collewaert, V. 151
commercial/commercialization 3–4, 12, 26, 38, 47, 57, 62; process 58; of technology 58; value 9, 14, 34, 37–38
common law systems 36
communication 41, 50, 52, 59, 69–71, 113, 114; channels 59, 122; marketing 120, 122; of startups 120; tools 121
competency/competencies 18; definition of 18; description of 18; frequency of **25**; notions of 18
competitor analysis: description of 91; research process 91–92; review on 96–98
competitors 97; building theory 100; exploratory phase 99–100; innovation phase 100–101; review on 96–98; validation of ideas 101–102
Constable, G. 62
consumers 4, 91, 100, 113, 123, 126
contemporaneity 171
contract obligations 144–145
control rights 132–133
convergent thinking methods 58
Cooper, R.G. 177
copyright: protection 35–36; system 36
core competencies 23, 67–69, 71
corporate: development 145; engagement 161–162; investment schemes 13
Costa, R. C. 74
cost-plus pricing 117
CQ *see* cultural intelligence (CQ)
creativity: space and energy for 169–170; techniques 50
creditors 132–133
Creswell, J. 93
Crossing the Chasm (Moore) 107
cross-licensing 39
crowdfunding 14, 133
Crown ElectroKinetics 38
cultural/culture 68, 160–161; limitations 164–165; of organization 161; and values 69, 160
cultural intelligence (CQ) 171
customer: acquisition channels **123**, 123–124; based pricing 117–119; behavior 94; cost structures 118–119; discovery 96, 105, 106, 108, 110–111; empathy 110; engagement 125;

groups 180; learning 119; relationship 125; segments 108; willingness-to-pay 117

daily leadership activities 167
Darwin, C. 159–160
data 75; analytics 178; driven business models 75
debt 132; financing 132; securities 133
decision-making 81, 109, 144–145, 151–152; combined approach in 85–87; effectiveness 70; elements required for 82; entrepreneurial self-efficacy on 81–82; evidence-based 115; implementing 170–171; literature about 85; process 81–85, 167
Delmar, F. 85
demand pull 9
design thinking 48, 58, 109–110; models 58–59; process 100–101
digital/digitalization 52–54; ecosystem for vehicles 164; entrepreneurship 76; innovations 52; startups 52; technologies 52, 75; transformation 164, 172; venture business model 78
"direct sales" approach 122–123
discovery view 9
divergent thinking 58, 62
diversity 68, 159, 162, 167, 168, 170
Donaldson, L. 176
donation-based crowdfunding 133
Dong, J. 178
Douglas, E. J. 140
Downey, D. 175
D printing 3
Drucker, P. 125, 160
due diligence 143
Durand, C. 37
dynamic business environment 86

economics: development 164–165; globalization 41; rights 36
ecosystems 68, 159–162, 179; entrepreneurial 8; of workers 159; workforce 157–159
Edutech startup 180
effective leadership 166, 170
effectual: *vs.* causal logic 85; entrepreneurs 83–85
effectuation 8, 11, 82; causation *vs.* 82–83, *83*; hybrid approach combining 86, *86*; logic 8, 83
effectuators 84–85
efficient marketing 120–121
electronics 3, 46
emerging markets (EMs) 40, 41
emotional intelligence (EQ) 171
empathy 100–101, 110, 169–170; and iteration 58; map *101*
EMs *see* emerging markets (EMs)
EntreComp 19, **20–21**, 25
entrepreneurial competencies **22**, 25–27, 68; definition of 19; description of 17–19; development of 23–27; EntreComp 19;

frameworks 19, 22–23, **24**, 27; KEEN
engineering entrepreneurial mindset and
skillset framework 19–22; measuring 23–25,
27; models 18, 19; potential methods for
assessing **26**; self-perception of 25; taxonomies
of 19
entrepreneurial decision-making: causation
vs. effectuation 82–83; combined approach
in 85–87; description of 81–82; effectual
entrepreneurs and 83–84
entrepreneurial/entrepreneurs 3, 4, 12, 14, 17, 81,
85–87, 91, 141–143, 149–152, 164, 178–181;
definition of 176; ecosystems 8; effectuation
logic 83; environment 164; expectations from
148–149; funding-seeking 147; incentives
144; innovation 161–162; literature and
practical approaches 175–176; marketing
communication 122; mindset 23; perception
by 149; persistence and resilience of 67;
perspective 148–149; practical tools for 82;
processes 8; requirements for 148; strategy 69;
teams 10; theory and practice for 4; values 68;
ventures, survival and success of 147; vision
69–70
entrepreneurial leadership: concept of 165–
166; description of 164–165; knowledge
management potential of 168–169; questions
in 166
entrepreneurship 18, 62, 74, 81–82, 165; benefits
of 17; education 17–18, 26, 27; hands-on
experience in 27; practice of 5; research 133;
studies in 69, 82
environmental dynamism 52
EQ *see* emotional intelligence (EQ)
equity 132; crowdfunding 133; financing 133;
investor risk management 132–133; theory 166
ethics, codes of 166
ethnography 110
European Parliament and Council 18, 68
exclusivity 10
existential intelligence (XQ) 171
exiting, timing for 151
expectancy theory 166
expectation management 165
experimentation 110
experiment/experimental/experimentation: groups
114–115; marketing 114–116, *115*; run 115;
stimuli 114
expertise 179
explicit knowledge 168
exploration/exploratory: methods 99–101;
processes 177; techniques 99
external equity financing 148

Fassin, Y. 151
Fayolle, A. 68
feasibility 47, 51, 58, 64, 69, 76, 96, 106

FFE *see* fuzzy front end (FFE)
financial/financing 13; cycle 133–134; phases **134**;
risk 76; theory 132
firms 175; boundaries 176–177; capital providers
and entrepreneurs 151–152; characteristics
and value 141–142; for collaboration 179;
description of 150; efforts to develop
innovative products 176; external partnerships
with 177; financial state and fundraising time
141; heterogeneity 150; innovation 43; internal
and external data 75; literature 177; long-term
sustainability 173; marketing activities of
established 114; mission 71; operations 13;
performance 125; preferences of valuation
model 150–151; products 178; reputations 177;
strategies and business models 175; timing
for funding and exiting 151; valuation 141,
143–144; websites 178
5G patent technologies 38
Flatten, T. C. 119
flexibility 177, 178; definition of 177; in
practice 179–180
fund/funding: process 139, 140, *140*; provider 142;
risks 136; sources of **134**, 147–148; timing for
151
funding challenge: asset classes 132; creditor risk
management 132; crowdfunding 133; debt
and equity 132; description of 131; equity
investor risk management 132–133; mezzanine
financing 133; risk and return 132
fundraising 4, 141, 143; campaign 139;
process 142
fuzzy front end (FFE) 106

Galbraith, J.R. 175
game-changing technologies 47
Gartner Hype Cycle 51
Garud, R. 177
Geevarghese, G. 93
Gheethu, J. 91
Ghezzi, A. 52
Ghosh, A. 41
Gianesini, G. 19, 27
Giones, F. 52, 75
global leadership theory 173
global value chain 37
goal theory 166
go-kill criteria 177–178
Goman, C. 167
Gomes, L.A.V. 177
governance rights 132–133
Grindley, P. C. 39

Haftor, D. M. 74
Hall, J. 149
Hartmann, P. M. 75
Hassan, M. 93

HCD *see* human-centered design (HCD)
heterogeneity 150
high-tech ventures 38, 148, 150
Hofer, C. W. 149
Homburg, C. 113
How-Wow-Now-Ciao Matrix 51
Hsieh, T. 157–160, 162
Hu, Z. 41
Huang, L. 151
HubSpot 123
human: resources 12, 69, 165–166, 170;
    sensors 159
human-centered design (HCD) 57–58; approach
    57–59; different processes of 59; framework
    58, 59, *59*, 63; mindsets in 58–60, **60**;
    processes 58–59, **60–61**, 64
hybrid models 133
hypothesis: development 77, 114; testing 122

IBM 38–39, 41
ideation: phase 51; process 62; techniques 100
identity 36, 121, 135, 171
infancy risk 131
infrastructure risk 76
initial public offering (IPO) 147
innovation-driven enterprises (IDEs) 162
innovative/innovation 69–70, 100–101, 107;
    entrepreneurial 161–162; exploration 176;
    firms 176; internal 162; management 51,
    176–177; open 52; process 48, 176; promotion
    35; space and energy for 169–170; strategy 52;
    and technology 7
integrative thinking 110
integrity in tech industry 169–170
intellectual capital (IC) 168
intellectual intelligence (IQ) 171
intellectual property (IP) 10, 14, 134, 145, 149;
    copyright protection 35–36; enforcement 41;
    institutional advantages 41; patent protection
    34–35; protection institutions 33–34, *34*; rights
    135; trademark protection 36–37
intellectual property rights (IPRs) 10, 11
intellectual property (IP) strategies 37; factors
    influence 37, **38**; licensing and cross-licensing
    39; location strategy 40–41; patent-based
    commercialization 37–38; roadmap of forming
    global 42, *42*; standard-setting strategy 41–42
intelligence, levels of 171
intercultural competencies 68
international new ventures (INVs) 37, **38**, 39, 42
International Standard Industrial Classification
    (ISIC) 51
Internet of Things 3, 41, 46
internships/co-op positions 27
interpersonal skills 168
intrapreneurship 22, 57
investability 140

investments 9–10; contract, negotiating 143–144;
    process 47, 143; risks 143–144
investors 13, 131, 142, 144–145; equity 132;
    financial objective of 131; investing strategy
    142; readiness 140; and venture 143–144
IP *see* intellectual property (IP)
Islam, M. 37–38
iteration 12, 58, 76–78, 111

Jelinek, M. 4
Jennings, D. 81
Jobs, S. 91–92
Job-to-be-done (JTBD) framework theory 97–98
Johnson, K. 157, 159
Jones, R. 158

Kahneman, D. 110
Kantabutra, S. 70
Kates, A. 175
Katila, R. 77, 105
Kearns-Manolatos, D. 158
KEEN (Kern Entrepreneurial Engineering
    Network) 19–20, 22, 23, **23**, 26, 27
Khanin, D. 151
Killian, J. 157–159
Kiron, D. 158
Klarmann, M. 118
Knight, A. P. 151
Knight, F. 8
Knockaert, M. 150
knowledge 168, 179
knowledge management (KM) 168–169
Kohavi, R. 178
Komarkova, I. 18
Kotter, J. 171
KPIs 145, 178
Kristinsson, K. 84
Kubica, T. 169
Kumta, G. 168
Kwok, J. 140

Lackéus, M. 26
LaForest, S. 169
laggards 107, 108
Land, Edwin "Din" 157
Larsen, I. B. 23, 48
Laskovaia, A. 85
late majority 108
Launchpad Venture Group 158
Lawrence, L. 58–59
Lawrence, Paul R. 175
leaders/leadership 69, 159–160, 166–168, 171;
    accountability for performance 170; adopting
    futuristic tech changes 171–173; behaviors
    167; capacities of entrepreneur 150; clarity of
    purpose 169; credibility of 166, 169; definition
    of 166; implementing decisions 170–171;

implementing tech principles 169; integrity in tech industry 169–170; principles of 165, 167, 168; self-awareness of 170–171; skills 166–167; values and practices 165

Lean Methodology 96

The Lean Startup (Ries) 105

Lean Startup Method 105, 108, 110, 111, 114; customer discovery and development 106; description of 105–106; fuzzy front end (FFE) 106; minimum viable product 106–107; product lifecycle, adoption, and diffusion curves 107–108

learning 172; capabilities 172; by doing 114

Leatherbee, M. 77, 105

LED technology 109

Lee, J.Y. 178

liability: of newness 113, 120; of smallness 113

licensing 39, 42

Liedtka, J. 110

Likens, S. 3

Liñán, F. 68

linear process 92, *92*

liquidation of corporation 144

Liu, T. 4

location strategy 40–41

Loch, C.H. 178

Lopez-Nunez, M. I. 25

Lorsch, Jay W. 175

MacroGenics 39

Madhavan, A. 34, 37

Madrid Agreement 33, 37

Madrid System 36–37

manpower resources 170

Manthey, S. I. 48–50

manufacturing 3, 10–12, 52, 136, 165

March, J. G. 81

Mares, J. 177

market/marketing 4; based economies 148; challenges 113; communication of startups 120; communication tools 121; competition 135; conditions 132; definition of 113; description of 91; environment 9; experimentation 114; for ideas 10–11; instruments 115–116; messages 121; mix 122; opportunities 175, 179; orientation 100; potential 10; review on 96–98; risk 135; types of research 93–96; *see also* market research

Market Pull (MP) innovation strategy 47

market research: categorization by objective 93–94, **94**; implementing 94–95; iteration process in 102, *102*; process 91–92, *92*, 98; qualitative *vs.* quantitative 93–94, **94**; sources of 93; systematic approach to 92; types of **93**, 93–96

Martin, R. 161

Mason, C. 140

Maurya, A. 11, 76

Mawson, S. 23

meta-cognitive intelligence (MCQ) 171

mezzanine financing 133

Milberg, W. 37

milestone payments 11

Miller, C. C. 85

minimum viable product (MVP) 11, 106–107

mission 70–71, 159–160

MIT Human Dynamics Laboratory 161

Moore, G.: *Crossing the Chasm* 107

moral intelligence (MQ) 171

moral rights 36

Morris, M. H. 25, 29

multi-sided revenue streams 75

Murray, F. 161

Musk, E. 105–106, 164

El-Namaki, M. 70

National Aeronautics and Space Administration (NASA) 158

National Science Foundation's Innovation Corps 26

naturalistic fallacy 114

Neff, J. 69

Netflix 78

new product development (NPD) 106

Newton, I. 93

niche markets 108, 177, 180

Nichols, S. P. 4

non-boundary performance 176–179

North, K. 168

Northouse, P. 167

Ogilvie, T. 110

open innovation 52

operational risk 136

opportunity: business model 10–11; experimentation and learning 11; identification 70; intellectual property 10; market size for 9–10; sources of 9; value propositions 9

optimism 110

organization 57; management 69; objectives 166; values 160; *see also* firms

organizational theory: classical principle of 176; conceptual lenses 176; description of 175–176; experimentation perspective 177–178, 180–181; flexibility 177, 179–180; importance of 175–176; non-boundary performance 176–179; *see also* startups

Osterwalder, A. 9, 11, 78; *Business Model Generation* 108

ownership 13, 42, 118–119, 144

Oxcart 157

Papageorgiadis, N. 40–41

partnerships 11, 13, 14, 23, 27, 34, 133, 144, 151, 162, 177

patent-based commercialization 37–38
Patent Cooperation Treaty (PCT) 35, 41
Patent Prosecution Highway program 41
patents/patenting 10, 42; development of 35, *35, 40*; protection 34–35; validity 34
peer-to-peer lending 133
Pentland, Alex "Sandy" 161
Perceived Behavioral Control 68–69
perceived feasibility 69
performance, accountability for 170
personal values 67–68, 71
PEST analysis *96*, 96–98
Pigneur, Y.: *Business Model Generation* 108
place 122
planning effectuator 85
Porter Five Forces 96–98, *97*
power relations, inequities in 151
pre-emptive rights 144
pre-profitability ventures 141
price differentiation 119–120; first-degree 119; second-degree 119; third-degree 119
Price Sensitivity Meter 118
pricing 113, 116; basic price differentiation 119–120; communication channels 122; cost-plus 117; customer-based 118–119; discounts for early customers 120; experimental marketing 114–116; marketing communication 120; marketing messages 121; price discounts for early customers 120; setting 116–117; startups, common marketing challenges of 113–114; target market 120–121
private equity (PE) 148
probability 8, 92, 102, 111, 120, 132
problem: framing and reframing 109–110; solution fit 135
product: continuous improvement of 108–109; definition 111; lifecycle 107–108; market 10–11; risk 136
product development 132; description of 57–58; human-centered design processes and mindsets 58–59; ideate space 62; and implementation decisions 63; implement space 62–63; implications for 63–64; process 111, 177, 181; prototype space 62; synthesize space 62; understand space processes 59
profit-sharing 133
prospect theory 151–152
protection: institutions 33–34; systems 43
prototyping 47, 58, 62, 108
public: funding 180; listings 13; organizations 135

qualitative research, advantages of 99, **99**

Radio Frequency Identification (RFID) technology 41–42
Ranganathan, R. 41
real-life market research 96

Reinig, B. A. 62
relationship 162; building 171; development 169; maintenance 151–152
return, risk and 132
revenue-sharing 133
rewards-based crowdfunding 133
Reymen, I. M. M. J. 85
Rich, B. 157, 159
Ries, E. 11, 176; *The Lean Startup* 105
Rimalovski, F. 62
risk 4, 8; assessment 84; categories of 75–76; in finance 131; and return 132; taking process 84
Roberge, M. 123
Robertson, C. 91
Robinson, F. 106–107
robotics 3, 158, 162
Rockefeller, J. D. 41
Rosenkopf, L. 41
Ruvio, A. 69
Ryder, R. D. 34, 37

sales: analytics 125; channel design 122–124; funnel setup *124*, 124–125
Sarasvathy, S. 8, 82
scalability 135, 140
Schein, E. H. 172
Schelfhout, W. 25
schisms 160, 162
Scholz, R. W. 81
Schwartz, J. 158
Schwartz, S. H. 67
search engine optimization (SEO) 122
securities 132–133
seed funding 13, 134
'seed' investment 134
self-organization 159–160
self-perception 25, 27
sense of urgency 171
setting prices 116–117, *117*
Shane, S. 85
shareholders 70, 145
Shepherd, D. 140
short-term wins 172
silent partnership 133
Simester, D. 178
Simon, H. A.: *The Sciences of the Artificial* 100
skill-based entrepreneurial competencies 23
smart business 78, 85
Smolka, K. 85
social media platforms 76, 99, 122, 178
software ventures 142
Sommer, A.F. 177
Sommer, S.C. 178
sprints 107
stakeholders 3–4, 59, 71, 86, 169, 170
standard-setting organizations (SSOs) 41, 42
standard-setting strategy 41–42

startups 114, 120, 122, 162, 176, 179; advantages
of 176; biotech 179; challenge for 116;
characteristic of 180; experimentation method
178; flexibility 180; incubators 27; internal
and external challenges 180; leaders of 173;
marketing 113–114, 116, 120; organizing
181; practical implications for 175; products
and services 176; resources and capabilities
required for 178; uncertainties of 177–179;
visual recognizability 121; vital marketing
principle for 114
strategic/strategy: clarity 140; initiatives 141;
intention 179; management 74, 172; operation
and implementation of 166; partnerships 121
subsidies 139, 148
sustainability 140, 148, 169–171
Sutherland, D. 41
SWOT analysis 98, *98*
systematic/system: data collection 77; literature
review 50; performance 170

target market 10, 82, 120–121
team: performance 132; risk 135
team building: corporate engagement with
entrepreneurial innovation 161–162; culture
160–161; description of 157–158; leadership,
mission, values 159–160; workforce
ecosystems 158–159
tech: industry 167, 169–170; leadership 173
Technological Capabilities Panel (TCP) 157
technological/technology 158, 164; adoption 169;
application selection 50–51; characterization
50; commercialization 57; description of 3;
development of 74; domains 3; entrepreneurs/
entrepreneurship 7–10, 53, 58, 60, 62, 140;
environment 172; innovation and 7; and
resources 4; risk 135; scale and institutional
knowledge to 172–173; turnovers 165, 170;
variations and forms 3
Technology Application Selection (TAS)
framework 46–49, *49*, 51
Technology Characterization Model 50
technology entrepreneurship 4, 8, 12, 46, 51–52,
57; description of 3; literature on 4; practice of
4, 5; structures and resources in 4
technology push (TP) innovation strategy 9,
46–48, *48*
Technology Readiness Level 47
technology readiness levels (TRLs) 135
technology ventures 3, 4, 52, 131, 139, 147;
capitalization strategy 141–142; capital
requirements 141; description of 12, 139–140;
financing 13, 133–134; funding risks 136;
fundraising post-closing 144–145; market risk
135; need for raising funds 141; negotiation
and closing 143–144; operational risk 136;
pitching and engaging 142–143; plans and

pitches 12; product risk 136; providing value to
fund provider 142; resourcing 12–13; stages of
133–134; team risk 135; technology risk 135;
see also ventures
tech stakeholders 165
Teece, D. J. 39, 53
Terzidis, O. 22, 23, **24**, 47–48, **48**
theoretical model 100, 151
theory construction process 100
theory of planned behavior (TPB) 68
Thomke, S. 178
Tittel, A. 22, 23, **24**, 47–48, *48*
total addressable (or total available) market
(TAM) 10
Total Quality Movement 108–109
trademarks 10; protection 36–37; registration
33–34
transformation, space and energy for 169–170
trust 168–169
Tuertscher, P. 177
Turel, O. 151
Tushman, M.L. 176
Tversky, A. 110
Twin, A. 91

Uber taxi application 52
uncertainty 4, 8, 86, 139, 177; degree of 151;
levels of 83, 84, 87, 181
Unified Process Model of Technology Push
(UPMTP) 47–49
upfront payments 11
user-generated content (UGC) 122
Usman, M. 177
US Small Business Administration 91

validation process 101–102
value proposition 48–49, 108, 113; application
50–51; business model approach 51–54;
definition of 53; description of 46; risks in 50;
TAS framework 48–49; through technology
push innovation strategy lens 46–48
Value Proposition Canvas 11, 14
value/valuation 9, 159–160; creation 4, 18, 161;
in-use approach 119; in-use pricing 118;
model, preferences of 150–151; pricing 118;
propositions 9; strategy 145
Van de Ven, A. H. 177
Vanhaverbeke, W. 177
Van Westendorp method 118, *119*
vehicles, digital ecosystem for 164
venture capital (VC) 14, 148, 150, 151; financing
141; funds/funding 38, 134, 141, 145; goal of
151; institutions 151–152; requirements 149
ventures 3, 150; advantages and disadvantages
149; capitalists 132, 134, 143, 149–151; debt
lending 148; development of 133–134, 139;
finance 141; financial needs 13; investor and

143–144; legal structure 14; needs and business model 13; performance and growth 144–145; science and engineering-driven 4; stakeholders 3; step-by-step roadmap for 42; success 3–4
vesting 144
virtual reality (VR) 3, 46, 110–111
vision: communicating 172; empowering 172; of organization 171–172

Watkins, M. D. 167
Wattam, S. 81
Weinberg, G. 123
Wickham, P. A. 81–82
willingness-to-pay 118

worker platforms 115
workforce ecosystems 157–159
World Intellectual Property Organization (WIPO) 33–34; official website 36; Performances and Phonograms Treaty 36
World Trade Organization 34

XQ *see* existential intelligence (XQ)
Xu, Y. 40–41

Yin, R. K. 93

Zacharakis, A. 12
Zappos 157, 160

Printed in the United States
by Baker & Taylor Publisher Services